Public Administration, Gove~~r~~ and Globalization

Volume 19

Series Editor

Ali Farazmand, School of Public Administration, Florida Atlantic University, Fort Lauderdale, FL, USA

The aim of Public Administration, Governance and Globalization (PAGG) is to publish primary research and theoretical contributions as well as practical reports on fieldwork to help advance the knowledge and understanding about public, nonprofit, private, and nongovernmental organizations and institutions. The governance, administration, and management of these organizations at local, national, regional, and international levels will be discussed in the context of this age of rapid change and globalization. This series on public management offers original materials that contribute to our better understanding of the critical issues as well as routine processes of governance and public administration, now more than ever because of the intricate forces of globalization that affect almost every nation-states and their policy choices at all jurisdictions across the world. The series covers a wide range of topics that address the key issues of interest to scholars, educators, practitioners, and policymakers in public administration capacities around the globe. Books in the series could be research monographs, edited volumes, textbooks, reference volumes or handbooks.

More information about this series at http://www.springer.com/series/8656

Michal Plaček · František Ochrana ·
Milan Jan Půček · Juraj Nemec

Fiscal Decentralization Reforms

The Impact on the Efficiency of Local
Governments in Central and Eastern Europe

 Springer

Michal Plaček
Charles University
Prague, Czech Republic

František Ochrana
Charles University
Prague, Czech Republic

Milan Jan Půček
College of Regional Development
Prague, Czech Republic

Juraj Nemec
Masaryk University
Brno, Czech Republic

Public Administration, Governance and Globalization
ISBN 978-3-030-46760-9   ISBN 978-3-030-46758-6   (eBook)
https://doi.org/10.1007/978-3-030-46758-6

This Springer imprint is published by the registered company Springer Nature Switzerland AG
The registered company address is: Gewerbestrasse 11, 6330 Cham, Switzerland

Preface

One of the problems of the current theory of public administration is examining the impact of factors influencing the efficiency of local governments. This book deals with the issue of the impact of fiscal decentralization reforms on the efficiency of local governments in Central and Eastern European (CEE) countries. Fiscal decentralization has been a problem in Western European countries and the United States for decades (see, for example, Oates 1972; Tiebout 1956) and remains a current question of theory.

The situation is different in CEE countries. These are countries where, until the fall of the communist regimes, there was a strong state centralism that also involved local governments. In these countries, public administration at all levels took the form of a centrally managed government. Problems related to fiscal decentralization in CEE countries were therefore only on the agenda after the fall of the communist regimes. This led to public administration being reformed. It includes the de-etatization (reversing the nationalizing of enterprises into privately or joint private-state owned enterprises) of local governments and the transition to fiscal decentralization. This change is known as the fiscal decentralization reform process. However, the process of fiscal decentralization in CEE countries has significant differences compared to other European countries that were not marked by the communist era. Following the idea of "path dependence" (Peters 2000; David 2007), previous practices have left their evolutionary footprint on the current evolution of public administration in CEE countries. This is a problem that has not yet been sufficiently explored. Therefore, the authors of this book aim to analyze the impact of fiscal decentralization reforms on the efficiency of local governments in CEE countries and to contribute to the scientific explanation of the relevant factors affecting local government efficiency. This corresponds to the selected book structure.

The book is divided into three parts. In the first part, we have created a theoretical-conceptual framework. Based on an analysis of current scientific discourse, we then present the concept of fiscal decentralization and define seven basic factors that we believe have an impact on local government efficiency. These are the factors of: Information asymmetry, rational ignorance and rational abstention, the behavior of bureaucracy, municipal competition, the fiscal illusion factor, inter-governmental grants and transfers, municipal size, and the environmental and institutional environment factor.

The second part examines local self-government in the following CEE countries: Bulgaria, the Czech Republic, Hungary, Poland, Romania, Slovakia, and Slovenia. An analysis of these countries is then carried out in terms of the quality of decentralization and the level of fiscal decentralization. From this (mostly qualitative) analysis, general theoretical conclusions are drawn.

The third part deals with empirical analysis of the impact of fiscal decentralization on the efficiency of municipalities in the Czech Republic. The Czech Republic was chosen for the following reasons: First, the availability of the necessary data. In the case of the Czech Republic (unlike other CEE countries) we were able to obtain all relevant data for empirical analysis. The second reason is that the Czech Republic is a country that, after the establishment of Czechoslovakia,[1] was one of the democratic countries with a Western European standard of democracy. After the communist regime came to power, the Czech Republic (or Czechoslovakia) became a typical country of Central and Eastern Europe, where a tough centralist regime ruled for 40 years. Similarly, the Soviet model of public administration was established in other CEE countries. After the fall of the communist regime, public administration was reformed. This included the decentralization of public administration. In this book, having a large data set, we examine the link between decentralization and the efficiency of local government. As other CEE countries have undergone and are undergoing similar developments, the Czech Republic is in a way a "social laboratory" where we can examine the impact of path dependence on the evolution of public administration and analyze the impact of fiscal decentralization on the efficiency of local governments. On the basis of quantitative data analysis (especially using DEA and second stage DEA) we seek the answer to the main research question, "What impact has fiscal decentralization had on the efficiency of municipalities in the Czech Republic and what impact do the identified factors have on local government efficiency? Conclusions and recommendations for public policy are formulated from the achieved results. The book therefore contributes to enriching the scientific debate on the decentralization of public administration and the factors affecting the efficiency of local government.

---

[1]Czechoslovakia was founded in 1918. In 1938, on the basis of the Munich Agreement signed by fascist Germany, Great Britain, France and Italy (without Czechoslovakia), Czechoslovakia was forced to withdraw from the border areas with a German population (the so-called Sudetenland), which went to Hitler's Germany. Subsequently, in 1939, Slovakia disconnected from Czechoslovakia and formed its own state. Regarding the rest of the Czech territory, the Protectorate of Bohemia and Moravia was founded under the patronage of fascist Germany. The post-war political development in Czechoslovakia was influenced by the fact that at the end of World War II, at a conference in Tehran and Yalta, the victorious powers agreed that Czechoslovakia (along with other CEE countries, where the communist regime later assumed power) would belong to the sphere under the Soviet Union. This predetermined further political developments in Czechoslovakia. The local communists took power in 1948 and ruled until 1989. Czechoslovakia was divided into two independent states in 1993 (the Czech Republic and the Slovak Republic). The Czech Republic became a successor state of Czechoslovakia.

The contribution of the book lies in the fact that it examines the unexplored issue of CEE countries (countries which are already part of the EU.) For non-European readers, it provides information on the development of self-government in the CEE countries and the factors affecting local government efficiency. We also see this publication as scientific.

Prague, Czech Republic   Michal Plaček
Prague, Czech Republic   František Ochrana
Prague, Czech Republic   Milan Jan Půček
Brno, Czech Republic   Juraj Nemec

Contents

Chapter 1
Fiscal Decentralization Reforms and Local Government Efficiency: An Introduction

1.1 Development of the Concept of "Decentralization"

The theory of fiscal federalism emerged in the 1950s and 1960s (Guziejewska 2018). In addition to Wallace Oates, Kenneth Arrow, Richard Musgrave, and Paul Samuelson were its main representatives at that time. The theory of fiscal federalism developed first in countries with a federal system (Guziejewska 2018). Federalism is a system of government characterized by semiautonomous states in a regime with a common central government; authority is allocated between levels of government (Bednar 2011). This system is composed of several governing units, each with its own preferences and decisions to make (Bednar 2011; Ostrom 1991, 1999, 2008). In federal arrangements, the center and subunits share sovereignty, as both have a constitutionally protected status and cannot be unilaterally disempowered by the other tier of government (Bolleyer et al. 2014).

For example, in Switzerland, the Federal Constitution guarantees the autonomy of the cantons; the principle of subsidiarity ensures that all tasks that are not explicitly assigned to the federal level are the responsibility of the cantons; and cooperative executive federalism, in which cantons are in charge of the implementation of federal law, makes the cantons important actors even in federal policy areas (Füglister and Wasserfallen 2014).

Many economic and political claims about federalism rely on two principles: the Tiebout hypothesis (1956) and Oates's Decentralization Theorem (1972). Tiebout notes that most models assume that all government spending is provided centrally; he considers these analyses to be too simplified and inapplicable at the local level, and therefore developed his own model (Špalek 2011). This model focuses on local spending associated with local provision of public goods and services. It empirically demonstrates that local public spending can exceed central public spending and suggests a model for addressing local expenditures that match local preferences, called "voting with your feet." This hypothesis asserts that when voters are fully mobile, they choose the community that suits their income and expenditure needs politically. Each community is expected to set its own level of spending, which is

© Springer Nature Switzerland AG 2020
M. Plaček et al., *Fiscal Decentralization Reforms*, Public Administration, Governance and Globalization 19, https://doi.org/10.1007/978-3-030-46758-6_1

financed by local taxes. The voters are fully rational and have accurate information on the level of public goods provided by each community. They can then identify the optimal community in which to reside. This creates homogeneous communities where people are willing and able to agree on a production of public goods and services that is optimal for all members of the community. It is therefore possible to determine the optimal level of production of public goods (Špalek 2011). The Tiebout model is based on assumptions that can be very difficult to achieve in reality:

- The consumer—the voter is fully mobile and moves into a community that fits their preferences.
- The consumer—the voter is perfectly aware of, and responds to, the differences in income and expenditures on individual goods.
- There are a large number of communities among which the consumer can choose.
- There are no barriers to the labor market.
- There is an "optimal community size," defined as the number of inhabitants to whom public goods are provided at the minimum average cost.
- The community situated under the optimal supply point seeks new residents to lower average costs. The community over the optimal point tries to reduce the number of its inhabitants. Where the level of goods is optimal, there is an effort to maintain the current size of the state (Špalek 2011; Čermáková 2006).

The preferred level of public goods varies. "All communities have a solid structure of income and expenditure that reflects the wishes of their residents. The allocation of public spending is performed by the 'city manager', whose job Tiebout compares to the work of a stockbroker offering public services (Čermáková 2006, p. 37). Because local governments are able to provide a wide range of public goods that are in line with local preferences, the result is an optimal provision of public goods and services. "This fact stems from the assumption that the goods provided are perhaps social/club-oriented rather than purely public, and therefore have a rather local character" (Špalek 2011, p. 98).

The issue of fiscal decentralization is related to the existence of economies of scale. If the cost of delivering public goods and services is recalculated per capita, there is a breakdown of fixed costs and fixed overheads among a larger number of people, and the cost of producing public goods and services per capita is lower. This is described by Buchanan's theory of clubs, which assumes that the club's purpose is to share the costs of securing an indivisible commodity or to satisfy the desire of individuals with similar preferences within the association. Within the club, there are economies of scale (Brennan and Buchanan 1980; Čermáková 2006, p. 38). This can be applied analogously to territorial units that will allocate public goods according to the preferences of their inhabitants. As a result of these preferences, the allocation of public goods and services will vary from place to place.

The mobility factor in the Tiebout model was criticized by Oates (1972). According to Oates, mobility leads to a conflict between economic efficiency and social justice (Špalek 2011). This critique served as the basis for Oates' decentralization theorem, which is a key theory in favor of decentralization. Oates' decentralization theorem assumes the existence of two levels of government—central and local. The local government reflects the population's demand for public goods and services. Oates compares the efficiency of the provision of public goods and services by local and central governments (Čermáková 2006). The central government may decide that certain public goods and services will be provided by local governments in a uniform amount to provide a single amount for a single price. As a result of this decision, there will be a loss of efficiency resulting from both inadequate consumption and over-consumption of public goods and services.

Oates' decentralization theorem has some problems, particularly in the reduction of revenue from scale due to decentralization and in the optimal size of the jurisdiction, which may vary according to the type of public good. The effect of spillover of consumption of public goods among jurisdictions bears mentioning (Čermáková 2006).

In their approach to the theory of fiscal federalism, Musgrave and Musgrave (1989) focused on which fiscal functions could be executed both centrally and in a decentralized way. In their view, the fiscal system in each country is mostly two or three levels, and this is primarily a consequence of historical development and geographical conditions (Čermáková 2006). They confirm that public goods and services should be provided in accordance with the preferences of the local population. However, public goods are decided by public choice, i.e. public goods benefiting all the inhabitants of a particular state; the central government should ensure that public goods benefit the inhabitants of the territory as decided by local governments. This approach necessarily requires a change in the financing of the production of public goods and services, as the population of each area should pay for the public goods provided by the local government. There is a differentiation of taxes between federal taxes, which finance public goods and services that are used throughout the territory, and local ones, which serve to finance public goods in a certain area (Čermáková 2006).

The public choice theory constituted a more realistic, normative view of fiscal decentralization, which considered the role of political processes and the fact that decision makers and politicians are opportunistic in their motivations, striving to maintain power and influence, and generating high wages for the administration (Guziejewska 2018). Jackson and Brown (2003) claim that the disadvantage of a centralized system is high decision-making costs and the risk of concentration of power. It is precisely decentralization that eliminates this risk. This is described in greater detail by Brennan and Buchanan's (1980) decentralization hypothesis, which states that the government tends to expand like a leviathan and, at the expense of its citizens, seeks to maximize its power and income from taxation. Decentralization can limit state expansion (Čermáková 2006). Competition is associated with superior performance by governmental organizations. Three forms of competition in local government are identified by theory: competition between local authorities, competition between councils and private contractors, and competition between parties for political power (Watt 1999). Competition between councils takes two forms: first, geographical competition between authorities in different areas for a share of the market in households and businesses; second, competition between different tiers of local governments for a share of local tax revenues in the same geographical area (Watt 1999). This view is supported by most recent empirical literature, which provides evidence in favor of a negative relationship between fiscal decentralization and government size (Di Liddo et al. 2018). Scholars claim that decentralized policy provision enhances governmental honesty and efficiency and gives governments the chance to innovate, rather than adopt a common policy. These forces lead directly to a belief in efficiency, policy specialization, and a reduction in corruption (Bednar 2011; Brennan and Buchanan 1980; Tanzi 1996).

Decentralization has not only an administrative value, but also a civic dimension (Vo 2010). Oates asserted that the intellectual roots of decentralization "are found in twentieth-century Catholic social philosophy". In point of fact, Oates's interpretation of decentralization is quite discordant with Catholic social philosophy, which may have its modern origins in *Rerum Novarum* (Drew and Grant 2017). Subsidiarity has its roots in the Catholic Natural Law tradition, which asserts that there are universally evident and universally binding existential ends for people that can be discerned by reason, the order of nature, and the ordinance of God (Drew and Grant 2017).

Since decentralization "increases the opportunities for citizens to take interest in public affairs, it makes them get accustomed to using freedom. And from the accumulation of these local, active, persnickety freedoms is born the most efficient counterweight against the claims of the central government, even if it were supported by an impersonal, collective will" (De Tocqueville 1961, p. 62). De Tocqueville insists that local and associational freedoms—political freedoms—are the only guards against despotism because they ensure the capacity of citizens to actively govern themselves by providing the training and the taste for freedom (Cruikshank 1993).

The concept of decentralization can be divided into three sub-components (Prud'homme 1995; Balaguer-Coll et al. 2010): spatial, market, and administrative decentralization. Spatial decentralization is perceived as a process of moving urban populations and activities from large agglomerations. Market decentralization is a process for creating conditions where the goods and services provided by decentralized market solutions exceed those of the public sector (Balaguer-Coll et al. 2010). Administrative decentralization is perceived as a transfer of responsibility for planning and management, and the acquisition and allocation of resources at lower levels of government. Administrative decentralization has three further sub-components: deconcentration, which is the distribution of decision-making power between lower levels within the central government; delegation, which is the transfer of power from the central government to autonomous organizations; and devolution, which is the transfer of power to lower levels of government (Balaguer-Coll et al. 2010, p. 577).

A similar view is offered by Freille et al. (2007), who distinguish between market decentralization, which is associated with traditional fiscal federalism; political decentralization, as a form of transferring decision-making power closer to citizens; constitutional decentralization, consisting of the creation of central institutions in the regions; and spatial decentralization, which consists of the development of regions outside the main urban agglomerations.

In their critical assessment of decentralization, Torrisi et al. (2011) stated that "decentralization" is a very ambiguous term that is often used in a misleading way, and that its simplest definition is a definition in the negative sense, namely that decentralization is not a transfer of decision-making power and resources to the central

Table 1.1 Forms of decentralization

Form of decentralization	Description
Fiscal decentralization	The way the central government provides resources to local governments
Political decentralization	This concerns the level at which the central government allows local governments to take on political functions, the degree to which political actors and themes are significant at the local level, and how independent they are from the central government
Administrative decentralization	This describes the degree of autonomy of local governments with respect to central governments
Deconcentration	This describes the transfer of decision-making power from the central government to the authorities in the regions, which are, however, responsible in the hierarchy to the central authorities
Delegation	Transfer of responsibility for public policy to local governments or semi-autonomous organizations that are not responsible to the local government
Devolution	The central government allows the quasi autonomous local units to exercise and control the delegated policy

Source Torrisi et al. (2011)

government. Their approach is based on the principal-agent relationship between the central government and the local government, which consists of the division of competences in the following areas: (a) finance, (b) provision of services, (c) human resources, (d) accessibility rules, and (e) governance rules. Each of these features is based on multiple choices. They provide a comprehensive overview of various forms of decentralization (Table 1.1).

Freille et al. (2007) identified indicators that can measure decentralization: local government revenue and expenditure as a percentage of GDP, the number of local governments and jurisdictions, and the existence of autonomous regions. The OECD and Korea Institute of Public Finance (2013) define fiscal decentralization using the following taxing power indicator: how to set shared taxes and changes to them, setting up subsidy relationships, and their goals. Another OECD and Korea Institute of Public Finance (2013) indicator is spending power, which can be broken down into the following categories:

- Autonomy in public policy—the extent to which local governments can decide on public policy goals and what targets are determined by local government;
- Budgetary autonomy—the extent of the freedom of local governments to use budgetary resources, and what control mechanisms on the use of budgetary resources from the central government exist;
- Autonomy of inputs—the control of local governments over public policy inputs, such as public-sector employees, whether they have the right to decide how public services will be provided, e.g. by outsourcing or in-house;

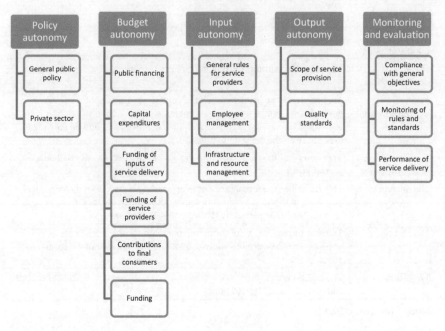

Fig. 1.1 Structure of the spending power indicator. *Source* OECD and Korea Institute of Public Finance (2013)

- Autonomy of outputs—the extent to which local governments have control over outputs in the form of public goods and services, and how quality standards are set for these outputs;
- Monitoring and evaluation—the extent to which local governments have the ability to evaluate public and policy outcomes and benchmarking, for example (Fig. 1.1).

The practical application of the spending power indicator was demonstrated in case studies from the USA, Germany, and Norway (OECD and Korea Institute of Public Finance 2013). Fiscal indicators of decentralization are used by the World Bank, with its indicators derived from the Government Finance Statistics used by the International Monetary Fund. Ladner et al. (2016) describe the conceptual framework for measuring autonomy designed by Clark (1984), who defined four types of autonomy. Each type of autonomy is based on a combination of specific powers; namely initiative and immunity. Initiative means the competence of local governments to realize their own interests. Immunity means the power of local governments to act without control from higher levels of government. Based on a combination of these competencies, the following ideal types of autonomy were identified:

Type 1—Local governments have both initiative and immunity.
Type 2—Decentralized liberalism, whereby local governments can act in their own interest, but their decisions are subject to the control of a higher level of government.

Type 3—Limited autonomy in the sense that local governments do not have the opportunity to act on their own but are not subject to control by a higher level of government.
Type 4—Local governments cannot act on their own account and are subject to control by higher government levels (Ladner et al. 2016).

According to Gurr and King (1987) Types 1 and 2 are augmented by a combination of local factors. In their view, "Type 1" autonomy is determined by the local economy and social factors such as the potential tax revenues from the local economy and the ability of the population to control local policies and prevent rent seeking. The lower the performance of the local economy, the more the local government will be dependent on resources from higher levels of government. "Type 2" is the key constitutional and legislative setting that defines the competencies of local governments. Within the scope of competencies, the wider the competencies of local governments, the more financial resources they should have to implement them.

Regarding this theory, Ladner et al. (2016) built their own set of indicators of autonomy. In their conception, these indicators cover a period from 1990 to 2014, so they were able to capture a temporal shift in autonomy. They define this as the Local Autonomy Index, which is based on the following indicators:

- Institutional anchoring—the range of formal autonomy of local governments and the choice of objectives to be implemented by local governments;
- Scope of policies—the range of functions that local governments implement within their policies, such as health, education, and local infrastructure;
- Real political power—the real influence the local government has on the extent of its policies;
- Fiscal autonomy—the extent to which local governments can impose taxes on their residents;
- Transfer system—the proportion of non-purpose financial transfers received by the local government out of all transfers received;
- Financial self-sufficiency—the proportion of local government revenue derived from local resources;
- Credit autonomy—the ability of local governments to obtain repayable resources;
- Organizational autonomy—the extent to which local governments can determine their organizational structure and electoral system;
- Law on self-government—the extent of legal protection of the right to self-government;
- Administrative supervision—supervision of local self-governments by the central government;
- Access to the central government—the extent to which central government public policies are consulted on with local authorities.

From a conceptual point of view, these approaches can be described as the first generation of fiscal federalism (Mookherjee 2015), as they are primarily concerned with the efficient establishment of fiscal relations among levels of government. The central government is still perceived as the single maximizer of welfare. The role of local governments is perceived to be that of a messenger of information about local needs to the central government and of a grant manager (Mookherjee 2015).

The theory of the first degree of fiscal federalism was summarized by Provazníková (2011) in several principles that should fulfill the optimal system of fiscal federalism:

- Principle of disparity—fiscal arrangements should respect differences in population preferences in the structure of public goods in a given territory.
- Principle of centralization of redistribution—the redistribution function of fiscal policy should be implemented by the central government, which has the necessary tools and information and can ensure uniform redistribution throughout the territory.
- Principle of ensuring a minimum level of basic public services—the central government should guarantee a minimum level of basic public goods and services to all citizens of the country, regardless of the area they live in.
- Principle of equalization of fiscal position—as there are significant territorial differences in both fiscal capacity as well as the differing needs of individual local governments, the central government should ensure that the minimum levels of basic public goods in individual areas are attained at a comparable tax rate.
- (Local) neutrality principle—the central government should strive to minimize the differences in taxes imposed by individual areas that would cause local distortions in economic decisions (Provazníková 2011, p. 52).

The idea of decentralization has become a part of public policy following the recommendations of the OECD and the World Bank. Decentralization was significantly expanded in the context of reforms in the spirit of New Public Management (NPM) (Alonso et al. 2015; Smoke 2015a, b). Smoke (2015a, b) notes that decentralization is viewed as a universal tool of reform, particularly in emerging economies such as Vietnam (Vu et al. 2014; Malesky et al. 2014), China (Mok and Wu 2013), Pakistan (Aslam and Yilmaz 2011), India (Singh 2008), Uganda (Deininger and Mpuga 2005), and Tanzania (Hulst et al. 2015). Reforms in the "one size fits all" spirit were criticized in the now classic article by Prud'homme (1995), followed by criticism from De Vries (2000). Smoke (2015a, b) summarized the complaints about decentralization as a complex process that is often realized in a dynamic environment characterized by apparent homogeneity. Applications of routine decentralization procedures often fail to produce the expected results due to the heterogeneous environment (2015a, b) Even non-critical advocates of decentralization have begun to express their frustration with the results of decentralization; in connection with this, the importance of this criticism is growing in academic debates as well as in the real policy of recentralization (2015a, b). The key argument is that this type of reform is much more diverse and complex than expected. To achieve efficient and sustainable decentralization, a much more sophisticated analysis and strategic approach is needed, which responds to the circumstances of a given country (2015a, b).

With the criticism of NPM and the emergence of new paradigms, a new perception of decentralization has developed that reflects the irreversible transformation of the traditional hierarchical form of governance while at the same time seeking to find efficient ways of coordinating decentralized structures. This can be summarized by the term "network governance" (Osborne et al. 2014). The basis of this approach is to identify the different actors in the network—their needs, interests, self-governing (managerial) capacities, subsequent involvement in decision-making, and resource allocation. The aim of governance is to reintegrate fragmented processes, prevent inefficient distribution of powers and resources, and, in the extreme case, prevent destructive decomposition of the governmental structure and system of management for the provision of public services and goods within the territory.

The second generation of the theory of fiscal federalism deals with political economy and the problem of corruption (Mookherjee 2015). It focuses mainly on the issue of inefficient allocation due to decisions made by coalition partners with minimal representation, who represent a certain district but do not fully acknowledge the impact on other districts. This leads to a reduction of the efficiency of centralized allocation. Another part of the theory deals with government agencies and related issues of optimal contract setting, corruption, and rent seeking (Mookherjee 2015). A very important part of the theory deals with accountability, the influence of local elites, and the contribution of decentralization to increased performance, the use of benchmarking and performance indicators, and competition among local governments.

This list of topics is, of course, not complete, as the volume of literature dealing with the impacts of decentralization has increased considerably in recent years. However, it is important to note that a large number of studies have produced very contradictory results. This is demonstrated, for example, by the influence of decentralization on corruption. Some studies argue that decentralization may lead to more corruption (Goldsmith 1999; Treisman 2000; Wu 2005); other studies claim that decentralization leads to less corruption (Ames 1994; Barenstein and de Mello 2001; Fisman and Gatti 2002). Few studies have considered the various aspects of decentralization (Enikolopov and Zhuravskaya 2007). The most complex concept of decentralization, within the context of corruption research, was reported by Freille et al. (2007), who tested the impact of decentralization on corruption in more than 100 countries and used 20 indicators of decentralization on the corruption perception index compiled by Transparency International (2019) and the World Bank. Their main findings confirmed that fiscal decentralization is associated with a lower level of corruption and that decentralization connected with the establishment of central government institutions in the region is associated with a higher level of corruption. Similarly, Neudorfer and Neudorfer (2015) maintained that countries with strong regional governments provide many more opportunities for networking and local collusive monopolies, which lead to higher levels of corruption.

For the second generation of the theory of fiscal federalism, the benefits of decentralization are as follows:

- On average, democratic decentralization helps to better align spending decisions with local consumption.
- The benefits of decentralization are considerably heterogeneous and vary across jurisdictions. Regions with high social capital benefit more from decentralization; less developed regions have a higher risk of corruption.

- The establishment and implementation of decentralization has a major impact on the ultimate benefits. Key areas include establishing accountability mechanisms, oversight mechanisms from citizens, and transparent budgetary procedures, or providing citizens with information on performance.
- Higher levels of government are a necessary complement to the success of reforms in the spirit of decentralization. Here, for example, there would be significant supervision via independent audits and independent media control.
- Community development projects work less reliably than local government projects, since they do not operate with the electoral and electoral sanction mechanisms that arise with an unpopular public policy.
- One way to remedy the failure of civil society is to include disadvantaged groups in the decision-making process. This inclusion can serve as an incubator for new political leadership by weakening traditional stereotypes.

Citizen engagement does not follow the predicted time trajectory. Instead of a balance of civic activity, long periods of civic inactivity may occur, alternating with short intervals of civic engagement. From a normative point of view, it is necessary to focus on a long period and a constant mechanism of learning, monitoring, experimentation, and evaluation (Mookherjee 2015; Mansuri and Rao 2013).

1.2   Current Research on Decentralization

This chapter presents a literature search. The methodology of Mookherjee (2015) was used for classifying resources, with the resources divided into literature exploring the first level of fiscal federalism and literature exploring the second level of fiscal federalism. Full classification is only applied to the analysis of sources for the Czech Republic. For international sources, the focus is on literature of the second level of fiscal federalism. Foreign studies were divided into the following categories: empirical cross-national studies, empirical studies on national data, and theoretical studies.

The empirical cross-national studies are mainly econometric studies which attempt to analyze the effects of decentralization on: the efficiency of public expenditures (Boetti et al. 2012; Adam et al. 2014), accountability levels (Papenfuss and Schaefer 2010) the volume of different types of expenditures such as education and healthcare (Busemeyer 2008), economic growth (Abdellatif et al. 2015; Cerniglia 2003), the size of the public sector (Alonso et al. 2015; Golem and Malešević Perović 2014; Fiva 2006) government budget deficits (Afonso and Fernandes 2006; Stegarescu 2005), corruption (Freille et al. 2007), and management of natural disasters (Escaleras and Register 2012). This type of approach is relatively comfortable in terms of data demands, mostly using the World Bank or OECD decentralization indicators. These studies, however, are a frequent target of criticism due to the data and methods used. Aslam and Yilmaz (2011) suggested that empirical explorations of the impact of decentralization on macroeconomic variables and the size of the public sector are mixed, as most of the conclusions are very sensitive to how decentralization has been defined and how it is measured.

Another form of empirical cross-national studies evaluates decentralization reforms across multiple countries. This is more of a qualitative analysis than an extensive econometric analysis. In one such study, social accountability is addressed by involving citizens and civil society in increasing pressure on policy and civil servants for more accountability (Brinkerhoff and Wetterberg 2016); it is perceived as an instrument that can improve the functioning of the public sector. The study focuses on the analysis of supply factors: the structure of the state and the nature of democracy. Their analysis covers four case studies from developing countries. The authors argue that the key factors impacting social accountability are the degree of decentralization and the amount of room for citizen involvement.

The area of developing countries has been addressed by Smoke (2015a, b), from the point of view of combating poverty (Bardhan and Mookherjee 2005), the creation of infrastructure and institutional framework design (Mookherjee 2006), and in the former Eastern Bloc (Aristovnik 2012).

Considering the direction of research referred to as empirical studies on national data, a significant part of the literature focuses on developing countries, such as the efficiency of public service provision in China (Mok and Wu 2013; Wu and Wang 2013), transport, health and repair of communications in Vietnam (Malesky et al. 2014), quality of basic education in Bali (Faozanudin 2014), services in Pakistan (Aslam and Yilmaz 2011; Singh 2008), the quality of primary education in Argentina (Galiani et al. 2008), accountability in Uganda (Deininger and Mpuga, 2005), and the role of the private sector in securing regional needs in India (Firman and Fahmi 2017).

Political devolution in the context of local governments was addressed by Hidayat (2017), who sees an opportunity to improve the level of provision of public services, especially education. The opposite approach can be seen in a study by Hoey (2017) that deals with the recentralization of planning activities needed to reform health care in Bolivia. Hoey describes the main obstacles to recentralization, such as the need to provide financial resources for the staff, the provision of the necessary competencies, and the restoration of trust and accountability. These issues were overcome through participatory planning and implementation based on negotiation. Negative experiences with administrative and fiscal decentralization, such as land renting from local governments in China, were described in the work of Huang and Du (2017). Local governments favor industrial tenants over tenants in the service sector. This preference is further enhanced by the economic cycle. Huang and Du present the need to rethink the competencies of local governments. A similar view is provided by China's business studies of local governments (Mei et al. 2016). These activities have often been seen as a source of economic growth, but critical voices are emerging, pointing out that these activities may be a source of future economic problems, primarily due to the resources being allocated to inappropriate sectors. Another negative impact can be caused by the boom of corruption and poor environmental management. A very interesting view of decentralization in the context of disaster risk elimination is provided in a study by Grady et al. (2016), which focuses on Indonesia, concluding that decentralization increases the risk of disasters. The causes are traditional, namely the low capacity of local governments, inadequate compliance with legislation, lack of policy, and lack of communication. This article demonstrates the great heterogeneity of the effects of decentralization. Other authors (Escaleras and Register 2012), in a study of mature countries, confirm the exact opposite conclusions.

Of course, there is evidence for advanced countries such as Switzerland as well. Wyss and Lorenz (2000) analyze the impact of decentralization on the coordination of health care between the central government and the regions. There have been other analyses of the impact of fiscal decentralization on the ability of local governments to respond to the demand for public goods and services in Norway (Borge et al. 2008), on the performance of the public sector in Canada (Aubert and Bourdeau 2012), and on voters and their influence on the efficiency of municipalities in Germany (Geys et al. 2010). The topic of devolution, or the impact of the transfer of administrative powers from the central government to local governments, in Italy, specifically in the transport sector and its impact on efficiency and corruption, is dealt with by Carlucci et al. (2017), who state that in Italy, it is necessary to take into account the considerable heterogeneity of the regions, expressed in terms of purchasing power parity. Andersen and Torsteinsen (2017) focus on the issue of reconciling strategic management and operational autonomy. In their case study, they focus on a municipality which has more than 10 years of experience in setting up agencies. According to the authors, it is very difficult to find an optimal degree of autonomy as it is actually a continuous process of negotiating between two levels. López Martínez et al. (2016) dealt with early school leaving in Spanish regions. According to the authors, apart from the economic crisis, the decentralized system of education in Spain, which is affected by the different economic levels of the regions, plays a significant role. The positive effects of decentralization on the example of social services provided by municipalities in Spain during the economic crisis are noted by Navarro and Velasco (2016). As a result of the economic crisis in 2013, the Spanish government decided to bring selected social services up to date. The authors consider the unintended positive effect of the new establishment of competencies with which the municipalities gained legitimacy by implementing public policies in areas the newly established competency had not originally counted on (e.g. in childcare). The impact of decentralization as part of the NPM reforms in the health sector in Italy is addressed by Sarto and Veronesi (2016), who state that more autonomous regions with a center-based government have been adopting a more managerial style of management in their healthcare facilities. In Central and Eastern Europe, this theme is linked to reforms in the spirit of NPM. The evaluation of the effects in this area is very much focused on government agencies; in this area the research evaluates how their higher autonomy and specialization leads to better results and higher efficiency (Randma-Liiv et al. 2011; Hajnal 2011; Sarapuu 2011).

Another important area is the analysis of local government efficiency through frontier techniques, namely data envelopment analysis (DEA) and free disposal hull (FDH). Later models use a two-stage technique: a combination of nonparametric analysis and a regression model. The nonparametric analysis serves to analyze the efficiency achieved and the regression model serves to verify the influence of control variables such as decentralization and socioeconomic factors. This approach is applied to countries with high territorial fragmentation, such as Spain (Benito et al. 2010), France (Seifert and Nieswand 2014), and the Lisbon region (Afonso and Fernandes 2006). An article by Balaguer-Coll et al. (2010) is considered very important in this area. The authors examine the link between the efficiency of municipalities in Spain and decentralization. They use non-parametric models to evaluate efficiency. The finding that some municipalities can manage their resources more efficiently if they have more room for decision-making has significant implications. A sample of small municipalities in Spain was investigated by Arcelus et al. (2015). In their view, the efficiency of providing public services between municipalities increases the level of joint service provision among municipalities, the share of local taxes in operating funding compared to financing by grants, the presence of external control, and accumulated past infrastructure investments.

An important part of empirical studies is the analysis of economies of scale that are related to differences in the size of municipalities. Each study tries to prove the existence of economies of scale in the production of selected public services and goods or to calculate the optimal size of the municipality. The results of these studies are often different, depending on the type of production of public services and goods, as well as on the country (see, for example, Dahl and Tufte 1973; King 1984; Mouritzen 1989; Sharpe 1995; Goldsmith and Rose 2000; Swianiewicz 2014).

The methods used in these articles are discussed in terms of the suitability of their application. For example, using a Flemish municipality dataset, Geys and Moesen (2009) confirmed that the use of the method has a significant effect on performance measurement results, so it is important to evaluate the robustness of the methods used and compare the results of these methods with each other.

The last category studied is theoretical studies. As Mookherjee (2015) noted, contemporary theoretical concepts deal primarily with the second generation of fiscal federalism. The researchers focus on the agency's problem in terms of tradeoff between the internalization of externalities in the centralized system and accountability as an advantage of the decentralized system (Tommasi and Weinschelbaum 2007). Another approach, represented by Mookherjee (2006), focuses on the benefit of delegation and notes that perhaps the most significant benefit is a more efficient distribution of information that leads to better tasks. Less progress has been made in analyzing the costs of communication and measuring the complexity of contracts. However, this theory needs to build stronger foundations. Another research direction is the influence of decentralization and its associated strategic or operational autonomy on management and organizational culture oriented towards performance (Verbeeten and Speklé 2015). Aubert and Bourdeau (2012) similarly argue that agencies benefit from greater freedom and the ability to make financial and personnel decisions. This is also related to the autonomy of management. The organization works better with greater autonomy in management. Decentralized leadership, which relies on the ability of local governments to set their own public policy and the resulting opportunism, is dealt with by Silva (2016). The impact of information production in decentralized systems is analyzed by experimental design (Livermore 2017), concluding that decentralization may overproduce socially defective information. Livermore illustrates the point using the legal and economic impacts of two important environmental laws, the Clean Water Act and the Act restricting the production of greenhouse gases, in the sectors that deal with electricity generation.

1.3 Fiscal Decentralization and Local Government Efficiency

There is currently a relatively significant stream of literature that focuses on assessing efficiency in local governments. It has started to be promoted more intensively since 1980 in the context of reforms in the spirit of New Public Management. The main objective of these reforms was to increase the efficiency of the public sector through instruments such as privatization, decentralization, and implementation of modern managerial methods (Pollitt and Bouckaert 2011). Another important milestone for exploring this area is the economic crisis that began in 2008 (da Cruz and Marques 2014; Drew et al. 2015). From a wider perspective, efficiency is part of the concept of performance. Worthington and Dollery (2002) state that overall, performance creates efficiency, which describes how well an organization uses resources in producing services, and effectiveness, the degree to which a system achieves its program and policy objectives.

Fogarty and Mugera (2013) recognize the following types of efficiency: technical efficiency, allocation efficiency, dynamic efficiency, scale efficiency. Technical efficiency means producing maximum output with the inputs available for the given technology (Narbón-Perpiñá and De Witte 2017a, b). Allocative efficiency means that resources are allocated to producing the items most valued by society. Cost efficiency is a measure that combines allocative and technical efficiency (Fogarty and Mugera 2013). Dynamic efficiency means that resources are used efficiently over time (Fogarty and Mugera 2013; Drew et al. 2015). Scale efficiency considers whether an organization is operating at the correct scale (Fogarty and Mugera 2013; Drew et al. 2017).

According to Aiello et al. (2017), these parametric and non-parametric methods are most often used in the field of efficiency literature (Table 1.2).

We can identify the following efficiencies in the context of local governments (D'Inverno et al. 2018): individual public services, solid waste, sewage disposal, water, energy provision, hospitals, municipal savings banks, public libraries, road maintenance, fire protection, the elderly care sector, local police services, public transportation, and pre-school education. The second branch deals with studies that analyze global municipal efficiency for various countries. Basically, the concept of efficiency of local governments can be represented graphically as follows (Fig. 1.2).

The figure shows a system approach to investigating the efficiency of selected services provided by local government. Local governments act as production units

Table 1.2 Overview of parametric and non-parametric methods for calculating efficiency according to Aiello et al. (2017)

	Nonparametric and determinist approaches		Parametric and stochastic approaches		
	DEA (data envelopment analysis)	FDH (free disposal hull)	SFA (stochastic frontier analysis)	DFA (distribution free approach)	TFA (thick frontier approach)
Functional form of the frontier	Not specified	Not specified	To be specified	To be specified	To be specified
Erratic disturbance	Not allowed	Not allowed	Composite term—inefficiency, random error,	Composite term—inefficiency, random error,	Composite term—inefficiency, random error
Efficiency	Time variant, point estimates	Time variant, point estimates	Time variant, point estimates	Time variant, point estimates	Time variant, only general estimate
Advantages	No constraint to assign a functional form to frontier, no constraint regarding error distribution, point estimates of each decision making unit (DMU)	No constraint to assign a functional form to frontier, no constraint regarding error distribution, point estimates of each DMU, no assumption of production set convexity	Composite error split into a component relating to efficiency and another due to randomness, point estimates of each DMU	Composite error split into a component relating to efficiency and another due to randomness, point estimates of each DMU	Composite error spit into a component relating to efficiency and another due to randomness
Caveats	No randomness, no parametric test for inference	No randomness, no parametric test for inference	Arbitrary choice of distribution for the error term, arbitrary choice of functional form of frontier	Arbitrary choice of functional form for the frontier, efficiency is assumed to be time-invariant	Arbitrary choice of functional form for the frontier, arbitrary choice of distribution for the error term, no point estimates

Source Aiello et al. (2017, p. 37)

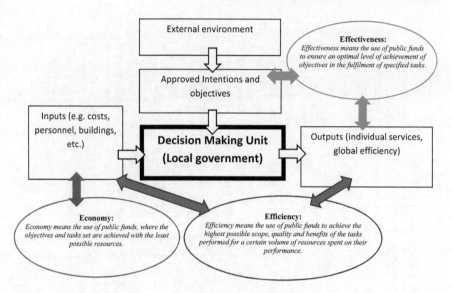

Fig. 1.2 Concept of efficiency in the local government environment. *Source* Authors

(or providers of public goods and services). Local governments are looking for ways to allocate resources efficiently, create allocation variants and decide which option to choose. Local government therefore seeks and chooses the most economically viable option for securing services. We use the term "Decision Making Unit" to indicate this fact of economic choice and the rationality of local government decision-making.[1]

Decision-Making Units have a "set" behavior for their input. The goal is the anticipated state of the system. Resources (human, material, and financial) are needed to reach the target. These form the entrance to the system. Inside the system, these resources are transformed into outputs and results. Because resources are scarce

---

[1] A Decision Making Unit is a production system. The elements of this system are individual actors of local government. These include, for example, individual representatives of local governments (mayor), municipal councils and officials. Relationships between system elements have the character of activities. These movements have a dual character ("routing"). This concerns both the activities that take place in the Decision Making Unit/local government system and the activities where local government actors interact with the external environment. Activities have both a formal character and an informal character. The formal character of the activities is influenced by individual legal regulations coming from the external environment. These include, in particular, the Municipalities Act, the Act on Financial Control, the Act on Taxes (Tax Purpose), and possibly other government regulations and government decrees governing the implementation of laws binding for the Decision Making Unit/local government. Formal activities are also influenced by regulations (decrees and regulations). These are internal regulations that elaborate local government as binding ordinances and regulations for the given municipality. In addition to formal activities, the behavior of the Decision Making Unit also affects informal activities. These are unplanned (originally unintended, spontaneous) activities that arise between individual local government actors. These activities take the form, for example, of networks created on the basis of personal sympathy or lack of sympathy. Both types of activities affect the resulting functioning and condition of the system. They affect the functioning of local government and have an impact on efficiency.

(hence limited), the rational actors of the Decision-Making Unit seek a way to transform available resources that respects the principles of economy, efficiency, and effectiveness. Based on the 3E indicators, we can compare individual municipalities. Formally we can express the production of Decision-Making Units as follows:

$$P = f(I) \tag{1.1}$$

$$C = g(P) = g(f(I) = h(I), \tag{1.2}$$

where

P = Production
I = Input variables (inputs)
C = Costs.

These relationships can be interpreted as requiring inputs (defined by input variables I) to produce, transforming them into outputs of the described output P, costing C. The process of resource transformation is expressed by the fact that:

(a) For the input, we identify certain resources (human, material, financial);
(b) For the output we identify services and goods that can potentially bring satisfaction to their users.
(c) The "interior" of the production system is the transformation of inputs into outputs, and we are interested in the economic connection between inputs and outputs.

It is clear from the figure that the needs of society and the applicable legislation determine the main objectives and goals of the local government. With the help of efficiency analysis, the local government can fulfill this assignment in three basic ways. The first is input-oriented (input-oriented model), where the local government seeks to achieve a given amount of output (e.g. population to which it provides a certain service, etc.) using a minimum amount of inputs (costs, labor, etc.) The second way is output-oriented, where the local government tries to maximize its output with a predetermined amount of input. The last approach is a combination of both previous models, where the local government maximizes outputs and minimizes inputs. This fulfills the assumptions of 3 E.

This area is critical to achieving unbiased results and there is currently a big debate about what variables should figure in inputs and outputs. Da Cruz and Marques (2014), Lo Storto (2016), and Drew et al. (2018) state that input variables may be similar for all countries, but inputs must be country specific.

In the case of defining outputs, the situation is more difficult. Šťastná and Gregor (2015) and Walker et al. (2017) point to the problem of the great complexity of local government activities. In the research of Narbón-Perpiñá and De Witte (2017a), the following are the most common outputs: the global output indicator (compiled as an index containing the public services provided by the municipalities), total population of the municipality, followed by the area of the municipality and the built-up area. The following are the number of issued permits or processed documents, which express the administrative tasks that the municipality must perform. According to Narbón-Perpiñá and De Witte (2017a), outputs can also be defined by the type of services provided by municipalities, including the following: the number of street lighting points, the length of roads, the amount of processed municipal waste, the number of sports facilities, the number of cultural facilities, the number of recreational facilities, parks, and green areas. Great emphasis is placed on public services in the field of education and provision of social services, such as the number of children attending nursery and elementary schools, the number of elderly, and the number of facilities providing social services to the elderly (Narbón-Perpiñá and De Witte 2017a).

Criticism of this approach comes from Lo Storto (2016), who states that the inclusion of multiple inputs into the analysis can lead to inconsistent results. First, it is very difficult to assign a given input to a particular output. Secondly, the measurements of indicators used as outputs can be affected by a number of factors which cannot be managed and controlled by the municipal government. The whole relationship is also affected by socio-demographic conditions, etc. (Lo Storto 2016).

McQuestin et al. (2018) and Lo Storto (2016) suggest the use of proxy variables; these variables make it possible to reduce the complexity while respecting Nunamaker's rule. Proxies are not precise measures of service output—although they are probably a good reflection of the minimum service need. Lo Storto (2016) argues that proxy indicators used as outputs serve as indirect approximations of the demand for public services delivered to citizens. A suitable proxy variable is the population of the municipality, the size of the municipality, or the number of economic subjects. The great advantage of this approach lies in the possibility of obtaining data from databases of statistical offices in a given country. On the other hand, this approach also has its shortcomings. Drew et al. (2017) argue that using the population as a proxy variable overestimates outputs. We can also work with the number of economic subjects as a proxy variable. Both variables, population and economic subjects, may consume the same public services, based on specific institutional settings in a particular country. In some cases, utilization of both variables could distort the results (Drew et al. 2017).

Table 1.3 summarizes the input and output indicators for efficiency analysis.

Basic fiscal federalism literature aimed at local governments assumes that local politicians operate in a competitive environment. As a result, cities are assumed to produce a level of output that we can consider efficient (Grossman et al. 1999). In particular, we consider the spending option with the lowest costs to be efficient. This assumption makes sense assuming heterogeneous preferences between jurisdictions, in the absence of economies of scale from centralized service provision, and in the absence of interjurisdictional spillovers (Bönisch et al. 2011). The impact of fiscal federalism lies in a better establishment of the relationship between public spending and its funding (Boetti et al. 2012).

The first generation of fiscal federalism perceived this problem as a tradeoff between two kinds of inefficiency (Boetti et al. 2012). The first source of inefficiency is the central provision of public goods and services. Individual communities are assumed to have heterogeneous preferences. A second source of inefficiency is

Table 1.3 Summary of input and output indicators for efficiency analysis (Narbón-Perpiñá and De Witte 2017a; Lo Storto 2016; Drew et al. 2017; Da Cruz and Marquez 2014)

Inputs	
Input category	Input (input types)
Finance	Total expenditure, current expenditure, capital expenditure, financial expenditure, net current expenditure (current expenditure—interest and amortization), personnel expenditures, issued bonds, municipality rating, expenditure on purchases of services, equipment and inventory, expenditure on maintenance of buildings, expenditure of a budget linked to a specific public service or a good for output, value of assets in the balance sheet, value of the municipality's assets, average prices of real estate in the municipality, municipal income, tax revenues, transfers from central government, income from property tax, fees, charges
Non-financial inputs	Number of hospitals, infant mortality rate, number of municipal employees, number of employees allocated for implementation of the given output, area of municipality
Outputs	
Output category	Output (types of output)
Basic Public services: Administrative Infrastructure Communal service	Administrative services (population, civil affairs, number of certificates, requested documents, number of receipts processed, electoral services, the number of planning applications, amount of internal reports issued, number of building permits issued, taxes on construction, square feet of city building space) Street lighting (number of lighting points) Municipal roads (length of roads in the town, pavement, pavement shortage, pavement condition, numbers of vehicles) Waste collection (amount of waste in kg, quintals, tons, populace, number of waste producers) Sewerage services (number of properties receiving sewerage services, number of sewerage connections penetration rate of seweraage, share of households with sewage, waste water treated, sewerage network shortage, sewerage network condition) Water supply (number of properties consuming water services, penetration rate of water supply, share of households with water supply, amount of water, treated flow, water tank capacity, quality condition, water shortage) Electricity (number of consumers, number of households)
Parks, sports, culture and recreational facilities	Sport facilities (surface of indoor and outdoor sporting facilities, quality of sporting facilities) Cultural facilities (number of visits to municipal museums, number of monuments, number of museums and galleries, area of cultural facilities and their quality) Parks (surface area of public parks, area of parks per person, acres of park space in use, number of trees planted, size of urban green area) Recreational facilities (surface area of parks, sports, leisure and other recreational facilities, number of cultural buildings, congress centres, number of sports facilities, e.g. municipal pools, sports halls, courts, race tracks)

(continued)

Table 1.3 (continued)

Health, education, social services	Health (number of health centers, the number of beds, number of visits and bed wards, emergency response time in minutes, number of food handling premises) Kindergartens or nurseries (kindergartens, nurseries, number of students in kindergartens, child population, ratio of the number of children at kindergartens to population) Primary and secondary education (number of students enrolled in primary and secondary schools, ratio of the number of students to population, literate population, number of public schools in a municipality, number of hours of teaching comprehensive and senior secondary school, number of school institutions, the enrollment per school, student attendance per school, students who get promoted to the next grade per school, students in the right grade per school) Social services (number of minimal subsistence grants, retirements or geriatric homes, general assistance for the elderly, medical assistance in public hospitals, number of senior citizens, share of population older than 65 years, days of institutional care for the elderly, elderly patient population) Care for children (children´s day care centers and family day care, the number of approved places in childcare) Social services and organizations (number of social organizations, surface area of assistance centers, seating capacity of social welfare institutions per 100 persons, unemployed population, immigrant population, social protection users in total resident population, number of homes for the disabled, number of days in social centers)
Other (public safety, markets, public transport, environmental protection, business development)	Public safety (existence of municipal police, area of territory police must patrol, number of crimes registered in the municipality, number of interventions and detentions, number of police vehicles in circulation, number of civilian fire deaths, total losses caused by fire) Market (market surface area, number of business lots and stall spaces) Public transport (number of bus stations in a municipality) Environmental protection (urban ecosystem quality, number of economic activities, heavy industrial activities, environmentally degraded areas, built up area and arable land, annual emissions of ozone and sulfur dioxide) Business development (number of employees paying social security, number of jobs in a municipality, unemployment rate, area of industrial region, percentage of inhabitants employed in manufacturing) Others (average house area, aggregate market value of residential and business property, cemetery area)
Global output indicators, quality index	Global output indicators (For example, national administrative data is used, which evaluates the quality of public services or the quality of life in a given municipality, e.g. Comprehensive Performance Assessment in the United Kingdom) Quality index (number of votes as an indicator of citizen satisfaction, number of employees per 10,000 residents)

(continued)

Table 1.3 (continued)

Proxy variables	They are often used to measure global efficiency. There are often cases where we are unable to find a suitable indicator for a given public service or good that would describe the service or the good directly. We therefore use variables that are assumed to have a high correlation with the given output we want to describe. As a classic example, we can use the site's population as a proxy variable for the minimum amount of public goods and services provided. The proxy variable can also be the area of the municipality. This proxy variable expresses the scope of space that the municipality must maintain. The most common proxy variable is the population in a given age category, as a proxy variable for securing public goods and services in the field of education, social and health services

Source Narbón-Perpiñá and De Witte (2017a), Lo Storto (2016), Drew et al. (2017), Da Cruz and Marquez (2014)

the decentralized provision of goods where the local government cannot consider spillovers from other jurisdictions (Boetti et al. 2012).

The new second-generation theories of fiscal federalism perceive tradeoffs between centralization and decentralization as an issue now based on a comparison between the higher degree of policy coordination under centralization (which guarantees the internalization of externalities) and the higher degree of *accountability* of local politicians under decentralization. In this model, we are no longer trying to minimize spending, but to achieve technical and allocation efficiencies (Boetti et al. 2012).

1.4 Key Factors Influencing Local Government Efficiency

In this part, we will try to analyze key factors that influence the efficiency of local governments in the second generation of fiscal federalism.

Information asymmetry, rational ignorance and rational abstention

The first factors to be addressed are information asymmetry (Boetti et al. 2012; Agasisti et al. 2015; Bönisch et al. 2011), rational ignorance and rational abstention (Grossman et al. 1999).[2]

---

[2]Information is a key prerequisite for efficient decision making. Neumann and Morgenstern (2004) show that when decision-makers decide in a case of uncertainty, they are guided by two basic principles in the selection and decision-making, the principle of the magnitude of the utility that a certain decision will give them and the probability of the given variant. Also, local government decisions are usually made under conditions of uncertainty. On the voter's side, we notice a phenomenon for which we use the term "information illusions". Citizens (voters) believe that more information can reduce the uncertainty in decision making. Voters "incorporate" this assumption into their choice of principals (politicians). They are looking for competent politicians whom they think have sufficient information, and the professional and moral potential to perform their public office.

Ideally, voters want the classic principal-agent setting. Principals, who are the residents, want the government to provide as many public goods and services as possible at a given cost. That is why they want competent politicians in office. Citizens rationally assume that competent politicians have (compared to incompetent politicians) a higher capacity for quality decision-making which benefits the citizens. Their competent decision-making brings additional benefits compared to incompetent politicians. Competent politicians can therefore provide more public goods and services at a given level of tax and private consumption. Grossman et al. (1999) consider the government being governed by benevolent politicians as a prerequisite for such government functioning. However, in order to fully exploit the potential of these politicians, it is desirable that they have feedback from their citizens, both with sufficient information and with enough input from citizens. The problem, however, is that there may be situations where citizens provide few incentives for government participation in terms of monitoring government performance.

Empirical research (Ochrana et al. 2007) shows that this condition was typical of the Czech Republic in the first decade of the twenty-first century. Its residues remain evident not only in the Czech Republic but also in other Central European countries of the former Soviet bloc. The method of providing public services takes the form of a so-called 'supplier approach'. Public authorities, as providers of public services, play a decisive role in this, considering insufficiently, if at all, the empirically determined and evaluated demand of citizens for individual public services. Such a way of providing public services leads to inefficient allocation because local government (decision making unit) faces inadequately defined demands from citizens. Local governments do not have the necessary information to adequately determine the priorities and demands of citizens for public services in a given municipality. It is actually a peculiar case of inefficiency, which we can explain on the basis of inspiration from Oates' theorem. This time, however, the allocation inefficiency is not caused by decisions of the central government, but rather by the local government's decisions, where the local government, because of a lack of information, chooses the inefficient option[3] without realizing it.

Inefficiencies could arise because of limited and uninformed participation by citizen voters. In large cities, for example, voters face a very low probability of influencing electoral performance and consequently their motivation to participate is low (Grossman et al. 1999). Those who participate are mostly motivated by special

---

[3]The way to remedy this is to create a customer approach in the provision of public services. In it, citizens have a decisive role as actors who demand public services of a certain quality and quantity. A prerequisite for the functioning of this method of providing public services is the existence of an element (employee of the municipal office) responsible for determining the requirements (demands) of citizens for public services in the given municipality. Query methods and techniques can be a tool for this. The ideal (target status) is such that the given employee of the office, based on the information from the questionnaire, then performs the operationalization of the identified requirements of the public for the qualitative and quantitative parameters of public services. The output is a (variant) recommendation (together with cost-benefit evaluation) on how to appropriately provide the required public services for the given municipality. This proposal is the basis for the council's deliberations and the final decision. This can be improved (especially in the case of larger fiscal units) by implementing the electronization of public administration.

interest and their preferences may be at odds with the preferences of median voters (Grossman et al. 1999). These groups may prefer a higher level of provision of public goods than is considered socially optimal (Grossman et al. 1999). On the other hand, vote maximizing politicians prefer the inefficient use of resources for prestigious investments (state of the art technology) or overlook it for social reasons (Bönisch et al. 2011).

Some studies also mention the importance of the ideological orientation of politicians (Agasisti et al. 2015). Basic intuition states that left-wing governments tend to spend and create inefficiencies (Grossman et al. 1999). One study (McLure 2007) also talks about the existence of a political electoral budget cycle. This theory claims that with upcoming elections, public spending increases inefficiently to prove competence (Boetti et al. 2012) and secure re-election (Plaček et al. 2016). Ineffective expenditures can be manifested, for example, by investments in projects that are due to be completed shortly before the elections, or by non-investment transfers to citizens, sports clubs and associations (Plaček et al. 2016).

The citizens' only defense are the so-called Exit and Voice mechanisms. However, these mechanisms work better in small jurisdictions where there is more competition between municipalities and lower transaction costs for moving to another municipality. In smaller municipalities, the transaction costs of obtaining government performance information can also be considered to be smaller and the weight of the voice to be greater. This reduces information asymmetry between principals and agents and limits the possibility of wasteful spending and rent extraction. Some other models consider the options as incomplete contract. In this approach, centralization vs. decentralization is a tradeoff between the possibility of internalizing spillover effects and the loss of accountability in the sense that wealth in a given jurisdiction can affect election results.

For this problem, we must also take into account the opportunistic behavior of the central government, which may discriminate against certain regions as a result of so-called pork barrel policy (Boetti et al. 2012). It should be noted that this "discrimination of the government" (and its inefficiency) is not necessarily deliberate by the government. It may be caused by other factors that may have a negative impact on the efficient decision making of local government. We can mention, for example, the factor of "time constraints." Local governments operate under significant time constraints. They simultaneously solve a number of problems, which are not finite. Time constraints thus limit both the range and the number of variants offered. Policymakers are under constant pressure when deciding, creating, and selecting options. This can have a negative impact on allocation efficiency.

Bureaucratic behavior
Another factor that affects the resulting efficiency is the behavior of bureaucrats. The term "bureaucracy" (in public administration) is used with three basic levels of meaning. First, it means the actions (procedures) performed by these officials. Secondly, the term "bureaucracy" means a layer of public administration officials, hierarchized according to delegated power over officials. Third, bureaucracy means the exercise of power resulting from the delegation of powers to officials.

Fig. 1.3 Bureaucracy, voter
and politics as a relationship
of principal and agent

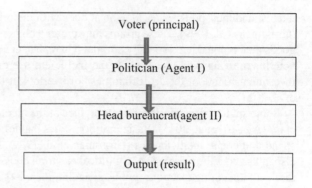

There are several theoretical approaches that we can apply to problem analysis. The main streams include the classic Niskannen model of bureaucracy (Niskanen 1975; Tullock 1965), the aforementioned principal agent theory, stewardship theory, and resource dependency theory. We can consider social network theory, transaction costs, and life cycle theory as complementary theories.

Niskanen's model (1975) argues that bureaucrats try to maximize their institution's budget and, as a result, become inefficient. In terms of public choice, bureaucracy acts as a special interest group. It is a rational actor that strives to maximize its own utility function. Bureaucracy has a monopoly on information and has information superiority over politicians (principals). It can therefore relatively easily enforce decisions that pursue the preferences of bureaucracy in public elections. This is reflected, for example, in the fact that bureaucracy tends to maximize the budget of the public organization in which the bureaucracy is employed.[4] The bureaucrat can also influence the agenda, i.e. determine the process and order of discussion of the problems to be solved. As a result, bureaucrats can influence the outcome of the public choice by their strategic behavior.

As Agasisti et al. (2015) show, bureaucrats also tend to create a so-called pillow. This involves creating artificial reserves in the organization's budget, which will enable the organization to run without the need to implement efficiency measures. Bureaucrats also tend to prefer a higher labor/capital mix than what would be optimal. Bureaucrats also reveal preferences for tangible rather than intangible inputs. Ultimately, the bureaucracy's behavior resembles that of a monopoly, thus producing fewer public goods and services at a higher cost than is socially optimal.

The principal agent theory applied to the behavior of bureaucracy is very similar to that of a policy voter relationship. Graphically, we can illustrate the problem of the relationship between the principal (tenant) and agent as follows (Fig. 1.3).

The voter (citizen) acts as a principal. He is a tenant who, in the public election, chooses his proxy to assert his interests. The agent is a politician. The voter "chooses"

---

[4]This, for example, results in bureaucracy trying to spend all available resources by the end of the budget year, regardless of the criterion of the efficiency and effectiveness of such an allocation. A characteristic feature of bureaucracy is that it "quasi-identifies itself with the system," and thus the public interest or the actual mission of the organization can be ignored.

him in the public election, assuming that he will promote his interests. The politician is in the role of "Agent I." He entrusts the head bureaucrat, acting as Agent II, with the realization of his intentions. The head bureaucrat has other bureaucrats as subordinates. They are "end-of-the-line officials" who execute the politician's decisions (Agent I) and the orders of their supervisor (Agent II). The bureaucrat is therefore the final link in the whole process of realizing the output of the public choice. Thus, a bureaucrat (having an information monopoly) can significantly influence the outcome of a public choice by their strategic behavior. Their behavior may have a negative impact on allocation efficiency.

Again, we encounter the problem of information asymmetry and the resulting transaction costs required for agent control (Nordberg 2011). We assume that bureaucrats tend to be opportunistic. This opportunistic behavior manifests itself in the above-described efforts to maximize budget, create pillows, rent annuities or corruption (Aras and Crowther 2010). Thus, information asymmetry arises not only in relation to voters but also in relation to politicians who bear ultimate responsibility for results. The resulting information asymmetry can lead to moral hazard, where an informed actor can maximize his benefit at the expense of the public sector (the uninformed actor). On the basis of information asymmetry, there may be inefficient choice of the variant, which will displace the higher quality offered service with a lower quality service. This is a manifest breach by the public sector of the VFM (Value for Money) principle, which, however, is difficult for the principals to discern because they do not have sufficient information and monitoring tools. To some extent, this negative consequence can be eliminated provided that the standard of the required service is clearly defined by the principal. In practice, however, in some cases it is difficult to fully fulfill this assumption. This applies in particular to cases where the government purchases a good or service the quality of which can only be demonstrated with a longer time lag. In such cases, the quality of the service will only be reflected ex post, i.e. after it has been purchased.

Contrary to principal agent theory, stewardship theory is based on a psychological and sociological approach (Madison et al. 2016). This theory does not regard bureaucrats as individuals whose main goal is to maximize benefits, but as servants whose real desire is to serve. The interests of bureaucrats are therefore in line with the interests of politicians and voters. Inefficiency arises from honest incompetence according to (Kauppi and Van Raaij 2015), who claim that information asymmetry arises on both sides of the principal agent relationship. A case of honest incompetence can be induced by a number of factors, such as the aforementioned decision making under conditions of bilateral uncertainty or time constraints. It can also be caused by the "paradox of exhausted professional competence".[5] The consequence is a negative impact on efficiency.

---

[5]These are cases known from the Czech Republic, when politicians ascend to higher floors (functions) until they reach a place where they no longer have the professional capacity. The system (and practices) are set up in the Czech Republic so that politicians do not return to a "lower level," i.e. to the previous function, which corresponds to their professional capacities, but after a certain time can move on to a higher position within the EU office (even as a commissioner …).

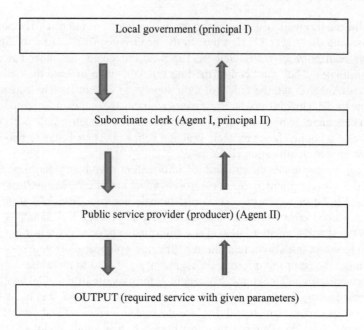

Fig. 1.4 Acquisition of a service as a principal-agent relationship

Not even bureaucrats have a perfect idea of what the demands of politicians and citizens are. According to source dependency theory, bureaucrats face pressure from external actors. The theory seeks to build legitimacy and acceptance for these actors (Hessels and Terjesen 2010). The decisive factor is their dependence on different sources. This determines their final actions. Organizations seek to raise additional resources and minimize reliance on existing resources. In the case of a lack of resources, organizations are forced to innovate and increase their efficiency. However, this is not the case in the public sector environment because organizations are not at risk of extinction due to a lack of resources. The pressure on innovation and efficiency is therefore lower.

Efficiency losses can also occur as a result of the so-called administrative effect. This arises from the activity of a bureaucrat who is entrusted by the politician with the task of "administering" the public service tender. Principal-agent theory (Pratt and Zeckhauser 1986) provides a conceptual framework for explanation. Graphically, the problem can be expressed as follows (Fig. 1.4):

Local government authorities act as principal I. They make the initial decisions on how to provide a particular service. They choose between their own production and external contracting. If the local government decides to provide external security services, it entrusts a subordinate official (bureaucrat) to execute its decision. The latter acts as agent I with regard to his superior. Principal I empowers him to prepare documents for external outsourcing of the purchased service and for the subsequent implementation of the procurement process. The official thus acts in a dual role. In relation to a tenderer for a given service, the official is a principal (principal II) because it is he who prepares, organizes, and administers the whole process. In relation to the politician, he is agent I. In relation to an external public service provider, he is also the principal (principal II), who was authorized by his superior to carry out the process required for the external acquisition of the service.

This dual position of bureaucrats may lead to efficiency losses, either because of the aforementioned information asymmetry (Niskanen 1975) or due to the lack of transparency of the award procedures (Strand et al. 2011) and induced higher cost of procurement (Stehlík 2018). Losses in efficiency may also arise as a result of low monitoring of award procedures by the principal (principal I), who focuses primarily on adherence to formal aspects of award procedures. The economic side of 3E tracking is secondary or is significantly lacking. The consequence is a negative impact on the efficient provision of public services.

Competition among municipalities
Local government efficiency studies show that competition among municipalities is another important factor affecting efficiency. According to Tiebout (1956) and Brennan and Buchanan (1980), this is a phenomenon that manifests itself through the mechanism of voting with one's feet. According to Grossman et al. (1999), the level of competition faced by local politicians lies not only in the number of competing municipalities, but also in the degree to which these municipalities are perceived as efficient substitutes. We consider the mobility costs, transaction costs as well as the characteristics of the locality such as the location, climate, amenities, state of the public infrastructure, security, recreational areas, and the range of services provided by the city. For example, the decision to move to a big city reveals a demand for the goods and services this big city provides. We can assume that a large city provides, for example, better infrastructure, and greater access to educational, cultural and health services. An efficient substitute must offer a similar number of services (Grossman et al. 1999). In the short term, there is a choice of cities in close proximity but in the longer term we can consider all cities in the country as competitors.

Another possible manifestation of competition among cities is mimicking the provision of public goods of their neighbors (Šťastná 2011). There are two ways to do this. First, it is explained by the yardstick competition. If incompletely informed voters evaluate the performance of their government, they can take policies pursued by its neighbors as a yardstick that helps to improve information on the costs of running the office or public service provision (Šťastná 2011, p. 63). The second option is that the local government itself lacks perfect information. To avoid information costs such as the cost of analyzing the demand of its residents or elaborating cost-benefit analysis, local government tends to mimic the decisions of its neighbors (Šťastná 2011, p. 63).

The new phenomenon of big data also strengthens the competitive effect. There are currently several projects that will allow a comparison of cities in a given country or region; for example, in the Czech Republic there is the project "Municipalities in Data," which uses publicly available information to assess cities according to quality of life. Citizens are provided with indices describing cities in terms of health and the environment, material security, relationships and services. The project also offers an algorithm that is able to find the optimal location according to predefined preferences.

Such a benchmarking option creates a market mechanism (Nemec et al. 2008; Plaček et al. 2014), which leads to improvement in performance and the setting of standards in an environment where these standards are not set (Meričková et al. 2009). "Implementation of this method to a system of public management contributes to the development of a competitive environment not only in public administration, but also between public administration and private institutions in the provision of public services." (Meričková et al. 2009). In the municipal environment, the implementation of the quasi-market mechanism leads to the following effects:

- Increases average performance;
- Improves the situation for those with lower levels of performance;
- Decreases performance differences (Tillema and Van Hellden 2005).

A mechanism that impedes the implementation of these quasi-competitive mechanisms is the "Naming and Shaming" phenomenon (Kuhlman and Jäkel 2013). Political representation resists these mechanisms because good results are valued by the public and bad ones panned. This leads to resistance and an attempt only to prove performance at the level of "good enough" (Plaček et al. 2014). This behavior obscures the real problem. In general, a "problem" only becomes a problem when it is perceived as a mismatch between the ideal (expected) state and what the government needs to do to resolve it (Béland and Howlett 2016, p. 222). But the proclaimed level of "good enough" does not correspond to reality. On the part of the political representation, it is a masking of the problem, where it remains unnamed and avoided. The consequence is to remain in the existing inefficient state.

Fiscal illusion

Other aspects that might influence municipal efficiency could be subsumed under the term "fiscal illusion" (Boetti et al. 2012). Fiscal illusion refers to systematic misperception of fiscal parameters—a recurring propensity, for example, to underestimate one's tax liability associated with public programs (Oates 1972, p. 67). According to Dollery and Hamburger (1996, p. 262) the concept of fiscal illusion revolves around the proposition that the true costs and benefits of government may be consistently misconstrued by a citizenry in a given jurisdiction. At first glance, the term "fiscal illusion" appears to be a synonym for imperfect information. However, imperfect information is only a necessary, but not sufficient condition for fiscal illusion.

Imperfect information alone might well give rise to a random pattern of over or underestimation of such tax liabilities (Oates 1972, p. 67). Fiscal illusion in contrast, implies persistent and consistent behavior (Oates 1972, p. 67). It will lead to recurring, and presumably predictive biases in budgetary decisions (Oates 1972, p. 67). Therefore, fiscal illusion leads to a public sector of excessive size, since the cost of public programs is systematically underestimated, not the benefits of public programs. It should also be noted that fiscal illusion can inherently occur only to a limited extent. A certain type of taxation can remain hidden for taxpayers if it affects only a small part of their income. As this taxation increases, affects an increasing portion of the taxpayer's income, or becomes progressive, it is very difficult to hide

(Oates 1972, p. 68). Oates (1972) notes that there are the following five forms of fiscal illusion:

(1) complexity of the tax structure
(2) renter illusion with respect to property taxation
(3) income elasticity of the tax structure
(4) debt illusion
(5) the flypaper effect.

In the case of the complexity of the tax structure, misperception of the tax price occurs as a result of the fragmentation of the revenue system (Dollery and Hamburger 1996). The total tax revenue from the taxation of an individual may be higher if a greater number of smaller taxes are imposed than with a high tax burden resulting from only one or more taxes, without being perceived as such. As the complexity of the tax system increases or the simplicity of this system decreases, the perceived price of public goods decreases. It is very difficult for the taxpayer to identify the price of public goods and services. Even if the taxpayer is still able to do so, the cost of finding the necessary information outweighs the benefits (Dollery and Hamburger 1996). The more complex the tax system is, the greater the fiscal illusions and the public spending.

The second form of fiscal illusion is the so-called renter illusion. In this case, an increase in the share of renters in the jurisdiction leads to an increase in public spending. We assume that one of the main revenues of local budgets is property tax. Property tax falls directly on property owners, who as a result are able to calculate the price of the local public good. Of course, a higher property tax will affect tenants through increased rents. However, the theory argues that a disjunction exists between rental voter's perception of the level of public goods and services and the level of rents paid (Dollery and Hamburger 1996). This illusion does not last forever, but as long as tax prices are underestimated, renting voters will support higher levels of public expenditure. The ability of the renting voters' group to influence the growth of public spending will depend on the size of the group.

Another form of fiscal illusion is the revenue elasticity hypothesis. Revenue systems assessed with a high degree of income elasticity will attract larger increments in general income, and this increase will be automatically funneled into increased expenditure (Dollery and Hamburger 1996). Taxpayers are not interested in increasing public expenditure unless they are funded by an increase in tax rates, i.e. where they are financed solely by an increase in revenue. However, if tax rates are raised, they will stop supporting the increase in public spending. Taxpayers therefore perceive their tax rate more than their actual tax bill (Dollery and Hamburger 1996).

It is also worth mentioning a significant form of fiscal illusion called debt illusion. This theoretical approach states that voters are more aware of the cost of public sector programs paid through taxes than through public debt. Individuals are unable to calculate the future benefits and costs of governmental activity at any given time. Debt is a claim against future public tax revenues. Therefore, this way of financing public spending programs will only be reflected in future tax increases. However, the taxpayer is not able to convert future debt payments to present value.

The taxpayer does not have adequate knowledge ("awareness") of the debt. If the taxpayer is aware, it is a distorted view of debt. Debt then appears to the taxpayer as an illusion, a misinterpreted phenomenon. That's why debt illusion is worth mentioning.

Theory distinguishes two types of debt illusion (Dollery and Hamburger 1996). The first is called Vickrey type decision illusion, where an individual subjective assessment of debt on future tax liabilities was undervalued (Dollery and Hamburger 1996). The second case of debt illusion is the so-called Puviani-type behavioral distinction where the subjective assessment of the diminution of the value of assets is not treated (Dollery and Hamburger 1996). It is argued that in local government environments where property tax is the dominant source of income, property prices may decrease as a result of the increase in the debt of the site. That occurs, however, provided mobility of voters between jurisdictions will not fully capitalize debt into property prices.

The last form of fiscal illusion is the flypaper effect of grants and utility profits. In the case of the flypaper effect, categorical lump sum grants increase public spending by more than the equivalent increase in income from other sources (Dollery and Hamburger 1996). Politicians hide the lump-sum nature of grant revenues. Instead of increasing income tax burdens indirectly, e.g. through tax credits or a reduction in tax contributions, they use grants to increase public budgets (Dollery and Hamburger 1996). This is used by politicians to spread the illusion that in addition to actual average tax rates falling, there has been a reduction in the marginal tax price of public goods (Dollery and Hamburger 1996). In general, the results have indicated that intergovernmental grants are an important determinant of the level of public goods expenditure (Dollery and Hamburger 1996). These grants therefore reduce the average price for recipients of public goods, and voters make their allocation decisions more on the basis of this price than on the marginal tax price. Another effect of grants is that grants cause voters to consider their tax burden as being transferred to other jurisdictions. The utility profit illusion also works very similarly. Utility or public domain profits are used in internal subsidization to reduce the perceived tax price of public goods expenditure (Dollery and Hamburger 1996). The result is very similar to the flypaper effect as it also leads to an increase in the level of expenditure. The only difference is that grants will be exogenous rather than endogenous to local government ownership, in contrast to utility profits (Dollery and Hamburger 1996).

The previous section devoted to the description of individual types of fiscal illusions explained how public expenditures are increasing due to fiscal illusions. The amount of public expenditure is necessarily linked to the concept of efficiency, where public expenditure creates inputs on the part of the public sector. Increasing inputs when outputs are not increased necessarily leads to efficiency losses. It is true that the cost effect relation is given by the relation C/E, where C is the cost (expressed in monetary units) and E is the output effects (number of natural units of output). Rising inputs and unchanged outputs mean higher costs per unit of output, which means lower efficiency.

Efficiency literature (Narbón-Perpiñá and De Witte 2017a, b) pays attention only to some forms of fiscal illusion. Bönisch et al. (2011), Kalb (2010), (Balaguer-Coll et al. 2007), Da Cruz and Marques (2014), Doumpos and Cohen (2014), Pacheco et al.

(2014), Agasisti et al. (2015), Peréz-Lopéz et al. (2015), Šťastná and Gregor (2015), and Yusfany (2015) focus on debt illusion and intergovernmental grants. In the case of debt illusion, there may be two opposite effects on efficiency. The first effect is positive. We assume that the municipality has a low fiscal capacity and therefore increases its debt to cover its expenses. Increasing indebtedness makes municipalities more vulnerable and also forces them to seek operational savings. This is the so-called fiscal stress approach (Narbón-Perpiñá and De Vitte 2017a, b; Balaguer-Coll et al. 2007). Higher indebtedness may also be the result of previous investments, which may increase the efficiency of the municipality. The negative effect of indebtedness can manifest itself in lower pressure from citizens to achieve efficiency on the part of municipalities (Balaguer-Coll et al. 2007). Another possibility is that expenditure related to repayment of principal and interest on debt reduces the possibility of financing the goods and services provided by the municipality (Narbón-Perpiñá and De Vitte 2017a, b).

Intergovernmental grants and transfers

Intergovernmental grants and transfers can affect the efficiency of municipalities in several ways. In addition to the aforementioned fiscal illusion, the principle of fiscal equivalence is violated through intergovernmental grants. Fiscal equivalence means that the local government has the right to decide how many public goods and services will be produced and how they will be financed (Bönisch et al. 2011). In many systems, the central government (e.g. education, social services) determines the production of public goods and services at the local level, which determines the volume of production and the standards of delivery of these services. The central government pays intergovernmental grants to local governments on the basis of the "he who gives the orders, has to pay" rule. Municipalities tend to treat these grants differently than the money they receive through local taxes from citizens. If output quantities are more or less fixed, the municipality tends to use those large input quantities inefficiently, for example by investing in large prestigious buildings. Another source of inefficiency in this area may be the so-called "soft budget constraints" if most of the activities of local governments are funded through inter-municipal grants (Bönisch et al. 2011).

On the other hand, intergovernmental grants can increase efficiency as central governments can place more emphasis on controlling the use of this money. In this case, this means that the greater the central government's control over the use of funds, the greater the pressure on local governments to be efficient (Narbón-Perpiñá and De Vitte 2017a, b). However, central governmental control may be effective if there is a functional control system that monitors both the formal (accounting and documenting) aspect of expenditure activities and the economic effect of the expenditure incurred based on performance audits. In the Czech Republic (and most of the Central and Eastern European countries of the former Soviet bloc) no such system has worked yet. Generally accepted auditing as practiced in the public sector of the Czech Republic focuses primarily on the formal (accounting and documentation) aspect of expenditure activities. There are no performance audits. This is also one of the factors affecting inefficient allocation of centrally provided expenditures.

Municipality size

In the previous sections, we described in great detail how asymmetry of information and the behavior of politicians and bureaucrats have an impact on efficiency. We assumed that the problem of information asymmetry and the demand for account-ability of politicians and officials in large municipalities is greater than in smaller municipalities and should lead to lower efficiency. On the other hand, the theory points to the advantages of larger municipalities in relation to the possibility of increasing efficiency through economies of scale (McQuestin et al. 2018; Bönisch et al. 2011; Drew et al. 2015; Peréz-Lopéz et al. 2018; Doumpos and Cohen 2014).

Drew et al. (2015) describe the logic of how economies of scale work with state-ments like "bigger is cheaper" and "bigger is better." These statements can be inter-preted as meaning that larger municipalities providing public goods and services to larger populations have the advantage of lower administrative costs and greater pur-chasing power (Drew et al. 2015). Reduced costs can result either from economies of scale from production technologies, or from economies of sharing. Under economies of sharing, we can imagine the benefit of the non-rivalrous consumption of public goods and services (e.g. land) (Bönisch et al. 2011).

Economic theory argues that to a certain point the cost curve is U-shaped because increasing outputs reduce average fixed costs, but only up to a certain size of pro-duction, as coordination costs can outweigh reduced average fixed costs and average costs begin to rise again. It is also important to monitor the components of costs. Labor-intensive services generate few economies of scale because their idiosyncratic nature means that increased volume of services may require correspondingly large numbers of personnel (Drew et al. 2015, p. 6) whereas other services involve capital intensive production, such as water supply and other utilities.

This theory is also reflected in public policy through the merger of municipali-ties (McQuestin et al. 2018), the main motive of which is achieving cost-efficiency. Other benefits include better recruitment, greater employee specialization, a change in boundaries that is determined by the true nature of work processes, for example in recreation and education, rather than by historical roots. Other benefits are more effi-cient planning and provision, reduced interjurisdictional spillovers when individuals benefit from public spending of neighboring jurisdictions (McQuestin et al. 2018). Last but not least, it is necessary to mention that the connected municipalities have greater bargaining power when negotiating with the central government. On the other hand, problems arise in merging municipalities. Among the most serious is the loss of local identity and accountability.

From the economic point of view, there are also problems with the cost of coor-dination. McQuestin et al. (2018) also say that the very process of merging munici-palities, which is involuntary and without the participation of the actors involved, is very problematic.

Peréz-Lopéz et al. (2015), Campos-Alba et al. (2019) talk about the possibility of using managerial models based on New Public Management theory as an alternative to merging municipalities. These models are based on economies of scope. Economies of scope means achieving savings through joint operation of selected public services (Campos-Alba et al. 2019). This can be done through privatization, contracting out, mixed firms, agency and municipal cooperation.

Privatization is the first of these managerial schemes to make sense if demand for public goods and services is aggregated. If the private sector offers similar services to more municipalities, the scale of production and cost saving will increase (Peréz-Lopéz et al. 2015). However, the municipality loses control over the provision of these goods and services as they are provided on the basis of a market mechanism.

This negative can be addressed by a variant associated with contracting out, where the municipality retains control over the production and financing of the public goods and services. Only the realization of the public goods and services is transferred to the private sector. The benefit of this option should be greater efficiency of production assurance, provided at lower cost due to competition among suppliers.

A possible alternative to the previous two options is the creation of mixed firms. This is a collaboration between the public and private sectors, which will result in the creation of a joint company that provides selected public goods and services. Private sector partner funds could be used for financing public service delivery. Risks are also shared.

Another option is to create municipal agencies that operate on the same principles as private companies, achieving greater efficiency primarily through management autonomy and the provision of personalized services (Peréz-Lopéz et al. 2015).

However, the above approaches remain inaccessible to small municipalities. The reason for this is that, for example, public contracts announced by a small municipality may not be of sufficient interest to the private sector due to their size and expected profit rate. Another risk is that the municipality does not have sufficient resources at its disposal and does not perform public service to the extent that it would make sense to create agencies. Therefore, no benefit from economies of scale is available (Peréz-Lopéz et al. 2015). Inter-municipal cooperation seems to be the optimal solution. Specific forms of inter-municipal cooperation depend on the national context. Often, neighboring municipalities agree to create a common entity that is jointly managed, share common resources and pursue a common goal of providing public goods and services. This achieves economies of scale and provides public goods and services efficiently. This approach also makes cooperating municipalities more attractive to private suppliers, allowing municipalities to benefit from the competitive advantage (Peréz-Lopéz et al. 2015).

On the other hand, it is also necessary to mention the negatives of all the above approaches. Potential efficiency is limited by transaction costs; moral hazard, adverse selection or poor-quality services may be difficult to measure for public utilities (Bönisch et al. 2011, p. 5). Risks also arise for services with high capital costs and high risk of sunk cost, as these services are mainly realized through long-term cooperation and both sides strive for strategic behavior and try to transfer as much risk as possible to the counterparty. It is also worth mentioning the problem of

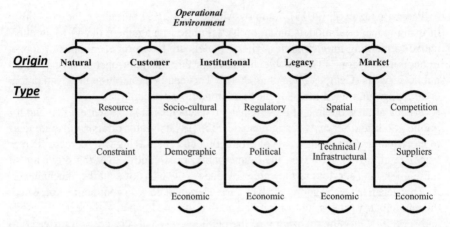

Fig. 1.5 General taxonomy of the operational environment of municipalities. *Source* Da Cruz and Marquez (2014, p. 93)

coordination costs, which rise along with the number of actors involved (Bönisch et al. 2011).

Environmental and institutional environment

Efficiency literature also discusses other factors that may have an impact on the efficiency of local governments, and which are not directly related to the theory of fiscal federalism, but ultimately may have a significant impact on efficiency. However, research in this area is very fragmented and the classification of these factors often differs. Da Cruz and Marquez (2014) propose a general taxonomy of the operational environment of municipalities. This taxonomy is represented in the following Fig. 1.5.

The scheme describes external factors that influence the performance of local governments according to the origin and type of factors. Natural conditions, customers, institutions, legacy, and market can be considered as factors of origin. This results in determinants such as resources and constraints.

Natural conditions represent factors influenced by natural conditions such as climate, topography, geology, and biodiversity (Da Cruz and Marquez 2014). Customer related aspects affect the behavior, characteristics of service end users, clients, population, and major stakeholders. The resulting determinants are socio-cultural, demographic, and economic (Da Cruz and Marquez 2014). Institutional origin describes determinants that originate in the capacity and behavior of institutions. These are mainly factors linked to regulation, policy and the economy (Da Cruz and Marquez 2014). Other determinants can be considered legacy-related, which can be seen as results of past decisions. The resulting determinants are spatial, technical, infrastructural, and economic. The last agent of the determinants is the market, respectively the behavior of the markets in which local governments operate. Competition, suppliers, and economics can be considered as determinants (Da Cruz and Marquez 2014).

Narbón-Perpiñá and De Vitte (2017b) propose the following general breakdown into six main categories: social and demographic, political, financial, economic, geographical or natural, institutional or managerial. Unlike Da Cruz and Marquez (2014), this breakdown is narrower. Both authors then provide a concrete list of determinants of efficiency. Table 1.4 summarizes the efficiency determinants of Da Cruz and Marquez (2014) and Narbón-Perpiñá and De Vitte (2017a, b).

Da Cruz and Marquez (2014) and Narbón-Perpiñá and De Vitte (2017a, b) state that it is not possible to fully describe the effect of all these variables on efficiency. According to these authors, empirical studies often report conflicting results. Da Cruz and Marquez (2014) and Narbón-Perpiñá and De Vitte (2017a, b) state that the interpretation of these results should be based on individual country conditions.

1.5   Lesson Learned from the Theory of Fiscal Decentralization and Efficiency Literature

In this section of the book, conclusions will be presented from a literature analysis dealing with factors influencing local government efficiency.

In general, the so-called literature of efficiency in municipalities can be divided into several streams, namely empirical, theoretical and meta-analysis. Within the empirical stream, the following types of studies were identified (D'Inverno et al. 2018) including individual public services, solid waste, sewage disposal, water, energy provision, hospitals, municipal savings banks, public libraries, road maintenance, fire protection, the sector of care for the elderly, local police services, public transportation and pre-school education. The second branch is in studies that analyze global municipal efficiency for various countries. Another possibility of categorizing empirical studies is the following types of studies from the point of view of public policy assessment (McQuestin et al. 2018): (1) compare the relative efficiencies of municipalities and make inferences regarding the optimal size of these councils, (2) identify which councils in particular are relatively technically inefficient, (3) evaluate the impact of council mergers, and (4) determine the impact of environmental factors on the efficiency of councils.

The theoretical branch of literature is currently centered mainly on modifying methods, e.g. Walker et al. (2018) focus on effects of information about effectiveness, which can depend on its combination with information about efficiency or equities; a similar trade off was dealt with by Lo Storto (2016). Others are enhancing efficiency analysis with other levels such as four stage DEA (Zheng et al. 2018), six stage DEA (Wang and Geng 2017), or hybrid window DEA (Halkos and Polemis, 2018) which integrates radial and non-radial efficiency measurements in DEA using the hybrid measure, while extending the proposed model by considering desirable and undesirable outputs as separable and non-separable. The application by Peréz-Lopéz, et al. (2018) of a new method for calculating time-invariant and time-variant scale inefficiency using DEA panel data estimates an approach that allows for the

Table 1.4 Summarization of the efficiency determinants

Da Cruz and Marquez (2014): Revisiting the determinants of local government performance

Natural determinants	Citizen related determinants	Institutional determinants	Legacy determinants
Resource (heritage, number of tourist-accommodation facilities, tourism)	Socio-cultural (democratic participation, development index, educational level, existence of free voters unions, newspaper reach, index of well being, primary education, secondary education, share of local lists in the council, tertiary education, voter turnout)	Regulatory (budgetary institutions, decentralization level)	Spatial (amalgamation, area, distance to the district capital, number of neighboring cities, scale)
Constraint (environmental sensitivity)	Demographic (age group, commuter share, eligible voters, immigrant share, population, population density, population growth, population over 65, population under 14, religious population, share of workers, share of homeowners, unemployment, urban population, household size)	Political ideology (Ideology, liberal and socialist parties, number of municipal council seats, number of years of mayoral term, political fragmentation/concentration, shares of votes received by the strongest party, type of government	Technical/Infrastructural (existence of libraries, information index, infrastructure investment, number of police officers)

(continued)

Table 1.4 (continued)

Economic (income, purchasing power)	Economic (commerce, establishments, fiscal autonomy, fiscal capacity, industry, service related establishments, share of block grants, share of expenditure of service costs, size of block grants)	Economic (debt service, fees and charges, financial deficit, financial liabilities, property tax rate, tax burden)

Narbón–Perpiñá and De Vitte (2017a, b): Local government efficiency: A systematic literature review—part II

Category	Factors
Social and demographic determinants	Population density, population growth, population size, age distribution of population, education level, immigration share and ethnic diversity, share of homeowners, other related social and demographic characteristics
Economic determinants	Unemployment, citizen income, economic status, tourism, commercial activity, industrial activity, other related economic characteristics
Political determinants	Ideological position, political deconcentration/fragmentation and strengths, voter turnout and potential electors, re-election and number of years until the next election, other related political characteristics
Financial determinants	Self-generated revenues, transfers or grants, debt or financial liabilities, fiscal surplus, infrastructure investment, other related financial characteristics
Geographical and natural determinants	Distance from the center and localization effects, area, type of municipalities, other factors related to geographical or natural characteristics
Institutional and management determinants	Informatization or level of computer usage, characteristics of mayor and local government employees, amalgamation, managerial forms, other factors related to institutional or management characteristics

Source Da Cruz and Marquez (2014), Narbón–Perpiñá and De Vitte (2017a, b) analysis of the evolution of scale inefficiency over a period of time. Galariotis et al. (2016) follow a benchmarking perspective and introduce a multi-attribute financial evaluation model that allows peer assessments to be made, including comparisons over time, while differentiating between managerial performance and the effect of the external environment.

Another part of the studies is a summary analysis of the application of nonparametric methods in municipalities. Narbón-Perpiñá and De Witte (2017a, b) offer a comprehensive review of the existing literature on local government efficiency from a global point of view covering all articles from 1990 to August 2016. The authors deal with efficiency studies of local governments in each country, assess data used, sample sizes, and results. In the second part of their study, they deal with techniques for calculating efficiency, then summarize the inputs and outputs used to evaluate efficiency and the main determinants of efficiency. Aiello et al. (2017) use Meta Regression Analysis (MRA), examining 360 efficiency scores retrieved from 54 papers published from 1993 to 2016 in order to evaluate the role played by the features of each paper (i.e. estimation method, sample size, dimension, returns to scale) in explaining the differences in results. The main conclusions include that focusing on technical efficiency provides higher efficiency scores than cost-effectiveness evaluators, researchers using panel data report higher efficiency, using panel data means reporting higher efficiencies than cross-sectional data, and FDH studies yield, on average, higher efficiency scores than DEA papers. A more specific research study by Emrouznejad and Yang (2018) focuses primarily on the use of DEA and evaluates the academic experience with this tool over the last 40 years.

Unlike the existing literature review, our review focuses more closely on articles that examine the efficiency of local governments in the context of variables related to the theory of fiscal federalism. So we have focused primarily on financial and secondary political variables. Our approach is based on a literature review (Da Cruz and Marquez 2014; Narbón-Perpiñá and De Witte 2017a, b) and our own research in the Web of Science database. We entered the keywords "Local Government" and "Fiscal Decentralization" into the Web of Science database. A total of 628 results (or outputs) were found. These results were then narrowed by adding another keyword, "Efficiency," which yielded a total of 76 articles. From these articles, the articles that correspond to the search objectives, i.e. a total of 21 articles, were selected based on a full reading.

Table 1.5 presents the summary results of the review literature.

The results of the research show that in the area of fiscal decentralization's impact on the efficiency of local governments, the results provided by current articles are considerably mixed. Differences in the concept of variables that describe fiscal and political variables, as well as primarily the resulting influence of these variables, are strongly country specific. Very often, the results contradict the theoretical assumptions and therefore differ not only geographically but also over time.

Table 1.5 Summary results of the review literature

Variables	Possibility of expressing	Mechanism of action	Impact on efficiency/country/reference
Amalgamation	Combination of DEA inputs and outputs	Efficiency, economies of scale, better strategic capacity	Negative/Australia/(Drew et al. 2015), Negative/Australia/(McQuestin et al. 2018)
Fiscal autonomy	Local tax and service charges as percentage of total revenue, expenses covered by income tax, tax burden (local taxes)	Better match expenditure with revenue needs, matching produced level of public goods and services with preference of citizens, higher accountability	Positive/South Africa/(Monkam 2014), positive/Belgium/(De Borger and Kerstens 1996a, b), positive/Italy/(Boetti et al. 2012), positive/Portugese/(Da Cruz and Marquez 2014), negative/Greece/(Doumpos and Cohen 2014), positive/Spain/(Benito et al. 2010)
	Grants from upper level of government per capita, log (grants/per population), independent vs dependent municipalities according to grants, grant revenues greater than median, revenue/subsidies, equalization of transfers as percentage of total adjusted current income	Fly paper effect, a greater share of central government grants means a lower ability to control for voters	Negative/Belgium/(De Borger and Kerstens 1996a, b), negative/Spain/(Balaguer-Coll et al. 2010), negative/Germany/(Geys and Moesen, 2009), negative/Italy/(Boetti et al. 2012), Negative/Chile/(Pacheco et al. 2014), negative/Indonesia/(Yusfany 2015), negative/Spain/(Peréz-Lopéz et al. 2015), positive/Norway/(Kalb 2010), negative/Spain/(Balaguer-Coll and Prior, 2009), negative/Italy/(Porcelli, 2014), negative/Czech Republic/(Štastná and Gregor 2015), negative/Greece/(Doumpos and Cohen 2014), positive/Germany/(Bönisch et al. 2011), negative/USA, (Grossman et al. 1999),

(continued)

Table 1.5 (continued)

Variables	Possibility of expressing	Mechanism of action	Impact on efficiency/country/reference
	Tax revenue–Log (tax revenue/population), tax revenue larger than the median	A government, which receives a large amount of tax revenues is not motivated to spend effectively	Negative/Spain/(Balaguer-Coll et al 2010), negative/Italy/(Boetti et al. 2012), negative/Chile/(Pacheco et al. 2014), positive/Belgium/(De Borger and Kerstens 1996a, b)
	Fiscal capacity–Log (own revenues/population), dependency on common municipal fund relative to self generated income, fiscal capacity > fiscal need, working capital	The greater the acceptance, the less motivation to deal with them more efficiently, this can be mitigated by higher control by citizens	Negative/Spain/(Balaguer-Coll et al. 2010), negative/Italy/(Boetti et al. 2012), negative/Italy/(Agasisti et al. 2015), negative/Spain/(Peréz-Lopéz et al. 2015), positive/Germany/(Kalb 2010), negative/Norway/(Borge et al. 2008), negative/Spain/(Balaguer-Coll and Prior, 2009), positive/Italy/(Porcelli, 2014), negative/Czech Republic/(Štastná and Gregor 2015), not statistically significant/Spain/(Benito et al. 2010)
	Financial liabilities–Log (financial liabilities/population), net debt	Loans received reduce citizens' control over expenditure	Positive/Spain/(Balaguer-Coll et al. 2010), negative/Portugese/(Da Cruz and Marques 2014), negative/Spain/(Peréz-Lopéz et al. 2015), positive/Spain/(Balaguer-Coll and Prior 2009), positive/Germany/(Bönisch et al. 2011), positive/Spain/(Benito et al. 2010)

(continued)

Table 1.5 (continued)

Variables	Possibility of expressing	Mechanism of action	Impact on efficiency/country/reference
	Deficit (total expenditure/total revenue, management surplus per capita)	Financial vulnerability is created either by inefficient management or structural insufficiency in resources	Negative/Spain/(Balaguer-Coll et al. 2010), negative/Italy/(Agasisti et al. 2015), negative/Spain/(Peréz-Lopéz et al. 2015), positive/Italy/(Porcelli, 2014)
Political leadership	Herfindal index	Efficient decision-making without fractionalism, low level of control	Negative/Germany/(Geys et al. 2009), positive/Chile/(Pacheco et al. 2014), positive/Indonesia/(Yusfany 2015), positive/Germany/(Kalb 2010), positive/Norway/(Borge et al. 2008), positive/Greece/(Doumpos and Cohen 2014)
	Liberal party, progressive party	Liberal parties have a greater tendency to reach efficiency	Negative/Belgium/(De Borger and Kerstens 1996a, b), positive/Spain/(Benito et al. 2010), not statistically significant/Belgium/(De Borger and Kerstens 1996a, b)
	Socialist party, share of left wing party in %, left wing mayor	Tendency towards inefficiency	Positive/Belgium (De Borger and Kerstens 1996a, b), negative/Germany/(Geys et al.. 2009), positive/Italy/(Boetti et al. 2010), positive/Italy/(Agasisti et al. 2015), positive/Spain/(Peréz-Lopéz et al. 2015), positive/Germany/(Kalb 2010), negative/Norway/(Borge et al. 2008), negative/Czech Republic/(Štastná and Gregor 2015), not statistically significant/Spain/(Benito et al.., 2012), positive/Belgium/(De Borge and Kerstens 1996)

(continued)

Table 1.5 (continued)

Variables	Possibility of expressing	Mechanism of action	Impact on efficiency/country/reference
	Right wing mayor, right wing party	More focused on achieving efficiency	Negative/Czech Republic/(Štastná and Gregor 2015), positive/Spain/(Benito et al. 2012)
	Votes held by governing party, % of council seat held by majority party, strong/weak left/right mayor	If the prevailing party has a majority, the other parties may be difficult to control and there is room for inefficiencies	Negative/Spain/(Balaguer-Coll et al. 2010), positive/South Africa/(Monkam 2014), positive/Chile/(Pacheco et al. 2014), negative/Spain/(Peréz-Lopéz et al. 2015), negative/Czech Republic/(Štastná and Gregor 2015)
	Voter turnout %	Greater involvement of voters leads to greater efficiency, reduces the negative impact of flypaper effect and fiscal illusion	Positive/Germany/(Geys et al. 2009), negative/Portugese/(Da Cruz and Marques 2014), positive/Norway/(Borge et al. 2008), negative/Czech Republic/(Štastná and Gregor 2015)

Source Authors

References

Abdellatif L, Atlam B, Aly H (2015) Revisiting the relation between decentralization and growth in the context of marketization. Eastern Eur Econ 53(4):255–276

Adam A, Delis MD, Kammas P (2014) Fiscal decentralization and public sector efficiency: evidence from OECD countries. Econ Gov 15(1):17–49

Afonso A, Fernandes S (2006) Measuring local government spending efficiency: evidence for the Lisbon region. Reg Stud 40(1):39–53

Agasisti T, Dal Bianco A, Griffini M (2015) The public sector fiscal efficiency in Italy: the case of Lombardy municipalities in the provision of the essential public services. Technical report no. 691, Società Italiana di Economia Pubblica, Università di Pavia, Pavia

Aiello F, Bonanno G, Capristo L (2017) Explaining differences in efficiency: the case of local government literature. Working Paper no. 04-2017, Università Della Calabria, Rende. Available via http://www.ecostat.unical.it/RePEc/WorkingPapers/WP04_2017.pdf

Alonso JM, Clifton J, Diaz-Fuentes D (2015) Did new public management matter? An empirical analysis of the outsourcing and decentralization effects on public sector size. Public Manag Rev 17(5):643–660

Ames B (1994) The reverse coattails effect: local party organization in the 1989 Brazilian presidential election. Am Pol Sci Rev 88(1):95–111

Andersen OJ, Torsteinsen H (2017) "The master of the house"—agencies in municipal service provision: balancing autonomy and accountability. Admin Soc 49(5):730–752

Aras G, Crowther D (2010) A handbook of corporate governance and social responsibility. Gower Publishing, Aldershot

Arcelus FJ, Arocena P, Cabasés F et al (2015) On the cost-efficiency of service delivery in small municipalities. Reg Stud 49(9):1469–1480

Aristovnik A (2012) Fiscal decentralization in Eastern Europe: trends and selected issues. Transylv Rev Adm Sci 37E:5–22

Aslam G, Yilmaz S (2011) Impact of decentralization reforms in Pakistan on service delivery—an empirical study. Public Admin Develop 31(3):159–171

Aubert BA, Bourdeau S (2012) Public sector performance and decentralization of decision rights. Can Public Admin 55(4):575–598

Balaguer-Coll TM, Prior D (2009) Short- and long-term evaluation of efficiency and quality. An application to Spanish municipalities. Appl Econ 41(23):2991–3002

Balaguer-Coll MT, Prior D, Tortosa-Ausina E (2007) On the determinants of local government performance: a two-stage nonparametric approach. Eur Econ Rev 51(2):425–451

Balaguer-Coll TM, Prior D, Tortosa-Ausina E (2010) Decentralization and efficiency of local government. Ann Regional Sci 45(3):571–601

Bardhan P, Mookherjee D (2005) Decentralization, corruption and government accountability: an overview. Boston University—Department of Economics—The Institute for Economic Development Working Papers Series

Barenstein M, de Mello L (2001) Fiscal decentralization and governance: a cross-country analysis. IMF Working paper no. 01/71, International Monetary Fund, Washington D.C. Available via https://www.imf.org/external/pubs/ft/wp/2001/wp0171.pdf

Bednar J (2011) The political science of federalism. Annu Rev Law Soc Sci 7:269–288

Béland D, Howlett M (2016) The role and impact of the multi-streams approach in comparative policy analysis. J Comp Policy Anal 18(3):221–227

Benito B, Bastida F, García JA (2010) Explaining differences in efficiency: an application to Spanish municipalities. J Appl Econ 42(4):515–528

Benito B, Albadalejo F, Vincente C (2012) Political budget cycles in local governments. Lex Localis 4(4):341–361

Boetti L, Piacenza M, Turati G (2012) Decentralization and local governments' performance: how does fiscal autonomy affect spending efficiency? FinanzArchiv 68(3):269–302

Bolleyer N, Swenden W, McEwen N (2014) A theoretical perspective on multi-level systems in Europe: constitutional power and partisan conflict Introduction. Comp Eur Polit 12(4–5):367–383

Bönisch P, Haug P, Illy A et al (2011) Municipality size and efficiency of local public services: does size matter? IWH Discussion Paper no. 18/2011, Halle Institute for Economic Research (IWH), Halle

Borge L-E, Falch T, Tovmo P (2008) Public sector efficiency: the roles of political and budgetary institutions, fiscal capacity, and democratic participation. Public Choice 136(3):475–495

Brennan G, Buchanan JM (1980) The power to tax: analytical foundations of a fiscal constitution. Cambridge University Press, Cambridge

Brinkerhoff DW, Wetterberg A (2016) Gauging the effects of social accountability on services, governance, and citizen empowerment. Public Admin Rev 76(2):274–336

Busemeyer MR (2008) The impact of fiscal decentralisation on education and other types of spending. Swiss Polit Sci Rev 14(3):451–481

Carlucci F, Cira A, Immordino G, Ioppolo G, Yigitclanar T (2017) Regional heterogeneity in Italy: Transport, devolution and corruption. Land Use Policy. 66(2017):28–33

Campos-Alba CM, la Higuera-Molina D, Emilio J, Pérez-López G, Zafra-Gómez JL (2019) Measuring the Efficiency of Public and Private Delivery Forms: An Application to the Waste Collection Service Using Order-M Data Panel Frontier Analysis, Sustainability, MDPI, Open Access Journal, 11(7):1–15.

Čermáková H (2006) Regionální kontext daňové politiky. Optimalizace rozpočtového určení daní se zaměřením na kraje. Dissertation, Masarykova Universita

Cerniglia F (2003) Decentralization in the public sector: quantitative aspects in federal and unitary countries. J Policy Model 25(8):749–776

Clark GL (1984) A theory of ocal autonomy. Ann Assoc Am Geogr 74(2):195–208

Cruikshank B (1993) Revolutions within—self-government and self esteem. Econ Soc 22(3):327–344

da Cruz NF, Marques RC (2014) Revisiting the determinants of local government performance. Omega-Int J Manage Sci 44:91–103

Dahl RA, Tufte ER (1973) Size and democracy. Stanford University Press, Redwood City

De Borger B, Kerstens K (1996a) Cost efficiency of Belgian local governments: a comparative analysis of FDH, DEA, and econometric approaches. Reg Sci Urban Econ 26(2):145–170

De Borger B, Kerstens K (1996b) Radial and nonradial measures of technical efficiency: an empirical illustration for Belgian local governments using an FDH reference technology. J Prod Anal 7(1):41–62

De Tocqueville A (1961) Democracy in America. Schocken

De Vries MS (2000) The rise and fall of decentralization: a comparative analysis of arguments and practices in European countries. Eur J Polit Res 38(2):193–224

Deininger K, Mpuga P (2005) Does greater accountability improve the quality of public service delivery? Evidence from Uganda. World Dev 33(1):171–191

Di Liddo G, Magazzino C, Porcelli F (2018) Government size, decentralization and growth: empirical evidence from Italian regions. Appl Econ 50(25):2777–2791

D'Inverno G, Carosi L, Ravagli L (2018) Global public spending efficiency in Tuscan municipalities. Socio Econ Plan Sci 61:102–113

Dollery B, Hamburger P (1996) Modelling bureaucracy: the case of the Australian federal budget sector 1982–1992. Public Admin 74(3):477–507

Doumpos M, Cohen S (2014) Applying data envelopment analysis on accounting data to assess and optimize the efficiency of greek local governments. Omega 46:74–85

Drew J, Grant B (2017) Subsidiarity: more than a principle of decentralization—a view from local government. Publius J Federalism 47(4):522–545

Drew J, Kortt MA, Dollery B (2015) What determines efficiency in local government? A DEA analysis of NSW local government. Econ Pap 34(4):243–256

Drew J, McQuestin D, Dollery B (2018) Do Municipal Mergers Improve Technical Efficiency? An Empirical Analysis of the 2008 Queensland Municipal Merger Program. Aust J Publ Admin 77(3):442–455

Drew J, Kortt MA, Dollery B (2017) No Aladdin's cave in New South Wales? Local government amalgamation, scale economies, and data envelopment analysis specification. Admin Soc 49(10):1450–1470

Emrouznejad A, Yang G (2018) A survey and analysis of the first 40 years of scholarly literature in DEA: 1978–2016. Soc Econ Plan Sci 61:4–8

Enikolopov R, Zhuravskaya E (2007) Decentralization and political institutions. J Public Econ 91(11–12):2261–2290

Escaleras M, Register AC (2012) Fiscal decentralization and natural hazard risks. Public Choice 151(1–2):165–183

Faozanudin M (2014) Role of local leadership in providing quality of basic education (Study in Banyumas Regency). In: Rokhman A, Patchanee T, Ritthikorn S, et al (eds) Proceedings of the 2014 International Conference on Public Management (ICPM-14), Atlantis Press, Paris, pp 362–367

Firman T, Fahmi FZ (2017) The privatization of metropolitan Jakarta's (Jabodetabek) urban fringes: the early stages of "post-suburbanization" in Indonesia. J Am Plann Assoc 83(1):68–79

Fisman R, Gatti R (2002) Decentralization and corruption: evidence across countries. J Public Econ 83(3):325–345

Fiva JH (2006) New evidence on the effect of fiscal decentralization on the size and composition of government spending. Finanz Archiv 62(2):250–280

Fogarty J, Mugera A (2013) Local government efficiency: evidence from Western Australia. Aust Econ Rev 46(3):300–311

Freille S, Haque Mohammad E, Kneller RA (2007) Federalism, decentralisation and corruption, MPRA Paper 27535. University Library of Munich, Germany

Füglister K, Wasserfallen F (2014) Comparative European politics, the dynamics of multi-level systems. Comp Eur Polit 12(4–5):404–421

Galariotis E, Guyot A, Doumpos M et al (2016) A novel multi-attribute benchmarking approach for assessing the financial performance of local governments: empirical evidence from France. Eur J Oper Res 248(1):301–317

Galiani S, Gertler P, Schargrodsky E (2008) School decentralization: helping the good get better, but leaving the poor behind. J Public Econ 92(10–11):2106–2120

Geys B, Moesen W (2009) Measuring local government technical (in)efficiency: an application and comparison of FDH, DEA, and econometric approaches. Public Perform Manag 32(4):499–513

Geys B, Heinemann F, Kalb A (2010) Voter involvement, fiscal autonomy and public sector efficiency: evidence from German municipalities. Eur J Polit Econ 26(2):265–278

Goldsmith AA (1999) Slapping the grasping hand: correlates of political corruption in emerging markets. Am J Econ Sociol 58(4):866–883

Goldsmith M, Rose LE (2000). Constituency, size and electoral politics: a comparison of patterns at local elections in Norway and the UK. Presented at the IPSA 18th World Congress, Quebec, 1–5 Aug 2000

Golem S, Malešević Perović S (2014) An empirical analysis of the relationship between fiscal decentralization and size of government. Finance a úvěr 64(1):30–58

Grady A, Gersonius B, Makarigakis A (2016) Taking stock of decentralized disaster risk reduction in Indonesia. Nat Hazard Earth Syst 16(9):2145–2157

Grossman PJ, Mavros P, Wassmer RW (1999) Public sector technical inefficiency in large U.S. cities. J Urban Econ 46(2):278–299

Gurr TR, King DS (1987) The state and the city. University of Chicago Press, Chicago

Guziejewska B (2018) Normative versus positive approach to fiscal decentralisation and the measures of decentralisation. An analysis based on the example of selected countries of Central and Eastern Europe. Comparative economic research. Central and Eastern Europe 21(1):101–117

Hajnal G (2011) Agencies and the politics of agentification in Hungary. Transylv Rev Adm Sci Special Issue: 74–92

Halkos GE, Polemis ML (2018) The impact of economic growth on environmental efficiency of the electricity sector: a hybrid window DEA methodology for the USA. J Environ Manage 211:334–346

Hessels J, Terjesen S (2010) Resource dependency and institutional theory perspectives on direct and indirect export choice. Small Bus Econ 34(2):203–220

Hidayat R (2017) Political devolution: lessons from a decentralized mode of government in Indonesia. Sage Open 7(1):215824401668681

Hoey L (2017) Reclaiming the authority to plan: how the legacy of structural adjustment affected Bolivia's effort to recentralize nutrition planning. World Dev 91:100–112

Huang Z, Du X (2017) Government intervention and land misallocation: evidence from China. Cities 60:323–332

Hulst R, Mafuru W, Mpenzi D (2015) Fifteen years after decentralization by devolution: political-administrative relations in Tanzanian local government. Public Admin Develop 35(5):360–371

Jackson PM, Brown CV (2003) Ekonomie veřejného sektoru. Eurolex Bohemia, Praha

Kalb A (2010) The impact of intergovernmental grants on cost efficiency: theory and evidence from German municipalities. Econ Anal Policy 40(1):23–48

Kauppi K, Van Raaij EM (2015) Opportunism and honest incompetence—seeking explanations for noncompliance in public procurement. J Publ Adm Res Theor 25(3):953–979

King D (1984) Fiscal tiers: the economics of multi-level government. George Allen & Unwin, London

Kuhlmann S, Jäkel T (2013) Competing, collaborating or controlling? Comparing benchmarking in European local government. Public Money Manage 33(4):269–276

Ladner A, Kueffer N, Balderschein H (2016) Measuring local autonomy in 39 countries (1990–2014). Reg Federal Stud 26(3):321–357

Livermore MA (2017) The perils of experimentation. Yale Law J 126(3):636–708

Lo Storto C (2016) The trade-off between cost efficiency and public service quality: a non-parametric frontier analysis of Italian major municipalities. Cities 51:52–63

López Martínez M, Reverte GM, Palacios Manzano M (2016) School failure in Spain and its regions: territorial disparities and proposals for improvement. Rev Estud Reg 107:121–155

Madison K, Holt DT, Kellermanns FW et al (2016) Viewing family firm behavior and governance through the lens of agency and stewardship theories. Fam Bus Rev 29(1):65–93

Malesky EJ, Nguyen CT, Tran A (2014) The impact of recentralization on public services: a difference-in-differences analysis of the abolition of elected councils in Vietnam. Am Polit Sci Rev 108(1):144–168

Mansuri G, Rao V (2013) Localizing development: does participation work? World bank policy research report. Available via http://siteresources.worldbank.org/INTRES/Resources/469232-1321568702932/8273725-1352313091329/PRR_Localizing_Development_full.pdf. Accessed 13 Mar 2017

McLure M (2007) The Paretian school and Italian fiscal sociology. Palgrave Macmillan, London

McQuestin D, Drew J, Dollery B (2018) Do municipal mergers improve technical efficiency? An empirical analysis of the 2008 Queensland municipal merger program. Aust J Publ Admin 77(3):442–455

Mei C, Chen K, Wu X (2016) Local government entrepreneurship in China: a public policy perspective introduction. China Int J 14(3). https://doi.org/10.2139/ssrn.2928230

Meričková B, Fantová Šumpíková M, Rousek P (2009) Benchmarking na úrovni miestnej samosprávy—vybrané problémy. In: Klazar Stanislav (ed) Teoretické a praktické aspekty veřejných finance. Nakladatelství Oeconomica, Praha

Mok KH, Wu XF (2013) Dual decentralization in China's transitional economy: welfare regionalism and policy implications for central-local relationship. Policy Soc 32(1):61–75

Monkam NF (2014) Local municipality productive efficiency and its determinants in South Africa. Dev So Afr 31(2):275–298. https://doi.org/10.1080/0376835X.2013.875888

Mookherjee D (2006) Decentralization, hierarchies, and incentives: a mechanism design perspective. J Econ Lit 44(2):367–390

Mookherjee D (2015) Political decentralization. Ann Rev Econ 7:231–249

Mouritzen PE (1989) City size and citizens' satisfaction: two competing theories revisited. Eur J Polit Res 17(6):661–688

Musgrave RA, Musgrave PB (1989) Public finance in theory and practice. McGraw-Hill Education, Maidenhead

Narbón-Perpiñá I, De Witte K (2017a) Local governments' efficiency: a systematic literature review—part I. Int T Oper Res 25(2):431–468

Narbón-Perpiñá I, De Witte K (2017b) Local governments' efficiency: a systematic literature review—part II. Int T Oper Res 25(4):1107–1136

Navarro C, Velasco F (2016) "In wealth and in poverty?" The changing role of Spanish municipalities in implementing childcare policies. Int Rev Adm Sci 82(2):315–334

Němec J, Meričková B, Ochrana F (2008) Introducing benchmarking in Czech Republic and Slovakia. Public Manag Rev 10(5):673–684

Neudorfer B, Neudorfer SN (2015) Decentralization and political corruption: disaggregating regional authority. Publius 45(1):24–50

Niskanen WA (1975) Bureaucrats and politicians. J Law Econ 18(3):617–643

Nordberg D (2011) Corporate governance: principles and issues. SAGE, Los Angeles

Oates WE (1972) Fiscal Federalism. Harcourt Brace Jovanovich, San Diego

Ochrana F, Fantová Šumpíková M, Pavel J et al (eds) (2007) Efektivnost zabezpečování vybraných veřejných služeb na úrovni obcí. Oeconomia, Praha

OECD, Korea Institute of Public Finance (2013) Measung fiscal decentralisation: Concepts and policies. In: Kim J, Lotz J, Blöchliger H (eds). OECD Fiscal Federalism Studies, Paris. Available via http://www.oecd.org/eco/public-finance/measuring-fiscal-decentralisation-concepts-and-policies.htm. Assessed 10 May 2017

Osborne SP, Radno Z, Vidal I (2014) A sustainable business model for public service organizations? Public Manag Rev 16(2):165–172

Ostrom V (1991) The meaning of American federalism: constituting a self-governing society. Institute for Contemporary Studies Press, San Francisco

Ostrom E (1999) Crossing the great divide: coproduction, synergy, and development. In: McGinnis MD (ed) Polycentric governance and development: readings from the workshop in political theory and policy analysis. University of Michigan Press, Michigan

Ostrom V (2008) The political theory of a compound republic: designing the American experiment. Lexington Books, Lanham

Pacheco F, Sanchez R, Villena M (2014) A longitudinal parametric approach to estimate local government efficiency. Technical Report no. 54918, Munich University Library, Munich

Papenfuss U, Schaefer Ch (2010) Improving public accountability by aligning reporting to organizational changes in publicservice provision—an empirical Internet study of all Austrian, German and Swiss towns and states from an agency-theory perspective. Int Rev Adm Sci 76(3):555–576

Peréz-López G, Prior D, Zafra JL (2015) Rethinking new public management delivery forms and efficiency: long-term effects in Spanish local government. J Publ Adm Res Theor 25(4):1157–1183

Pérez-López G, Prior D, José L. Zafra-Gómez LJ (2018) Temporal scale efficiency in DEA panel data estimations. An application to the solid waste disposal service in Spain, Omega, 76:18–27

Plaček M, Matějová L, Křápek M, et al (2014) Decentralization vs economies of scale: expenditure on maintenance of municipalities' property. In: Sedmihradská L (eds) Proceedings of the 19th International conference: theoretical and practical aspects of public finance 2014, 1st edn. Wolters Kluwer, Praha, pp 228–236

Plaček M, Půček M, Ochrana F et al (2016) Political business cycle in Czech Republic, Case of municipalities. Prague Econ Pap 25(3):304–320

Pollitt C, Bouckaert G (2011) Public management reform—a comparative analysis: new public management, governance, and the Neo-Weberian States. Oxford University Press, Oxford

Porcelli F (2014) Electoral accountability and local government efficiency: quasi-experimental evidence from the Italian health care sector reforms. Economis of Governance 15(3):221–251

Pratt JW, Zeckhauser J (1986) Principals and agents: the structure of business. Harvard Business School Press, Boston

Provazníková R (2011) Financování měst, obcí a regionů teorie a praxe, 2. aktualizované a rozšířené vydání. Grada Publishing, Prague

Prud'homme R (1995) The dangers of decentralization. World Bank Res Observer 10(2):201–220

Randma-Liiv T, Nakrošis V, Hajnal G (2011) Public sector organization in Central and Eastern Europe: From agencification to de-agencification. Transylv Rev Adm Sci (Special Issue):160–175

Walker RM, James O, Brewer GA.(2017) Replication, experiments and knowledge in public management research. Public Manag Rev 19(9):1221–1234. https://doi.org/10.1080/14719037.2017.1282003

Sarapuu K (2011) Post-communist development of administrative structure in Estonia: from fragmentation to segmentation. Transylv Rev Adm Sci (Special Issue):54–73

Šťastná L (2011) Three essays on local public finance. Dissertation thesis. Faculty of Social Science. Charles University, Prague

Sarto F, Veronesi G (2016) Clinical leadership and hospital performance: assessing the evidence base. BMC Health Serv Res 16(2):169

Seifert S, Nieswand M (2014) What drives intermediate local governments' spending efficiency: the case of French départements. J Local Gov Stud 40(5):766–790

Sharpe J (1995) Local Government: size, efficiency and citizen participation. In: The size of municipalities, efficiency and citizen participation. Council of Europe, Strasbourg, p 56

Silva DE (2016) Decentralized leadership. CESIfo Working Paper no. 6064. Ifo Institute—Leibniz Institute for Economic Research at the University of Munich, Munich

Singh N (2008) Decentralization and public delivery of health care services in India. Health Affair 27(4):991–1001

Smoke P (2015a) Rethinking decentralization: assessing challenges to a popular public sector reform. Public Admin Develop 35(2):97–112

Smoke P (2015b) Managing public sector decentralization in developing countries: moving beyond conventional recipes. Public Admin Develop 35(4):250–262

Špalek J (2011) Veřejné statky. Teorie a experiment, C. H. Beck, Praha

Šťastná L, Gregor M (2015) Public sector efficiency in transition and beyond: evidence from Czech local governments. Appl Econ 47(7):680–699

Stegarescu D (2005) Public sector decentralisation: measurement concepts and recent international trends. Fisc Stud 26(3):301–333

Stehlík P (2018) The competitive effect on public procurement for public service contracts: the case of the Czech Republic. J Econ 66(4):416–427

Strand I, Ramada P, Canton E et al (2011) Public procurement in Europe: cost and effectiveness. PwC, London

Swianiewicz P (2014) An empirical typology of local government systems in Eastern Europe. Local Gov Stud 40(2):292–311

Tanzi V (1996) Fiscal federalism and decentralization: a review of some efficiency and macroeconomic aspects. The World Bank, Washington, D.C

Tiebout CM (1956) A pure theory of local expenditures. J Polit Econ 64(5):416–424

Tillema S, Van Helden GJ (2005) Appreciation, acceptance and use of multidimensional benchmarking information by public sector organizations. In: Mellemvik F (ed) Bourmistrov A. International trends and experiences in government accounting Cappelen, Oslo, pp 230–247

Tommasi M, Weinschelbaum F (2007) Centralization vs. decentralization: a principal-agent analysis. J Public Econ Theory 9(2):369–389

Torrisi G, Pike A, Tomaney J et al (2011) Defining and measuring decentralisation: a critical review. MPRA Paper no. 51441. Munich Personal RePEc Archive. Munich. Available via https://mpra. ub.uni-muenchen.de/51441/1/MPRA_paper_51441.pdf. Accessed 10 May 2017

Transparency International (2019) Corruption perception index. Available via https://www. transparency.org/research/cpi/overview. Accessed 10 May 2017

Treisman D (2000) The causes of corruption: a cross-national study. J Public Econ 76(3):399–457

Tullock G (1965) The politics of bureaucracy. Public Affairs Press, Washington D.C

Verbeeten FHM, Speklé RF (2015) Management control, results-oriented culture and public sector performance: empirical evidence on new public management. Organ Stud 36(7):953–978

Vo DH (2010) The economics of fiscal decentralization. J Econ Surv 24(4):657–679

Von Neumann J, Morgenstern, O (2004) Theory of game and economics behavior. Princeton University Press

Vu TT, Zoukri M, Deffains B (2014) The interrelationship between formal and informal decentralization and its impact on subcentral governance performance: the case of Vietnam. CESifo Econ Stud 60(3):613–652

Walker RM, Lee MJ, James O et al (2018) Analyzing the complexity of performance information use: experiments with stakeholders to disaggregate dimensions of performance, data sources, and data types. Public Admin Rev 78(6):852–863

Wang Q, Geng Ch (2017) Research on financing efficiencies of strategic emerging listed companies by six-stage dea model. Math Probl Eng Article ID 3284657

Watt PA (1999) Public choice theory and local government: a comparative analysis of the UK and the USA. Local Gov Stud 25(3):95–97

Worthington A., Dollery B (2002) Incorporating contextual information in public sector efficiency analyses: a comparative study of NSW local government, Applied Economics, , 34(4):453–464

Wu X (2005) Corporate governance and corruption: a cross-country analysis. Governance 18(2):151–170

Wu AM, Wang W (2013) Determinants of expenditure decentralization: evidence from China. World Dev 46:176–184

Wyss K, Lorenz N (2000) Decentralization and central and regional coordination of health services: the case of Switzerland. Int J Health Plann Manage 15(2):103–114

Yusfany A (2015) The efficiency of local governments and its influence factors. Int J Technol Enhanc Emerg Eng Res 4(10):219–241

Zheng W, Sun H, Zhang P et al (2018) A four-stage DEA-based efficiency evaluation of public hospitals in China after the implementation of new medical reforms. PLoS ONE 13(10):e0203780

Chapter 2
The Fiscal Decentralization in Bulgaria

Bulgaria (officially the Republic of Bulgaria) has a long history. The peace treaty of the Khan Asparukh with the Byzantine Empire in 681 marked the foundation of the First Bulgarian Empire. This Empire existed until 1018, when the Byzantines conquered it. In 1185, Ivan Asen I and Peter IV organized a major uprising which resulted in the re-establishment of the Bulgarian state. The Asen dynasty died out in 1257, enabling the Mongols to establish suzerainty over the weakened Bulgarian state (until 1277). The Second Bulgarian Empire disintegrated into small feudal dominions by the fourteenth century and was occupied by the Ottoman Turks. In 1877, Russia declared war on the Ottomans and defeated them with the help of Bulgarian troops. The Treaty of San Stefano signed on March 3, 1878 by Russia and the Ottoman Empire set up the Third Bulgarian State. Bulgaria entered World War II in 1941 as a member of the Rome—Berlin—Tokyo Axis and was invaded by the USSR in September 1944. After this, the communist-dominated Fatherland Front took power and joined the Allied side until the war ended. In 1946, a one-party people's republic was instituted following a referendum. The Communist Party was forced to give up its political monopoly in November 1989 and the first free elections were held in June 1990. Bulgaria has been a member of NATO since April 2004 and a member of the EU since January 1, 2007.

Bulgaria occupies a portion of the eastern Balkan Peninsula, and it is bordered by Romania to the north, Serbia and North Macedonia to the west, Greece and Turkey to the south, and the Black Sea to the east. The land borders have a total length of 1808 km and the coastline has a length of 354 km. With a territory of 110,994 km^2, Bulgaria is Europe's 16th-largest country. Bulgaria has 7,050,034 inhabitants and the population density is 64 inhabitants/km^2.

The head of the executive branch is the President, elected by direct, popular vote for a five-year term, but with limited domestic powers. The head of government and the most powerful executive position is the Prime Minister. The Government is accountable to the Parliament, which elects the Prime Minister and the Council of Ministers. The administrative system consists of the central level and 28 regions—"oblasti" (plus six "planning regions" representing formally the level o f NUTS II).

© Springer Nature Switzerland AG 2020   51
M. Plaček et al., *Fiscal Decentralization Reforms*, Public Administration,
Governance and Globalization 19, https://doi.org/10.1007/978-3-030-46758-6_2

The central administration consists of the administration of the Council of Ministers, which includes the Chief Inspectorate, Ministries (currently 17 and varying with each government), State Agencies (currently 11 and varying over time), Executive Agencies (currently 29 and varying over time), the administrations of State Commissions (currently five and varying over time), as well as any administrative structures created by law (currently 43 and varying over time) or by a decision of the Council of Ministers (currently 19 and varying over time).

Regions are located at an intermediate level between the central government and the local authorities and headed by a regional governor who is appointed by the Council of Ministers and assisted by a regional administration, responsible for implementing state policies within the region, protecting the national interest, the rule of law, public order, and exerts administrative control.

The highest courts are the Supreme Administrative Court and the Supreme Court of Cassation—which deal with appeals and oversee the application of laws in subordinate courts. The Supreme Judicial Council manages the system and appoints judges.

The legislative powers are connected to two levels. The central level is represented by the unicameral Parliament—the National Assembly with 240 deputies elected to four-year terms by direct popular vote. The local level is represented by 265 municipalities and municipal administrations in the country, constituting the essence of local government (Zankina 2017).

The development of local self-government in Bulgaria

Bulgarian municipalities existed even before the restoration of Bulgarian statehood in the nineteenth century. At that time, the municipality was a church—school community and had no public legal powers. The municipality was established as a legal institution by the Constitution adopted on April 16, 1879. The Constitution of the People's Republic of Bulgaria in 1947 stated that the bodies of national self-government were the municipal, district and regional public councils, elected by the population of the respective administrative-territorial unit—a kind of symbiosis of state power and self-government, similar to other "socialist" countries (Hristova Stefanova 2018).

The recent foundations of the organization of government were set up in the Local Self-Government Act (1991), the Local Administration Act (1991), and the State Administrative Law (1998), all amended numerous times over the last 20 years. The development of the territorial structure of Bulgaria is shown by Table 2.1 (indicating that the number of municipalities did not significantly change over the last forty years).

The municipality today is a legal entity and is the basic administrative territorial unit through which self-government is implemented. Citizens participate in local affairs through municipal elected bodies of local self-government and also directly, through referendums or general meetings. The municipality consists of one or more

Table 2.1 The development of the territorial structure of Bulgaria

	Planning regions		Areas		Municipalities	
	Number	Average population	Number	Average population	Number	Average population
1950	x	x	14	516,300	2178	3300
1961	x	x	28	261,000	979	8000
1979	x	x	28	315,900	291	30,400
1987	x	x	9	997,400	273	32,900
1999	x	x	28	284,800	262	30,300
2006	6	1,280,000	28	280,000	264	30,000

Source Authors on the basis of data by Stoilova (2008)

settlements and the name of the municipality is the name of the settlement that is its administrative center. Municipalities manage their own municipal property and budgets. A municipality is a juridical person and a legal entity. Local self-government is performed through two elected bodies. The first is the municipal council, elected directly by the population, for a term of four years. The second is the mayor (body of executive power), elected directly, likewise for four years. However, mayors of quarters in the municipalities having quarter division are elected by secret ballot by the municipal council, following a proposal from the mayor of the municipality (Vodenicharov 2012).

According to the legislation, the local government is understood as a right of the citizens and the bodies elected by them to decide independently on all issues of local importance vested in them by the law. The main competencies of municipalities are municipal property, municipal companies, municipal finance, taxes and fees, and municipal administration; development of the territory of the municipality and of its settlements; education; health care; culture; public works and communal activities; social support; protection of the environment and rational use of natural resources; maintenance and the preservation of cultural, historic and architectural monuments; development of sports, recreation, and tourism. However, according to the opinion of the CoE monitoring report from 2011, the large majority of functions performed by the local authorities, relating to areas of great importance for citizens (education, public health and welfare), are delegated and not their own responsibilities (Vodenicharov 2012).

The Bulgarian government shows permanent interest in improving the quality of local democracy in the country. It adopted the Strategy for Decentralization in 2006 and a new strategy for 2016–2025, with the aim of improving territorial governance and coordination between government levels (Hristova Stefanova 2018).

2.1   The Level of Decentralization in Bulgaria from the Point of View of the Principles of the European Charter of Local Self-government

Bulgaria signed the European Charter of Local Self-Government on October 3, 1994 and ratified it on May 10, 1995 with entry into force on September 1, 1995, declaring itself bound by all the provisions of the Charter with the exception of Article 7, paragraph 2. This reservation was removed in 2012. Bulgaria is among the countries giving the Charter direct application, meaning that the Charter has been ratified and incorporated into its domestic legal system. In the event of a conflict between the Charter and an ordinary law, the provisions of the Charter prevail (Monitoring Report 2011).

The most recent Council of Europe monitoring visit to Bulgaria took place in 2010, and its monitoring report, entitled "Local and Regional Democracy in Bulgaria," was approved on September 21, 2011. The council expressed satisfaction with the overall positive developments of local democracy in the country, but also observed a number of points still deserving particular attention. The findings of this report (updated with more recent information—especially Hristova Stefanova (2018) are one of the core inputs for the following text.

The constitutional and legal foundation for local self-government
The core legal base for the existence of local self-government (LSG) in the country is the Constitution, namely Chapter VII (Local self-government and local administration). The Constitution declares that a municipality is the basic administrative territorial unit at the level of which self-government is practiced, that it is allowed property ownership and its own budget. Article 149 deals with the allocation of responsibilities between the central and local levels, article 10 stipulates that all elections, and national and local referendums be held on the basis of universal, equal and direct suffrage by secret ballot, and articles 140 and 17 explicitly provide for the right of municipal ownership.

The constitutional arrangements are framed by other existing legislation, especially the Law on Local Self-Government and Local Administration (1991), the Law on Administrative Territorial Structure of the Republic of Bulgaria (1995), the Law for the Territorial Division of the Capital Municipality and of the Big Cities (1995), the Law on Direct Citizen Participation in Government and Local Self-Government (2009), the Law on Spatial Planning (2001), the Municipal Budgets Law (1998), the Local Taxes and Fees Law (1997), the Municipal Debt Law (2005) and the Law on Municipal Property (1996).

The monitoring report states that, formally speaking, Bulgaria fully complies with Article 2, both at the constitutional level and at the level of the country's ordinary legislation.

The concept of local self-government
According to the monitoring report and existing academic studies, listed in the references, the independence of Bulgarian municipalities is relatively limited, especially

in practice. Formally, municipalities have their own budgets and assets and independently manage them, and may issue regulations, instructions and decisions that have a regulatory nature. The regional governor exercises control over the legality of such regulatory norms or other decisions of municipal councils, unless otherwise provided by law. The governor can recall unlawful measures for new consideration by the municipal council or to dispute them before the pertinent administrative court (Vodenicharov 2012).

The concern of the monitoring report is the level of the practical acceptance of the subsidiarity principle—according to the report, Bulgaria still remains a highly centralized state. From a legal point of view, the legislation should explicitly empower local authorities to take initiatives when the corresponding competencies have not been expressly attributed to them and when this is not explicitly prohibited by law (a similar problem is mentioned for Slovakia).

The scope of local self-government
According to law, municipalities in Bulgaria are equipped with a comprehensive set of responsibilities prescribed by law (see above). However, the monitoring report mentions the persistent lack of clarity in the division between delegated powers and the authorities' own powers. According to the OECD (2016a), municipal responsibilities are divided into two categories—delegated competencies, which include education (primary and secondary), social protection and health care, and municipal responsibilities, which include housing and community amenities, economic affairs, environmental protection, water supply and sewerage, waste, urban public transport, roads, culture, tourism, and leisure.

At the time of the monitoring visit there was no specific legislation in Bulgaria setting out the process of consultation with local authorities during the legislative process on issues that concern them. However, it seems that this gap was removed by the Law on Normative Acts from 2016, explicitly prescribing that in the process of legal drafting, ex ante impact assessment and public consultations with citizens and legal entities be carried out.

The protection of local authority boundaries
According to the monitoring report, the Bulgarian Constitution calls for a referendum on changes of municipal boundaries and the Law on the Territorial Administrative Structure describes in detail the procedure to be followed—consequently, this principle of the Charter is respected.

Administrative structures and resources for the tasks of local authorities
The existing legislation defines the core principles determining the structures and resources of LSGs in Bulgaria. The number of municipal council members is defined as follows (Vodenicharov 2012, pp. 76–77):

- up to 5000 inhabitants—11 councilors;
- up to 10,000 inhabitants—13 councilors;
- up to 20,000 inhabitants—17 councilors;

- up to 30,000 inhabitants—21 councilors;
- up to 50,000 inhabitants—23 councilors;
- up to 75,000 inhabitants—27 councilors;
- up to 100,000 inhabitants—29 councilors;
- up to 160,000 inhabitants—33 councilors;
- over 160,000 inhabitants—41 councilors;
- capital municipality—49 councilors.

As indicated, the mayor is the core executive body of the municipality. On the proposal of the mayor, the municipal council approves the total number of employees and the internal structure of the local administration. Municipal offices consist of two different categories of employees—civil servants and contractual (labour-code regulated) employees, who are responsible for the administrative and organizational aspects of municipal life as well as for other activities of municipal bodies—numbers depend on the size of a municipality. The monitoring report states that law regulates the political bodies at the municipal level (the council, the mayor) in a detailed way, but broadly leaves it up to them to determine the organization of the administrative structures.

Conditions under which responsibilities are exercised at the local level
The conditions of the office of elected local representatives provide for the free exercise of their functions. According to a recent OECD Report (2016b) in Bulgaria, the salaries of mayors and local employees are determined by the Municipal Council, but within the limits set out in national Decree No. 67 (salaries vary according to the population of the municipality). Municipal councilors are remunerated for their participation in plenary sessions and commissions. The remuneration varies according to the population of the municipality. This means that principles stated by this article of the Charter are fully respected in Bulgaria.

The administrative supervision of local authorities' activities
The monitoring report states that as far as supervision is concerned, three cases of possible conflict between the current Bulgarian legislation and the Charter principles could be highlighted: namely the excessive scope of delegated competences; the power of regional governors to directly annul a municipal act; and the lack of clarity on the grounds for the removal or dissolution of local elected bodies. The analysis of existing updated sources indicates that the situation has improved, but it still seems (Vodenicharov 2012) that the regional governor can suspend (not annul) illegal acts adopted by the mayors, within 14 days after being notified of the act.

The financial resources of local authorities and the financial transfer system
The "quality" of the fiscal decentralization in Bulgaria is rather problematic and the monitoring report was very negative in this area. According to the OECD (2016a) the local revenues of municipalities represent only 10.1%, but grants and subsidies were 81.5%. However, according to Savov et al. (2018, p. 103) the local revenues represent

35% of total municipal revenues (we return to this discrepancy later in the text). For grants, the core source is the general grant for state-delegated responsibilities (around 75% of all transfers), determined on the basis of standards and physical indicators—this grant has the character of a specific-purpose grant. The equalization mechanism is realized via unconditional general equalizing grants (around 10% of all transfers) to ensure a "minimum level" of local service provision by each municipality (source of finance capital and current expenditure).

The financial situation of municipalities in Bulgaria has recently been slowly improving because the macro-framework for the financing of municipalities had improved, with more funding being provided for education, social services, healthcare, etc. However, the debate about the necessary increase of local resources is at least temporarily frozen (Pavlov 2018).

Local authorities' right to associate
According to the monitoring report, the right to associate is recognized in a satisfactory manner both by the Constitution and the relevant legislation. Provision is made both for the right of association as such, i.e. the right to participate in national and regional associations, and for the right of association and cooperation among municipalities. The National Association of Municipalities of the Republic of Bulgaria, as the core representative association of municipalities, is well-established.

The legal protection of local self-government
The Constitution states that a municipality is a legal entity and may participate in judicial proceedings, this means that a municipal council is free to challenge before a court any act that encroaches on its rights. Civil cases in which the municipality is a claimant are under the jurisdiction of the district or regional lower courts. Municipalities may also file lawsuits against administrative decisions taken by the competent state bodies that affect their rights, freedoms or legitimate interests or unlawfully delegate duties—these proceedings fall under the jurisdiction of the administrative courts (Vodenicharov 2012). This article of the charter is well-respected in Bulgaria today.

The core challenges for fiscal decentralization in Bulgaria
According to the OECD (2016a), Bulgaria belongs to the European countries with the lowest percentage of local government expenditures to GDP—municipalities spent approximately 7% of GDP (the central level approximately 21% of GDP). Bulgaria seems to be one of the most centralized countries in the EU from the perspective of local government finance (the high percentage of municipal expenditures to GDP in 2015 was caused by EU funds absorption, especially in the housing area).

According to most available sources in English, financing local governments is based mainly on grants and transfers, while local tax revenues represent only a smaller

share of municipal financial resources, among the lowest levels in the OECD. Because
the recent regional publication on local governments in South East Europe delivers
a different picture (Savov et al. 2018), we checked the reality directly on municipal
web pages and consulted with local experts. According to 2017 and 2018 budget data
from selected cities (Varna and Silistra were investigated in depth), local revenues
may amount to up to 50% of total current revenues of municipalities in wealthy cities.
For example, the 2017 budget report of the city Varna shows that the total revenues
were 365,310,073 leva, of which local tax revenues amounted to 82,348,196 leva and
other local revenues 55,188,651 leva. However, smaller rural municipalities have far
lower local revenues and are highly dependent on state transfers. In any case, the
percentage of sectoral ear-marked grants is too high (more than 40% of total revenues)
and undermines the principle of local fiscal sustainability.

The following local taxes are sources for the municipal budget: real estate tax;
inheritance tax; donations tax; tax on onerously acquired property; tax on vehicles;
patent tax; tourist tax; other local taxes determined by law. The municipal council
issues an ordinance that determines the amount of taxes and related terms and conditions. The law defines the upper and lower limits of local taxes and allows the council
to establish the specific amount. Municipalities also collect local fees (the fees are
set in compliance with the following principles: reimbursement of full expenses to
the municipality for the services provided and the creation of conditions to expand
the offered services and improve their quality) for the following services: household
waste; use of public spaces, use of nurseries, baby food kitchens, kindergartens, specialized institutions that provide social services, campuses, dormitories and other
municipal social services, technical services, administrative services, acquisition of
a cemetery plot, owning a dog, and other local fees determined by law (Vodenicharov
2012).

Tables 2.2, 2.3 and 2.4 provide a statistical overview of Bulgarian local self-
government finances for the last few years (the data from 2015 may be influenced
by EU fund resources).

The indebtedness of the local level of government in Bulgaria is an important
problem. According to the data of the Ministry of Finance, the average level of
municipal debt for the country, as a percentage of revenues and subsidies, was 48.08
percent at the end of 2017. In 2018, 21 municipalities were taken off the list of
municipalities earmarked for financial recovery, though two new ones were added;
there are another nine municipalities that have been on the list consistently since
2016.

Table 2.2 The structure of transfers to municipalities 2017 (in thousands of leva)

Total	Delegated responsibilities	Lump sum transfers		Capital transfers	Other ear-marked transfers
		General	Snow cleaning		
3,449,280.6	2,609,730.2	274,000.0	30,228.1	269,016.9	271,338.1

Source Authors, based on Ministry of Finance data

Table 2.3 The structure of municipal expenditures: COFOG (mill. leva)

	2015	2016	2017
General administration	627	661	699
Defense	141	0	0
Public order and security	100	110	83
Economic functions	1,195	665	669
Environment	578	517	568
Housing	1,800	697	862
Health care	997	611	636
Recreation, culture, sports	831	542	550
Education	2282	2086	2424
Social protection	716	646	729
Total	9266	6536	7219

Source Authors, based on National Statistical Office data

Table 2.4 The structure of local government expenditures Bulgaria COFOG (%)

	2015	2016	2017
General administration	0.7	0.7	0.7
Defense	0.2	0	0
Public order and security	0.1	0.1	0.1
Economic functions	1.3	0.7	0.7
Environment	0.7	0.5	0.6
Housing	2.0	0.7	0.9
Health care	1.1	0.6	0.6
Recreation, culture, religion	0.9	0.6	0.5
Education	2.6	2.2	2.4
Social protection	0.8	0.7	0.7
Total	10.5	6.9	7.1

Source Authors, based on EUROSTAT data

References

Hristova Stefanova M (2018) Challenges of the implementation of the European charter of local self-government in Bulgarian legislation. Lex Localis 16(4):915–927

OECD (2016a) When size matters: scaling up delivery of Czech local services. In: Lewis C (ed). Available via https://oecdecoscope.wordpress.com/2016/07/26/when-size-matters-scaling-up-delivery-of-czech-local-services/. Assessed on 10 May 2017

OECD (2016b) Subnational Governments around the world: country profile Hungary (2016). OECD, Paris. Available via https://www.oecd.org/regional/regional-policy/profile-Hungary.pdf.

Pavlov S (2018) Financial situation of municipalities remains worrying, despite some improvement in 2017. Radio Bulgaria, Sofia

Pereira AT, Suwens J (2011) Local and regional democracy in Bulgaria. Monitoring report prepared by the Monitoring Committee of the Congress of Local and Regional Authorities. Strasbourg

Savov E, Stafa E, Dukič Ž (2018) Fiscal decentralization indicators for South-East Europe: 2006–2017. NALAS

Stoilova D (2008) Local government reforms in Bulgaria: recent developments and key challenges. 16th NISPAcee Annual Conference on Public Policy and Administration: Challenges and Synergies, Working Group on Local Government, Bratislava, Slovak Republic

Vodenicharov A (2012) Local government in the Republic of Bulgaria. In: Moreno Á-M (ed) Local government in the member states of the European union: a comparative legal perspective. Instituto Nacional de Administración Pública, Madrid, pp 69–90

Zankina E (2017) Public administration characteristics in Bulgaria. Unpublished report for EUPACK project

Chapter 3
The Fiscal Decentralization in the Czech Republic

The Czech Republic is a fully independent sovereign, democratic unitary state, established after the friendly split of Czechoslovakia on January 1, 1993. The Czech Constitution, which was ratified December 16, 1992, becoming fully effective on January 1, 1993, was changed several times between 1997 and 2001, to allow direct election of the president and application for NATO and EU membership.

The territory of the Czech Republic is 78,866 km^2, the total length of the borders of the state is 2290 km. The neighboring countries are the Slovak Republic, Poland, Austria, and Germany. The average density of population is 134 inhabitants per km^2. The Czech Republic has been a member of NATO from March 12, 1999, and a member of the EU since May 1, 2004. The Czech Republic includes the historical territories of Bohemia, Moravia, and Czech Silesia.

The Czech state was formed in the late ninth century as the Duchy of Bohemia under the Great Moravian Empire. In 1002, the duchy was formally recognized as an Imperial State of the Holy Roman Empire along with the Kingdom of Germany, the Kingdom of Burgundy, and the Kingdom of Italy; and became the Kingdom of Bohemia in 1198, attaining its greatest territorial extent in the fourteenth century. Prague was the imperial seat during the period from the 14th to the seventeenth century. Following the Battle of Mohács in 1526, the entire Crown of Bohemia was gradually integrated into the Habsburg Monarchy and in 1806 the Bohemian Kingdom became part of the Austrian Empire. The Republic of Czechoslovakia was formed in 1918 following the collapse of the Austro-Hungarian Empire after World War I. During World War II, the territory of Bohemia and Moravia was a protectorate of Nazi Germany established on March 16, 1939. Czechoslovakia was liberated in 1945 by the Soviet Union and the United States. The Communist Party of Czechoslovakia won the 1946 elections and after the 1948 coup d'état established a one-party communist state under Soviet influence. The 1989 Velvet Revolution peacefully ended communist rule and re-established democracy and a market economy.

The head of the executive branch is the President, elected by direct, popular vote for a five-year term. The head of government is the Prime Minister. The Cabinet is appointed by the President on the recommendation of the Prime Minister.

© Springer Nature Switzerland AG 2020
M. Plaček et al., *Fiscal Decentralization Reforms*, Public Administration,
Governance and Globalization 19, https://doi.org/10.1007/978-3-030-46758-6_3

The administrative system consists of central administrative bodies and specialized state administrative bodies on a subnational level (up to December 31, 2002, 76 districts also existed, i.e., deconcentrated branches of the national government in the Czech Republic, their existence ended as a part of the public administration reform). The central administration consists of a government office, ministries, central state administrative bodies and other central bodies (mainly agencies) with special status.

The judicial system in the Czech Republic consists of the Constitutional Court of the Czech Republic and the 'ordinary' court system. The ordinary court system consists of the Supreme Court, the Supreme Administrative Court, high courts, regional courts and district courts.

The legislative powers exist at three levels (all three levels have legislative powers, as defined by the Constitution)—the bicameral Parliament consists of two chambers, both elected in direct elections (the Lower House: Chamber of Deputies with 200 deputies and the Upper House: Senate with 81 senators), regional self-governments, and local self-governments.

The developments of local self-government in the Czech Republic
Self-government has a long tradition on the territory of the present Czech Republic, dating all the way back to 1848, with the old administrative feudal system losing its justification after the abolishment of servitude. Municipalities were organized as territorial self-governing bodies also partially exercising the state administration as part of their delegated powers.

After the Velvet Revolution in 1989 the first wave of administrative reform was oriented mostly towards creating real institutions of self-government, to divide executive and legislative powers on all levels, to change the territorial structure of Czechoslovakia, and to restructure the central government and the system of control in the public sector. The system of national committees was abolished on December 31, 1990, to create self-government structures in each municipality, to organize direct self-government elections in November 1990, and to split self-government and state administration functions at the local level.

Based on these decisions, self-governing municipalities with a high level of independence were established by the Law No. 369/1990 Coll. on Municipal Administration from January 1, 1991 (currently the Law on Municipalities 128/2000 and the Law on the Capital Prague 131/2000). Municipalities were established in the early 1990s with the same boundaries as the previous local administrative units. There are currently about 6250 municipalities in the country, and with this, the Czech Republic belongs to the group of countries with very high territorial fragmentation.

Municipalities operate independently of the central or regional level of government. The councils are elected in popular elections which are held every four years. The mayor is elected by the council from among the council members. The municipal manager is appointed by the mayor and this appointment (or removal) must be approved by the director of the regional office.

A basic right of local governments is to own and independently manage their own property. Property has been returned to municipalities in two waves. The first wave occurred in 1991 when most of their property was returned to the municipalities.

The second wave took place under the framework of the process of region creation in 2000 and the cancellation of districts in 2002 and the subsequent transfer of their responsibilities to the municipalities. Local self-governments are allowed to borrow or to issue bonds with only minor ex-post regulation.

Local government responsibilities are divided into two groups: independent (own) competencies and delegated powers. For independent competencies, local governments can implement their own policies. The independent competencies include, for instance, the management of the local government, the formulation and approval of the budget and final account, establishment of legal entities and organizations, management, personnel and material arrangement of the local government office, publishing of generally binding regulations of the municipality, local referenda, a municipal police force, imposing penalties for administrative offences, a program of development for the municipal cadastral district, municipal cadastral planning, and regulating plans and cooperation with other municipalities.

Independent competencies represent both a right and a duty of the municipality. There are defined services which a municipality must provide in the self-administration provision, e.g., elementary schools, kindergartens, children's homes, rest homes and social housing, theatres, libraries and museums, free-time activity facilities, water quality and delivery, gas and electricity delivery, public space cleaning, cemeteries, provision of public roads, public lighting, public transport, municipal police, firemen etc. Municipalities must finance these services from their own revenues, especially from tax revenues.

In the case of delegated powers, local governments execute central government policy. Due to the very fragmented municipal structure, not all municipalities exercise all types of delegated powers. Currently, municipalities are divided into three categories from this point of view: 5004 municipalities with basic competency—of these, 3445 municipalities have fewer than 500 inhabitants; 163 "second" category municipalities and 81 municipalities with extended competencies. The scope of the state administration is determined together with the grants for its provision. These grants are drawn from the state budget. The provision of the state administration, theoretically, should not financially burden the local government; however, in reality the grants finance only a part of the total expenses (Kadečka 2012).

3.1 The Level of Decentralization in the Czech Republic from the Point of View of the Principles of the European Charter of Local Self-government

The Czech Republic signed the European Charter of Local Self-government on May 28, 1998 and ratified it on May 7, 1999 with entry into force on September 1, 1999. It did not consider itself bound by Article 4, paragraph 5, Article 6, paragraph 2, Article 7, paragraph 2, Article 9, paragraphs 3, 5 and 6, and this position remains unchanged today.

The most recent finalized Council of Europe monitoring visit to the Czech Republic Slovakia took place in 2011, and in its monitoring report, entitled "Local and Regional Democracy in the Czech Republic," which was approved on March 8, 2012, the council expressed satisfaction with the overall positive situation of local and regional democracy in the country. The findings of this report are the core inputs for the following text, updated with more recent academic studies, especially information provided by Radvan et al. (2018).

The constitutional and legal foundation for local self-government

The core legal base for the existence of LSG in the country is the Constitution of the Czech Republic. Chapter 7 of the Constitution, entitled Territorial Self-Administration and including Articles 99–105, provides all of the main principles for the organization of local self-government, which are almost fully in line with the principles set out by the Charter. Article 99 defines the territorial structure of the Czech Republic (municipalities and self-governing regions). Article 100 deals especially with creating or abolishing municipalities—only on the basis of the constitutional law. Article 101 defines municipal elected bodies and sets the conditions when the state has the right to interfere with municipal activities. Article 102 defines the municipal election process; Article 103 was abolished; Article 104 gives the right to municipalities to decide on all aspects of their self-government. Article 105 deals with delegated competencies—the exercise of certain powers of local self-administration may be delegated to a municipality with a law.

The constitutional arrangements are framed by all the necessary legislation mentioned above. Therefore the Council of Europe monitoring visit concluded that "provisions enshrined in the 1992 Constitution take ample care of the requirement under Article 2 of the Charter that the principle of local self-government be recognized in the Constitution."

The concept of local self-government

The independence of Czech municipalities is high. Within the limits set by the law, municipalities have their own budgets and assets and independently manage them. Local governments may issue ordinances that bind all individual or corporate bodies within their jurisdiction. The Ministry of the Interior can suspend municipal ordinances which breach the law, but only the Constitutional Court has the right to invalidate these ordinances. Any modification of the powers of local authorities must be decided by parliament. Municipal councils are composed of members freely elected by secret ballot on the basis of direct, equal, and universal suffrage, and possess executive organs responsible to them. Taking this into account the monitoring report states, "The legal and financial regulations leave little room for doubt that local authorities in the Czech Republic enjoy a well-defined right to regulate and manage their part of public affairs, … on the other hand, whether the requirement that the share of public affairs devoted to the regulation and management of local is "substantial," may be open to some doubt… The right of self-government to be exercised by councils elected through free elections gives rise to no particular concern as far as the Czech Republic is concerned."

The scope of local self-government
Since their establishment in 1990 and especially after the 2000–2002 reform, municipalities in the Czech Republic have been equipped with a comprehensive set of
responsibilities prescribed by law (see above), and they also execute delegated state
administrative functions. Municipalities also have full discretion within the limits
of the law to execute these functions. Despite the fact that paragraph 5 of Article 4
of the Charter is not binding for the Czech Republic, the real legal situation is in
conformity with the Charter (municipal powers are full and exclusive). The duty to
consult local authorities for all relevant cases is stipulated by general laws (Act on
Municipalities, Act on the Capital City of Prague) and also by the Legislative Rules
of the Government. Many elected local officials hold parliamentary mandates, which
is a form of political influence and information.

Taking this into account, the monitoring report does not have any concerns
regarding all principles covered by paragraph 4 of the Charter.

The protection of local authority boundaries
Under Czech law, decisions to amalgamate two o r more municipalities are based upon
an agreement between the relevant municipalities and break-outs may be decided
following a referendum held in that part of the municipality that wishes to break
away. Taking this into account the report states: "There is no reason to believe that the
Czech obligation to consult before changes in the boundaries are made, as stipulated
under Article 5 of the Charter, is not respected."

Administrative structures and resources for the tasks of local authorities
The core principles determining the structures and resources of LSGs in the Czech
Republic are set by the Law on Municipalities, but details of implementation are to a
large extent left in "local hands." The major centrally determined issue is the number
of municipal council members, defined by the law as follows (Kadečka 2012):

- Up to 500 inhabitants: 5–15 councilors
- 501–3000 inhabitants: 11–15 councilors
- 3001–10,000 inhabitants: 11–25 councilors
- 10,001–50,000 inhabitants: 15–35 councilors
- 50,001–150,000 inhabitants: 25–45 councilors
- More than 150,000 inhabitants: 35–55 councilors.

In municipalities, the municipal office may be run by a "principal" appointed by
the municipal council upon the proposal of the mayor—the establishment of this
position is compulsory for second and third category municipalities. This person
is responsible to the mayor. Municipal offices may consist of different categories
of employees (civil servants, public servants, and labour-code regulated employees)
who are responsible for the administrative and organizational aspects of municipal
life as well as for other activities of municipal bodies—the numbers depend on
the size of a municipality. This means that, as a rule, Czech local authorities can
determine their own internal administrative structures with due respect to general
legislation. Municipalities are quite independent in the field of human resources,

and they can freely appoint and remove their own employees. The salaries of most municipal employees and of remunerated elected officials are pre-determined by law. Municipal employees may receive allowances and other types of compensation for expenses incurred in the fulfilment of their tasks. The salaries of the main municipal representatives are competitive in the light of the overall national economic situation and salaries that are paid in the public and private sectors.

The monitoring report states: "There is no reason to believe that Article 6 para. 1 of the Charter is not respected by the Czech Republic. On the other hand, the country has decided not to submit to Article 6 para. 2 of the Charter on the conditions of service for local (and regional) government employees. This fact may be understood in light of the wide discretion enjoyed by local and regional authorities in shaping their administrative and technical services and deciding about the staff needed to fulfil the different tasks."

Conditions under which responsibilities at the local level are exercised
The conditions of office of elected local representatives provide for the free exercise of their functions. Some elected council members may be "released" on a long-term basis in order to perform their office and are directly paid by the municipality. Other elected "non-released" members of the municipal council, if they are in an employment relationship, are granted leave by their employer with a salary compensation for performance of their office. The salary compensation is transferred by the municipality to the employer. Non-released members who are not employed receive a lump sum from the municipality as compensation for loss of earnings in relation to the performance of their office.

The list of functions and activities which are deemed incompatible with the holding of local elective office is determined by the Law on Conflict of Interest 159/2006. However, the list of such limitations is short and of general character.

Consequently, the monitoring report concludes that the current Czech system complies with the requirements of Article 7 of the charter. The Czech Republic is not bound by Article 7 para. 2 about financial compensation to elected representatives— according to the monitoring report opinion this is since such questions are left to the discretion of the local and regional council themselves.

The administrative supervision of local authorities' activities
In the Czech Republic, supervision of local and regional authorities' activities by the central government is systematically carried out according to the Constitution or statutory law (especially by the Ministry of Interior) and is basically limited to the legality of those activities. The Supreme Audit Office has the right only to control the use of means allocated by the central authorities. Municipalities call on external auditors for all activities that fall outside the competence of the SAO.

Consequently, the monitoring report concluded that the current Czech system fully complies with Article 8 of the Charter.

The financial resources of local authorities and the financial transfer system
The "quality" of the fiscal decentralization is the topic where some challenges still

can be found. The Czech Republic has decided not to ratify important parts of Article 9 (paragraphs 3, 5 and 6).

The real issue is the structure of revenues. A great part of municipal revenues still comes from the state level via the system of shared taxes. The monitoring report states on this: "In the Czech Republic, municipalities are highly dependent on financial redistribution by the State (which is based on population numbers and not on a population's wealth). This system of "shared taxation," according to which about 22% of state taxes are transferred to local and regional authorities, leaves the latter considerable freedom in deciding how these resources should be used within the field of their proper responsibilities." Municipalities have discretion over local fees, but limited discretion over the property tax—and this property tax autonomy of the Czech municipalities is to a great extent unused (Sedmihradská and Bakoš 2016).

This situation means that municipalities have rather limited power to determine the rates of their own revenues. The equalization is based on the number of residents and does not include other necessary aspects. Municipal representatives argue that the transfers for the execution of delegated powers are not commensurate with the size and nature of these powers and state that some municipalities have to subsidize the accomplishment of these tasks by drawing on their share of taxes in a way detrimental to their possibilities to exercise their proper powers according to their own decisions about the nature and size of these activities. Under the law, local and regional authorities are free to borrow under their own responsibility.

In the light of the above, we may argue that the Czech Republic meets the basic standards enshrined in Art. 9 of the Charter, with important reservations.

Local authorities' right to associate
In the Czech Republic, the right of local authorities to associate is defined in detail by the Municipal Law. The core professional organization of municipalities is the Union of Towns and Municipalities of the Czech Republic (http://www.smocr.cz/), which represents fewer than half of the local councils, but covers over 75% of the country's entire population. The report has no specific comments on this Article and its implementation in the Czech Republic.

The legal protection of local self-government
The central government cannot decide over local and regional authorities with legally binding effect. In cases of disagreement, they are bound to refer the question to the Constitutional Court for the final decision. The monitoring report states: "Local authorities' right of access to a judicial remedy according to Article 11 of the Charter is very well taken care of in the Czech Republic.

The core challenges for the fiscal decentralization in Czech Republic
As indicated above, the Czech local self-government situation, to a major extent, complies with the expectations set by the Charter principles—despite the fact that the Czech Republic is not legally bound by several principles of the Charter. Two core challenges could, however, be identified. The main problem is excessive fragmentation, and the second is municipal finance (this issue will be discussed in the last part of this text).

The territorial structure of the municipalities in the Czech Republic gained its current appearance in the seventeenth century. A t he beginning of the twentieth century, municipalities numbered approximately 11,000. Several waves of amalgamation were realised during the "socialist" period. In 1960, almost 20% of all municipalities were abolished and administratively merged with their larger neighbours; between 1970 and 1989, the number of municipalities was reduced by almost 50% to 4800 municipalities. However, after 1990, the number of municipalities started to grow again. And since 2001, the total number of municipalities has stabilized at about 6250 (Csachová and Nestorová-Dická 2011).

According to data from the Czech Statistical Office (2016), the absolute majority of municipalities are villages with a very small population: 77.1% of the municipalities have fewer than 1000 inhabitants; almost 24% of the municipalities have fewer than 200 inhabitants. The average size of the villages is 1685 inhabitants, and the median size is 425 inhabitants. There are only 19 cities that have more than 50,000 inhabitants. According to Thijs et al. (2017) the Czech Republic has the lowest average number of inhabitants per municipality—1690 (followed by France with 1885 and Slovakia with 1871).

The fragmented settlement structure in the Czech Republic is accompanied by a fragmented structure of local authorities. According to the Law on Municipalities, even very small villages have their own elected mayor and assembly, and every such village must provide at least basic public services, such as public administration, public lighting, waste management and community development. This fragmented structure has an impact on the implementation of delegated competencies (due to categorization of municipalities into three categories) and especially of own competencies. In 2004, the OECD pointed out that municipal fragmentation is a strong obstacle to better governance and the efficient delivery of policies because municipal self-government is not accompanied by measures based on the principle of "functional areas." According to Swianiewicz (2014) it quickly became apparent that territorial fragmentation was a major barrier to the decentralization and effective functioning of the local-government system.

Existing studies (for example Matějová et al. 2017, or Soukopová et al. 2014) indicate that the existence of small municipalities in the Czech Republic may be significantly "economically inefficient." Small municipalities (up to 1000 inhabitants) likely provide public services at higher costs (and lower quality) than municipalities with larger populations. Despite this fact, in the Czech Republic, due to the negative experiences from the period before 1989, there is still wide disagreement on amalgamation and changes cannot be expected in the short term perspective.

Most important data about the level of fiscal decentralization
Czech municipalities spend approximately 10–12% of GDP (the central level of government approximately 30% of GDP). Despite a strong decentralization process, the Czech Republic remains a centralized country from the perspective of local government spending. The level of LSG spending is bit more than half of the OECD average of unitary countries (OECD 2016).

Financing local governments is based mainly on shared taxes; tax revenues (except for shared taxes) represent only a small share of municipal financial resources, among the lowest levels in the OECD. The tax sharing system was introduced in 1993 and has twice been fundamentally changed. Until 1996, municipalities received a share of the personal income tax (PIT). Revenues from the PIT levied on dependent incomes were distributed among the municipalities based on the place of work; the distribution of revenues from the PIT levied on the incomes of the self-employed was based on the residence criterion. The system was adjusted in 1996: 30% of the PIT from dependent income and 20% of the corporate income tax (CIT) was received b y municipalities. As CIT revenues declined, another change was instituted in 2000 when the value added tax (VAT) was committed to revenue sharing. Currently, municipalities receive between 20.8% and 23.6% of the revenues from these three taxes and these resources are distributed among municipalities based on the population and area of the municipality, the number of school pupils and the size category. Revenues from shared taxes represent more than 50% of total municipal revenues.

Since 1993, municipalities have had the right to collect the real estate tax, with however only minimal decision-making power for the municipalities on the tax rate, i.e., municipalities can approve three different coefficients by which the tax rates are multiplied. The municipal revenues also include various fees, based on the Law on Local Fees 565/1990. Currently, there are eight local fees. Municipalities have discretion over the fee base, and fee rate, which has to respect the upper limits set by the law. Local fees are collected by the municipalities. Apart from local fees, municipalities collect fees for particular types of environmental pollution or damage and administrative fees. The current non-tax revenues amount to about 1% of municipal revenues and are composed mainly of rental incomes, incomes from own activity and incomes from interest. Capital revenues amount to about 3% of municipal revenues and their majority comes from property sales (Sedmihradská and Bakoš 2016).

The grant system is quite complex. Grants are provided for specific purposes and their usage is monitored. Some of them require matching funds. Current grants are usually formula-based and are provided to finance delegated responsibilities. The formulas are relatively stable; the changes in the parameters are approved in the Law on the State Budget. Capital grants are allocated using a case-by-case approach. Municipalities may also benefit from EU funds (as many operational programmes include eligible activities in fields related to municipal life) and many other foreign grant resources. The absorption capacity varies significantly; smaller municipalities in particular do not have their own capacity to draft projects and may outsource this (Kadečka 2012).

Concerning expenditures, the most important expenditure item is the salaries of teachers (delegated responsibility, financed by the above mentioned ear-marked transfer). Tables 3.1, 3.2 and 3.3 provide a statistical overview of the Czech local self-government finances for the last few years.

Municipalities are free to borrow or issue bonds without any restriction. Indebtedness, bailouts or bankruptcy are not a hot issue at the Czech municipal level—few

Table 3.1 Municipal revenues (million CZK, 1 EUR is approximately 26 CZK)

Revenue	2015	2016	2017
Total tax revenues	175,394	190,751	206,316
Shared personal income tax	38,924	44,781	47,846
Shared corporate income tax	41,200	45,762	47,071
Shared VAT	68,761	72,523	82,545
Property tax	10,334	10,586	10,765
Other local taxes and fees	16,175	17,099	18,089
Other current revenues	31,640	31,363	30,624
Capital revenues	5477	7878	6350
Total own revenues	212,511	229,991	243,290
Transfers	75,171	52,039	54,345
Total	287,692	282,031	297,635

Source Authors, based on Ministry of Finance data

Table 3.2 Structure of municipal expenditures: COFOG (mill. CZK, 1 EUR is app. 26 CZK)

	2015	2016	2017
General administration	50,655	52,834	55,446
Defense	0.0	0.0	0.1
Public order and security	8319	9139	11,163
Economic functions	72,134	60,420	69,304
Environment	21,617	18,593	20,566
Housing	28,669	28,109	32,835
Health care	2497	2086	2477
Recreation, culture, religion	26,989	25,080	28,562
Education	37,656	34,129	41,322
Social protection	9105	8858	11,114
Total	257,620	239,250	272,810

Source Authors, based on Ministry of Finance data

small villages and municipalities cope with a high insolvency risk—caused by specific mistakes, not by excessive borrowing. For example, the municipality Nebanice wanted to build twenty new family houses in the interest of municipal development and population growth. In 2001, the municipality received a subsidy of 8 million CZK from the Ministry for Regional Development. The municipality built utility lines and foundations of the houses, but potential buyers of the houses dropped their construction plans. The municipality was left with over 12.5 million CZK in debts linked to the construction (Hornek and Jüptner 2019).

Table 3.3 The structure of local government expenditures COFOG (%)

	2015	2016	2017
General administration	1.3	1.3	1.3
Defense	0.0	0.0	0.0
Public order and security	0.2	0.2	0.2
Economic functions	2.1	1.8	2.0
Environment	1.0	0.6	0.7
Housing	0.5	0.4	0.4
Health care	1.5	1.4	1.5
Recreation, culture, religion	0.8	0.7	0.8
Education	3.1	2.9	3.0
Social protection	0.8	0.8	0.8
Total	11.3	10.2	10.7

Source Authors, based on EUROSTAT data

References

Csachová S, Nestorová-Dická J (2011) Territorial structure of local government in the Slovak Republic, the Czech Republic and the Hungarian Republic—a comparative view. Geogr J 63(3):209–225

Hornek J, Jüptner P (2019) Endangered municipalities? Empirical inquiry into the functioning of small and critically indebted. J Publ Adm Policy 12(1)

Kadečka S (2012) Local government in the Czech Republic. In: Moreno Á-M (ed) Local government in the member states of the European union: a comparative legal perspective. Instituto Nacional de Administración Pública, Madrid, pp 111–135

Matějová L, Nemec J, Křápek M et al (2017) Economies of scale on the municipal level: fact or fiction in the Czech Republic? NISPACEE J Publ Adm Policy 10(1):39–60

OECD (2016) When size matters: scaling up delivery of Czech local services. In: Lewis C (ed). Available via https://oecdecoscope.wordpress.com/2016/07/26/when-size-matters-scaling-up-delivery-of-czech-local-services/. Assessed on 10 May 2017

Radvan M, Mrkývka P, Schweigl J (2018) Challenges of the implementation of the European charter of local self-government in Czech legislation. Lex Localis 16(4):895–906

Sedmihradská L, Bakoš E (2016) Municipal tax autonomy and tax mimicking in Czech municipalities. Lex Localis 14(1):75–92

Soukopová J, Nemec J, Matějová L et al (2014) Municipality size and local public services—do economies of scale exist? J Publ Adm Policy VII(2):30–43

Swianiewicz P (2014) An empirical typology of local government systems in Eastern Europe. Local Gov Stud 40(2):292–311

Thijs N, Hammerschmid G, Palaric E (2017) A comparative overview of public administration characteristics and performance in EU28. EU Commission, Brussels

Chapter 4
The Fiscal Decentralization in Hungary

Hungary is democratic unitary state with a long history. The freshly unified Hungarians led by Árpád settled in the Carpathian Basin and established the Principality of Hungary in 895. The Kingdom of Hungary was established in 1000, when Saint Stephen I, became the first King of Hungary. From 1526 (with part of the country temporarily occupied by Ottomans) Hungary was part of the Habsburg Monarchy and the Austrian Empire with different statuses. After World War I, Hungary underwent a period of profound political upheaval (1918–1919: Hungarian People's Republic, 1919–1920: Hungarian Soviet Republic and 1919–1920: Hungarian Republic). In 1920, the Kingdom of Hungary was established, becoming a puppet state of Nazi Germany from 1944 to 1945. After World War II, the first Hungarian Republic was re-established, soon becoming a satellite state of the Soviet Union (1949–1989: Hungarian People's Republic). June 1989 is widely considered the symbolic end of communism in Hungary, the Hungarian Republic (Third Republic) was re-established, which was renamed Hungary in 2012.

Hungary is a country in Central Europe with an area of 93,030 km^2. It borders Slovakia to the north, Ukraine to the northeast, Austria to the northwest, Romania to the east, Serbia to the south, Croatia to the southwest, and Slovenia to the west. The total length of its borders is 2242 km. Hungary has 9.8 million inhabitants; the population density is 105 inhabitants per km^2. Hungary has been a member of the NATO since March 12, 1999 and a member of the EU since May 1, 2004.

The current Hungarian political system operates under a framework reformed in 2012. The president serves as the head of state and is elected by the National Assembly every five years. The president has primarily representative responsibilities and powers, but he is also invested with veto power, and may send legislation to the 15-member Constitutional Court for review. The prime minister is elected by the National Assembly, serves as the head of government and exercises executive powers. He selects Cabinet ministers and has the exclusive right to dismiss them (although cabinet nominees must be consulted with parliamentary committees, survive a vote in the National Assembly, and be formally approved by the president). The central government consists of ministries—the number of which has ranged between 8 and 18 between 1990 and 2017 (numbering eight in 2017) and a number of agencies.

© Springer Nature Switzerland AG 2020
M. Plaček et al., *Fiscal Decentralization Reforms*, Public Administration, Governance and Globalization 19, https://doi.org/10.1007/978-3-030-46758-6_4

State involvement (deconcentrated state administration) on the regional and local levels is extensive. Many of these agencies have field offices at the county or even lower (local) administrative levels employing a significant share of civil servants. Since 2011, county government offices were established in every county and in 2013 district administrative offices were created. Both levels took a lot of the previous competencies of municipalities and self-governing regions (almost all delegated responsibilities). Following this reform, the regional self-government lost almost all its functions.

The central legislative power is represented by the unicameral Parliament with 199 members (reduced from 386 in the 2010 elections), which is elected every four years in a single-round first-past-the-post election with an election threshold of 5%. As indicated, the regional self-government (elected assemblies) level has only symbolic powers and also the powers of local self-governments (3178 municipalities) are more limited that the EU standard.

The court system consists of local courts, regional appellate courts and the Supreme Court. There are 20 regional courts in Hungary (19 counties and Budapest). Beside them there are 20 administrative and labor courts located at the seat of regional courts (Hajnal 2017).

The development of local self-government in Hungary
The royal counties and free royal municipalities already existed on the territory of Hungary during the medieval era. The first ideas of modern local and regional self-government appeared in Hungary before the civic revolution of 1848 and the first local government laws were passed in 1870 (municipal and county self-governments with elected councils were established). The dual level structure of local government did not change significantly before 1950. In 1950 a Soviet-type council system was introduced, similar to other countries in the region and a two-and-a-half-tier system was created (local councils, counties and from 1950 to 1971 also district councils). Because of the forced amalgamation of municipalities, their number was gradually reduced in the 1960s and 1970s.

After the end of the "communist" regime in October 1989, the principles of new self-governments were incorporated into the Constitution. The first freely-elected Parliament passed the Act on Local Government in 1990. One specific feature of this period was the decision to counteract the earlier forced amalgamations of municipalities: all communes, including the smallest villages, were given the right to establish a separate local self-government with general competence. A relatively independent and intact system of local and county self-governments providing wide-ranging autonomy for the local authorities was created during this period (Szente 2012). An important proportion of the powers exercised by the State before 1990 were entrusted to local authorities—especially primary school education, water supply and wastewater services, road maintenance, local public transport, local development, environmental protection, land use, fire protection and protection of minority rights, which are all competencies that are vital to citizens' everyday lives.

From 2010 on, with the inauguration of the second Orbán cabinet, a broad and overwhelming state reform was initiated, with the aim of enhancing central control and coordination over the national public administration system. The continuing and very intensive striving to maximize top-down control continues even today (Hajnal 2017). Significant reverses were introduced at the self-government level by the Cardinal Act on Local Government in Hungary (of December 21, 2011), which has made sweeping changes to the pattern of administrative organization in Hungary, as already indicated. The relations between the national and local levels were redefined in Hungary, with the powers of the State highly expanding and those of local authorities highly contracting. The main principle of the reform—formally linked to expected cost savings—was that local governments should only deal with local issues and services, and anything else could be transferred to central government supervision.

Taking these changes into account, the CoE monitoring report of October 31, 2013 (used as the basis for the following text) declares: ... "there is a very strong recentralization of powers, which has led to the considerable reduction of competencies previously assigned to local authorities; the principle of the financial autonomy of local authorities is not respected."

4.1   The Level of Decentralization in Hungary from the Point of View of the Principles of the European Charter of Local Self-government

Hungary signed the Carpathian Charter of Local Self-Government (Charter) on April 6, 1992, ratified it on March 21, 1994, and it entered into force on July 1, 1994—without reservations. After the collapse of the centralistic regime in 1990, Hungary opted for an administrative and political organization that left an important role for local government, seen as an essential outlet for democracy. However, the changes after 2011 reversed the trends towards subsidiarity and are already reflected in the 2013 monitoring report, and especially by existing academic studies, listed in this text. We try to combine these sources in the following evaluation.

The constitutional and legal foundation for local self-government

According to the monitoring report, the principle of local self-government was present in the old Hungarian Constitution and adequately guaranteed by legislative texts. At that time, local self-government was regarded as a cornerstone of the Hungarian democratic system. The situation is very different in 2012. Article 31 (1) of the new Constitution stipulates that "in Hungary local governments shall be established to administer public affairs and exercise public power at a local level." Nevertheless, no explicit mention is made of the principle of local self-government.

Not only the Constitution—the Cardinal Act on Local Government from December 21, 2011 does not directly refer to the principle of local self-government either (the explanatory memorandum to the Cardinal Act expressly refers to the Charter, but it does so only to strike a parallel with the traditions of local government in Hungary and avoids citing the principle of local self-government). According to the position of the Venice Commission, the Hungarian Constitution guarantees only the existence of local authorities, not their powers. Moreover, the local authorities' powers are exercised "within the limits of the law" which leaves the legislature with considerable room for manoeuvre.

Following the text of the 2011 legislation, local self-government appears unfair and costly. Moreover, Balázs and Hoffman (2017, p. 12) argue that in the newly established system, "local governments are 'part of the state system,' and their main task is to 'contribute to the realization of the targets of the state.'"

From its beginning, the monitoring report already clearly regrets the fact that the principle of local self-government is explicitly enshrined in neither the Act on Local Government nor in the Constitution.

The concept of local self-government
Since 2011, the share of competencies entrusted to local government has decreased very significantly and the financial autonomy of local governments has been severely reduced (the government argues that this was necessary to improve the health of the national public finances, however most experts feel that financial problems of municipalities were the result of the constantly increasing tension between broad task portfolios on the one hand, and insufficient funding). Health and social care as well as education have now been almost completely centralized (these three sectors accounted for 86% of local expenditures—now, as official statements explain, local self-governments have been "relieved of this burden").

The monitoring report states as follows: "Local authorities are therefore losing fundamental powers, with no real compensation, while in the spirit of the Charter, both the adequate finance and the public service functions of local interest should be allocated to them." On the other hand, the manner of electing and organizing local government councils still complies with the Charter.

The scope of local self-government
The 2011 reform significantly reduced the scope of local self-government and the division of powers between the central tier and local government has been radically modified, to the exclusive benefit of the former. In addition, the State took back delegated responsibilities, including the powers delegated to local town hall clerks and created its own local deconcentrated structures. Municipal responsibilities are now of two types: compulsory and voluntary. Compulsory tasks include road maintenance, public transport, child protection support, and provision of social services tied to local government ordinances. Voluntary responsibilities can be carried out only if all compulsory tasks are already financed.

The systematic consultations between the state and the municipalities do not function. The important reason for this is the fact that the government has no single talking partner, which does not facilitate consultation with local authorities (seven different associations represent interests of local self-governments).

The monitoring report concludes: "It is clear that the movement towards centralization of competences under way in Hungary does not conform to Article 4 of the Charter. Where Article 4.6 is concerned, the consultation procedure is a simply formal one."

The protection of local authority boundaries
The new legislation has not changed much in this area and according to the report the Hungarian system respects the principles laid down by Article 5 of the Charter.

Administrative structures and resources for the tasks of local authorities
The local government law centrally determines the number of municipal council members and the election rules, specifically for municipalities below and above 10,000 inhabitants. For municipalities with fewer than 10,000 inhabitants, a combination method is used, allowing voters to compose their own list, placing in order as many candidates as there are seats. The candidates elected are those having received the highest number of votes (Szente 2012). The number of municipal council members is determined as follows:

- up to 100 inhabitants: 2 members;
- up to 1000 inhabitants: 4 members;
- up to 5000 inhabitants: 6 members;
- up to 10,000 inhabitants: 8 members.

In larger municipalities the situation is as follows:

- between 10,000 and 25,000 inhabitants: 8 members elected by a majority single-seat constituency vote and 3 members taken from compensation lists;
- up to 50,000 inhabitants: 10 members elected by a majority single-seat constituency vote and 4 members taken from compensation lists;
- up to 75,000 inhabitants: 12 members elected by a majority single-seat constituency vote and 5 members taken from compensation lists;
- up to 100,000 inhabitants: 14 members elected by a majority single-seat constituency vote and 6 members taken from compensation lists;
- over 100,000 inhabitants: one additional constituency must be defined for every additional 10,000 inhabitants and the number of members elected from compensation lists increases by one for every additional 25,000 inhabitants.

The electoral legislation provides for separate direct elections for the mayor. The head of administration is designated and remunerated by the county.

The law on local government from 2011 also defines that municipalities below 2000 inhabitants have to group their administrative services together in a "district" or "micro-region" (each municipality keeps its mayor and its municipal council, but the administrative structures, and the exercise of prerogatives, have to be pooled). Balázs and Hoffman (2017) provide details on this procedure: If the villages do not freely contract for this joint municipal office, it is the commissioner of the government who is empowered by the law to determine the villages taking part in the association and replace the agreement for its establishment. Municipalities tried to fight this central-ization process and several judges handling such cases turned to the Constitutional Court. The judicial applications accepted by the Court declared the regulation to be contrary to the European Charter of Local Government; however, the Constitutional Court did not annul the contested rules. After the resolution of the Constitutional Court, only a corrective amendment bill was submitted to the Parliament, and it has not been passed.

The monitoring report concludes: "The administrative structures and resources available to the local authorities in Hungary today do not appear to be commensurate with the tasks assigned to them—a situation which is not in compliance with Article 6 of the Charter."

Conditions under which responsibilities are exercised at the local level

The conditions of office of elected local representatives provide for the free exercise of their functions. The list of functions and activities which are deemed incom-patible with the holding of local elective office is determined by law, since 2014 mayors cannot simultaneously be members of the national parliament. The monitor-ing report concludes that the current Hungarian system generally complies with the requirements of Article 7 of the Charter.

The administrative supervision of local authorities' activities

The monitoring report mentions several issues that seem to be problematic from the point of view of Article 8. The new Constitution empowers the governmental offices of the capital and of the counties to issue municipal decrees, by court decision, where a local authority fails to fulfil its "obligation to legislate imposed on it by law" (Article 32.5). The state administration bodies monitor whether local authorities comply with the law in their activities; it may respond to any shortcomings by prosecuting the authority in question (without the clear distinction of own competences and those delegated by the central government). Parliament may dissolve an elected body on the grounds of a violation of the Constitution, after seeking the opinion of the Constitutional Court.

Hungarian local authorities are subject to supervision by the State Audit Office and this supervision has been radically overhauled in recent years; however, the points on which the audit was carried out were negotiated with local authority associations. Both compliance and performance audits are delivered.

The financial resources of local authorities and the financial transfer system

The Constitution provides that local governments "shall, to the extent permitted by law" "determine their budgets and perform independent financial management accordingly." However, the financial autonomy of local governments has been severely reduced since 2011. Municipalities' own revenues are generated from land taxes, municipal taxes and local corporate taxes (the most important sources), but the main source of revenues are earmarked grants, distributed according to the estimated service costs. Equalization mechanisms are nearly non-existent. Taking this into account, the monitoring report concludes: "the current situation is not in conformity with Article 9 of the Charter, except as regards paragraphs 3 and 8."

Local authorities' right to associate
The right of local authorities to associate is well recognized by the legislation (however, the specific problem is the high number of representative associations of local self-governments, mentioned above). The present situation is in compliance with the requirements of Article 10.

The legal protection of local self-government
Local authorities may apply to the Constitutional Court only in cases of conflict with another authority concerning their respective responsibilities. The local government law provides for the possibility of appealing to the court against decisions which go against their interests—but only in very specific cases (such as when the government takes away a development project which would have been of local interest for a municipality). In such situations effective legal remedy is not available to local authorities—the situation is not in compliance with Article 11 of the Charter (see also Hoffman 2018).

The core challenges for the fiscal decentralization in Hungary
Besides the extreme recentralization realized in a top-down direction, the specific challenge for Hungarian local self-government is high fragmentation. The aforementioned fact that after 1989, parts of previously amalgamated municipalities received the right to dissolve and become separate municipalities is the core cause of the current situation, where many municipalities are very small, and because of this lack the means to fulfil their local public services mission and to cope with the limited resources. In Hungary, there are 103 municipalities with fewer than 100 inhabitants, 473 between 100–300 inhabitants, 462 between 300–500 inhabitants, 683 between 500–1000 inhabitants and only about half have more than 1000 inhabitants. The state addressed this situation in the Local Government Act of 2011, stipulating that the administrative structures of these small municipalities with fewer than 2.000 inhabitants shall be grouped together.

The more effective response to fragmentation is connected with the pre-2011 period. New, additional state subsidies were introduced to accelerate the formation of voluntary inter-municipal associations and as a result of these changes, the number of inter-municipal associations radically increased after 1997 (Balázs and Hoffman 2017). However, this option is no longer followed today.

The third core challenge is local finance evaluated in the following part.

Most important data about the level of fiscal decentralization
The local government expenditures in Hungary fell from 12 to 13% of GDP before the 2011 reforms to the current approximately 6% of GDP, one of the lowest levels in the EU and approximately half of the OECD average for unitary countries (OECD 2016).

The most important revenue source for municipalities is the local business tax (approximately 75% of local tax revenue) which is imposed on companies located or registered in the municipal area and based on corporate gross margins (the exact rate is decided by the municipality, but it is centrally capped at 2%). Property taxes are the second most important source (approximately 20% of local tax revenue) and include a building tax and a land tax (paid by owners, based either on area or floor space or on the adjusted market value, tax rates are set by each municipality, up to certain limits). Communal taxes are a minor tax source. Other municipal revenues include primary user tariffs and fees for public services which represent around 9% of local revenues (Szente 2012).

The 2011 reform also modified the grants system and reduced the amounts of the grants, in accordance to the recentralization of several responsibilities, such as the decline in funds from the Health Insurance Fund. A stricter grant system was set up in 2013, going from an income-based system to a task-based, expenditure-oriented system. Grants are now earmarked. The reform included the tightening of distribution rules and new equalization criteria based on the tax capacity of each municipality.

Dobos' (2014) analysis is a representative story about Hungarian local public finance. Before 2011, local self-governments enjoyed a high level of financial independence, but they were under constant and increasing fiscal pressure to maintain their functioning because of insufficient financing. Thus, most Hungarian local governments issued bonds or took out credits/loans. As a result, the local governments' debt was constantly growing and municipalities regularly turned to the national force majeure financial fund for assistance. The situation worsened after the 2008 financial crisis, when several local governments could not ensure their functioning: they had to stop their development plans, compensate their loss from local tax revenues and deal with the falling social status of local communities. In such a situation, the reformation of local governments' finances was a vital point. One measure was merging the mayors' offices of municipalities with fewer than 2000 inhabitants. Second, the central government changed the method of calculating the level of the core transfer to the local government system. The subsidization from the central budget on a per capita basis was replaced with determining the level of funding based on activities. From 2013, local governments' transfer funding changed to activity-based financing, with the central government granting the municipalities sums based on the calculated cost of each activity. According to Dobos (2014) this new system is more transparent, but its main weakness is that it has the form of an earmarked transfer, to cover the difference between own revenues and expenditure needs (municipalities with a higher level of revenue may receive less). And if the revenues of a municipality are over-estimated by the state, such a municipality would lack resources to cover its core responsibilities.

New fiscal rules have been introduced:

- Local self-governments cannot plan a deficit in their yearly budget;
- Local self-governments can only provide voluntary services if this does not endanger the fulfilment of their mandatory tasks, and these voluntary services must be covered from local governments' own revenue;

- Conditions of issuing bonds and taking out loans are strictly regulated.

It is very problematic to find any reliable data about the structure of munici-pal revenue in Hungary (open central data deal only with transfers). If we look at the example of one town (Eger—a wealthy city with tourism and wine producing industries) the structure of current revenues in 2018 was as follows:

- Local non-tax revenues: 2973 million FT;
- Local tax revenues: 4939 million FT;
- Government transfers: 3857 million FT;
- Total current revenues: 11,913 million FT.

Tables 4.1 and 4.2 provide data on the main transfer structure and local government expenditures.

Table 4.1 Main transfers to support municipalities (million forints)

	2015	2016	2017
General support transfer	150,994.9	154,094.9	151,589.9
Education	165,485.3	179,795.1	184,378.4
Social affairs	195,174.4	187,719.7	127,137.6
Culture	30,765.3	31,015.3	31,247.6
Child care	113,624.7	119,594.7	73,910.4
Current expenditure support	150,994.9	2042.0	45,368.5
Capital expenditure support	x	154,094.9	40,540.8

Source Authors, based on Ministry of Finance data

Table 4.2 The structure of local governmental expenditures: COFOG (% of GDP)

	2015	2016	2017
General administration	1.8	1.5	1.6
Defense	0	0	0
Public order and security	0	0	0
Economic functions	1.4	1.2	1.2
Environment	0.9	0.1	0.2
Housing	0.8	0.4	0.5
Health care	0.3	0.3	0.3
Recreation, culture, sports	0.7	0.6	0.7
Education	1.1	1.1	1.0
Social protection	0.8	0.7	0.7
Total	7.8	6.0	6.3

Source Authors, based on EUROSTAT data

Borrowing must be authorized by the State which decides whether the investment project for a loan is financially viable. Most loans are granted to cities or counties, which means that borrowing is beyond the reach of small municipalities. In 2010, local government debt reached 1247.5 billion HUF, which is largely debt in foreign currencies. At the end of 2011, the government took over the responsibility for counties' debts originating from loans and bonds; at the end of 2012, the government also took over the debts of municipalities of 5000 or fewer inhabitants.

References

Balázs I, Hoffman I (2017) Can (re)centralization be a modern governance in rural areas? Transylv Rev Adm Sci 50E:5–20

Dobos G (2014) Changing local relations: effects of the 2010–2014 political and administrative reforms in Hungary. In: Kuć-Czajkowska K, Sienkiewicz MV (eds) Local government in selected Central and Eastern European countries: experiences, reforms and determinants of development. Marie Curie Sklodowska University Press, Lublin, pp 73–89

Hajnal G (2017) Public administration characteristics in Hungary. Unpublished report for EUPACK project

Hoffman I (2018) Challenges of the implementation of the European charter of local self-government in the Hungarian legislation. Lex Localis 16(4):929–938

Szente Z (2012) Local government in Hungary. In: Moreno Á-M (ed) Local government in the member states of the European union: a comparative legal perspective. Instituto Nacional de Administración Pública, Madrid, pp 283–308

OECD (2016) When size matters: scaling up delivery of Czech local services. In: Lewis C (ed). Available via https://oecdecoscope.wordpress.com/2016/07/26/when-size-matters-scaling-up-delivery-of-czech-local-services/. Assessed on 10 May 2017

Chapter 5
The Fiscal Decentralization in Poland

Poland (officially the Republic of Poland) is a democratic unitary state with a very long and rich history. Poland began to form into a recognizable entity around the middle of the tenth century under the Piast dynasty in the tenth century. In 1025, the Kingdom of Poland was established. In the seventeenth century, Poland covered an area of about 1 million km^2. At the end of the eighteenth century, the territory of "greater" Poland (Commonwealth) was partitioned several times by all three of its more powerful neighbors (Russia, Prussia and Austria) and with this, the Kingdom of Poland effectively ceased to exist. After World War I, in November 1918, Poland regained its independence as the Second Polish Republic. During World War II, Poland was occupied by Nazi Germany and in 1945 was liberated by the Soviet Army. Polish borders were shifted westwards, resulting in considerable territorial losses. The Communist government came into power in Poland, analogous to many of the other countries in the area, and the new Polish government accepted the Soviet annexation of the pre-war eastern regions of Poland, and agreed to the permanent garrisoning of Red Army units on Poland's territory. In the 1980s, the independent trade union "Solidarity" was formed, which over time became a political force and in June 1989 triumphed in Poland's first partially free and democratic parliamentary elections, starting the country's process of transforming its socialist-style planned economy into a market economy.

Poland is located in Central Europe and now covers an area of 312,696 km^2. The population of the country is approximately 38.5 million, which means that Poland is the sixth most populous member state of the European Union. The population density is 123/km^2. Poland is bordered by the Baltic Sea, Lithuania, and Russia's Kaliningrad Oblast to the north, Belarus and Ukraine to the east, Slovakia and the Czech Republic to the south, and Germany to the west. The country has been a member of NATO since March 1999 and of the European Union (EU) since May 2004.

Poland is a representative democracy, with a president as the head of state. The government center is the Council of Ministers, led by the prime minister. The president is elected by popular vote every five years and appoints the cabinet (Council of Ministers) according to the proposals of the prime minister. Other government

© Springer Nature Switzerland AG 2020

M. Plaček et al., *Fiscal Decentralization Reforms*, Public Administration, Governance and Globalization 19, https://doi.org/10.1007/978-3-030-46758-6_5

administration at the central level comprises individual ministries, central offices, and agencies. In addition, it also includes a state administration that supports the central authorities (e.g. the Chancellery of the House of deputies—the Sejm, the Chancellery of the Senate). Government administration also operates at the voivodship level. It includes voivodes (governors of regions) supported by voivodship (regional) offices, complex/general administration offices, non-complex/specialized deconcentrated administration (part of the field government administration not subject to voivodes but to ministers or other central government bodies) as well as services and inspectorates (Mazur et al. 2017).

The legislative branch of the government, the Parliament, consists of two chambers. The lower house (Sejm) has 460 deputies and the Senate has 100 deputies. The Sejm is elected under proportional representation, the Senate is elected under the first-past-the-post voting method, with one senator from each of the 100 constituencies. The self-government is represented by voivodships (16 regions), poviats (314 counties), and gminas (2478 municipalities). A peculiar situation exists at the regional (voivodship) level, where apart from the voivodship self-government (marshals and voivodship boards) there are voivodes (governors of regions) representing the central government in the region. They are appointed and dismissed by the Council of Ministers.

The highest judicial level consists of the Supreme Court, the Supreme Administrative Court, the Constitutional Tribunal, and the State Tribunal. The common courts are divided into appellate courts, district courts and regional courts and have competency in criminal, civil, economic, labor and family law (Mazur et al. 2017).

The development of local self-government in Poland

From the eighteenth century until 1918, Poland was a nation divided among three neighboring countries (Russia, Prussia and Austria) that had different administrative systems, including self-government schemes. After World War I, Poland started building uniform local government structures, and the constitutional foundations for local and regional self-government were established in the Constitution of 1921 (the structures of territorial government were not developed until later). After World War II, in 1950, local governments were replaced by the system of people's councils (similar to other countries in the region) and their assets were nationalized (Kulesza and Sześciło 2012).

The reconstruction of local government was one of the priorities of the 1989 political transformation in Poland. The fundamental amendments to the Constitution were passed on December 1, 1989 and in March 1990; local self-government in municipalities was legally restored by the Territorial Self-government Act. In May 1990, representatives from almost 2500 local councils were elected in fully democratic elections.

The second wave Polish self-government reform is connected with the legislative package passed in 1998, effective from January 1, 1999. This reform established the counties and the regions based upon pre-existing similar territorial demarcations. This legislative package was enacted under a "new" Constitution for Poland, passed in 1997, in particular in Chapter VII, Articles 163 to 172, entitled "Local Government."

The 1997 Constitution directly states that local authorities are considered as public legal entities, acting through their own governing bodies, possessing legal personality and having rights of ownership and other property rights (Wójcik 2013)

Local self-government in Poland today has two levels—the municipality and the county. There are three forms of municipalities—urban municipality (this type of local body covers the area of towns and there are fewer than 300), rural municipality (there are some 1500 such units) and urban-rural municipality (this type is a mixed or consolidated form covering towns or townships and the area of the villages adjacent to them—almost 600). Within the rural communes, the parishes represent the basic form of neighborhood self-organization of rural communities in villages, without legal status. Counties have existed since 1998 and include the group of the 65 largest towns (towns with county rights) and 314 counties covering the territory of several municipalities (Mazur et al. 2017).

5.1 The Level of Decentralization in Poland from the Point of View of the Principles of the European Charter of Local Self-government

Poland signed the European Charter of Local Self-government on February 19, 1993, ratified it on November 22, 1993, and it entered into force on March 1, 1994. Poland ratified all the provisions of the Charter without reservations. The Charter is applicable to the two different tiers of local self-government: municipalities and counties. The Charter has become part of the Polish legal order and it takes precedence over domestic statutes, pursuant to Article 91 of the Polish Constitution.

The most recent monitoring report about Poland is from 2015, based on the monitoring visit of May 2014. We will try to supplement the information from this report with the results from existing academic studies, listed in this text, especially by findings of Radwanowicz-Wanczewska and Dąbek (2018).

The constitutional and legal foundation for local self-government
As already indicated, in Poland, the principle of local self-government is explicitly recognized in the Constitution (Articles 163–172). The core is Article 165, according to which:

> "a. Units of local government shall possess legal personality. They shall have rights of ownership and other property rights.
> b. The self-governing nature of units of local government shall be protected by the courts."

The other core legal sources include, for example, the Municipal Government Act and the County Government Act, the Municipal Economy Act, and the Public Finances Act.

The monitoring report states that the present Polish constitutional and statutory arrangements fully satisfy the requirements of Article 2 of the Charter, and mentions that (according to the opinion of local experts) the Charter had provided inspiration for both the philosophy of the decentralization processes and the legislation regulating the local government.

The concept of local self-government
The preamble of the Polish Constitution directly mentions the principle of subsidiarity and Article 15 states that "The territorial system of the Republic of Poland shall ensure the decentralization of public power." In addition, Article 16 provides that "Local government shall participate in the exercise of public power. The substantial part of public duties which local government is empowered to discharge by statute shall be done in its own name and under its own responsibility." Finally, Article 163 of the Constitution provides that "Local government shall perform public tasks not reserved by the Constitution or statutes to the organs of other public authorities." According to Mazur et al. (2017), Poland is one of the more decentralized states in Europe and, moreover, this success cannot be attributed to widespread civic engagement because decentralization in Poland was clearly a "revolution from above." However, Kulesza and Sześciło (2012) report that the reality of the right of municipalities to perform all public tasks not reserved to other bodies is undermined by practice. Central government bodies (especially the Supreme Chamber of Control— as the monitoring report states) are often followers of the Weberian bureaucratic vision of government and request that every (fiscal) action be determined in detailed laws

The representative governing body at the municipal level is the municipal council, while the municipality's executive organ is the mayor. Municipal councils and mayors are directly elected by the local residents, in regular local elections that are held every four years. The mayor is vested with a large number of executive competencies (like implementing the policies, plans and guidelines approved b y the council, adopting the individual decisions and adjudications on the different sectors of municipal activity). The mayor also runs the different municipal administration offices or units ("strong mayor model"). In the case of counties, the basic institutional organization includes the elected council and the executive person ("starosta") appointed by council. In the cities with county rights, there are no separate county bodies—the tasks, duties and competencies of the county are discharged by the regular organs of the municipality. The existing legal framework provides municipalities and counties with the right to decide to set up specific organs or structures.

The monitoring report does not include any direct criticism concerning the application of Article 3 of the Charter in the Polish conditions.

The scope of local self-government
The powers and competences of municipalities and counties differ, and each has its own constitutional and legal framework. Polish municipalities enjoy many competences—the Law on Municipalities divides original municipal competences into "compulsory" and "optional" tasks. Currently, the responsibilities of municipalities

are exercised in the following core fields: environmental protection, public streets, squares and public gardens and parks, traffic and public transportation, water supply and sewage systems, urban waste (disposal), welfare, care homes, public education (primary and middle schools), cultural and leisure facilities, conservation of historic monuments, sport facilities and tourism, markets, housing, social assistance programmes, and culture. Municipalities are also endowed with important planning powers, for instance in the domain of spatial planning and urban development. Municipalities have legislative powers: the municipal councils can approve, with due respect to the national laws, by-laws and local ordinances for different purposes. Municipalities also execute delegated responsibilities. According to the monitoring report, the number and importance of delegated tasks have increased sharply, while the national legislation and administrative regulations are too detailed, resulting in over-regulation. The extra delegation of tasks from the central government is realized without adequate financial resources to perform them.

Counties have their scope of competences, but according to the legislation counties can only act in those areas and may discharge only those competences that are expressly attributed to them by law. The competences attributed to counties are public education, promotion and protection of health, social assistance, family policy, support for people with disabilities, public transport and public roads, culture and cultural heritage protection, sports and tourism, geodesy, cartography and cadaster, real estate management, architectural and building administration, water supply, environmental protection and nature, agriculture, forestry and inland fisheries, public order and citizen safety, flood protection, fire protection and prevention, extraordinary threats to human life and health and the environment, combating unemployment and activation of the local labor market, and the protection of consumer rights.

According to the monitoring report, the requirements of Article 4 of the Charter are met by the present legal and political situation in Poland, but it also draws two points of concern: "The level of autonomy enjoyed by local government is increasingly being eroded by central government regulation; competences delegated to the local and regional level are increasing but adequate concomitant funding to carry out the tasks is lacking, for example in the field of education."

The protection of local authority boundaries
The Council of Ministers may create, merge, and dissolve municipalities and counties. It also defines the boundaries of municipalities and counties by way of regulations. Such changes are made by the Council of Ministers upon its own initiative, or on a motion by the local bodies themselves, require an opinion of the organs of local self-government units and are subject to public consultation. The creation, merger, or division of municipalities as well as a re-definition of their boundaries may also be initiated by residents in a referendum, the results of which could form the basis for a motion by the local council. However, the will of the residents is not the only basis for changing the boundaries. The Ministry of Administration and Digitization takes care that the territory of the resulting local body: (a) is as uniform as possible in terms of the settlement pattern and spatial arrangement; (b) takes into account social, economic and cultural ties; and (c) will ensure the ability of the local body to carry out

its tasks. The changes concerning territorial division are also subject to consultation in the joint committee of the central and local governments and published online.

According to the monitoring report, the current legal framework in Poland fully complies with the requirements of Article 5 of the Charter.

Administrative structures and resources for the tasks of local authorities
The size of the municipal council depends on the size of the municipality, as follows:

- up to 20,000 inhabitants 1 5 councilors;
- up to 50,000 inhabitants 2 1 councilors;
- up to 100,000 inhabitants 23 councilors;
- up to 200,000 inhabitants 25 councilors.

In municipalities with populations exceeding 200,000 residents, the number of councilors increases by 3 for every 100,000 residents. A special regulation applies for Warsaw, which allows a fixed number of 60 councilors (Kulesza and Sześciło 2012).

Formally, Polish local self-government municipalities enjoy a fair degree of autonomy in the field of internal organization—within the limits of state legislation, the council and the mayor may decide to establish a wide array of different committees and internal structures. However, the monitoring report indicates that in reality, the existence of numerous laws and administrative regulations impose excessively rigid organizational structures on municipalities and counties.

Polish local self-governments have the power and the autonomy to recruit highly qualified staff on the basis of merit and competence, with due respect to public and competitive procedures. Consequently, the report states that the current Polish system meets the requirements of Article 6 of the Charter.

Conditions under which responsibilities are exercised at the local level
In Poland, the conditions of office of local elected representatives provide for the free exercise of their functions. Council members receive an allowance for their work, which is on a part-time basis, its level depends on the number of residents of the municipality. The municipal council sets the remuneration of its members by means of a resolution. The remuneration of the mayor follows similar rules. The council decides on the salary of the mayor, depending on the population. The deputy mayor is selected by the mayor and earns the same salary. The Anti-Corruption Act regulates the conflict of interest of persons heading local government authorities and members of local councils.

The monitoring report does not include any direct criticism concerning the application of Article 7 of the Charter under the Polish conditions.

The administrative supervision of local authorities' activities
The administrative supervision of local self-government activities is strictly regulated by law, and can only be enforced under law. The Polish Constitution states: "The legality of actions by a local government shall be subject to review. The organs exercising review over the activity of units of local government shall be: the Prime Minister and

'voivods', and regarding financial matters—regional audit chambers." Municipal and county councils have the duty to refer all resolutions to the "voivode," who reviews them. If the voivode finds that a given measure or decision goes against the law, they may declare it null and void, partially or in full (very rare practice). Regional Accounting Chambers under the supreme authority of the Supreme Chamber of Control of the Regional Accounting Chambers ensure that municipalities and counties manage their expenditures according to the law, and within the municipal/county budget approved, but cannot revoke local body decisions or measures.

The monitoring report does not include any negative comments concerning the implementation of Article 8 of the Charter, but the fact that "voivode" can declare local resolutions void is not the common practice at the local level.

The financial resources of local authorities and the financial transfer system
Funding for local authorities is derived from own revenues, general lump sum subsidies (approximately 25–30% of revenues) and specific grants from the state budget (approximately 20% of revenues). The most important own source is shared income taxes. Only municipalities (not counties) can levy local taxes.

Formally, the Polish Constitution states in Article 167: "Units of local government shall be assured public funds adequate for the performance of the duties assigned to them." However, the monitoring report indicates important implementation problems, especially the opinion of municipal leaders that their own income remains limited and that they are not fully compensated for the execution of central government tasks delegated to them. Local taxes are set by law and by the Minister of Finance; local governments can only introduce tax exemptions and relief. The financial equalization system does not take into account the differences in the financial burdens on urban local authorities; instead, it takes into account, twice, the specific nature of rural municipalities. The core practical problem is financing education—the state provides the subsidy calculated per student and for the maintenance of buildings, but with the decreasing number of pupils, the level of this subsidy goes down, while salaries continue to rise (Swirska 2013).

Local authorities' right to associate
There are five well-structured and active associations of local authorities in Poland: the Association of Rural Communes (Municipalities) of the Republic of Poland, the Association of Polish Cities, the Association of Counties, the Association of Metropolises and the Association of Polish Small Towns. These associations play an active role in the representation, defense and advancement of local interests, and they negotiate on a regular basis with the central government on major developments affecting local interests.

The law on local public administration allows local authorities to associate through different types of joint bodies or agreements. The monitoring report states that the situation in Poland is satisfactory as regards Article 10 of the Charter.

The legal protection of local self-government
The legal protection of local self-government is directly guaranteed by the Constitution. Article 165.2 stipulates: "The self-governing nature of units of local government

shall be protected by the courts." Article 166.3 stipulates: "The administrative courts shall settle jurisdictional disputes between units of local government and units of government administration." The local self-governments are the subject of judicial protection, especially the following mechanisms: protection by ordinary courts, protection by administrative courts and protection by the Constitutional Court. Taking this into account, the monitoring report states that the Polish legal system completely meets the requirements of Article 11 of the Charter.

The core challenges for the fiscal decentralization in Poland
According to the OECD (2016), the share of subnational government expenditure increased from 23% in 1995 to 31% in 2013, reaching the average level of OECD unitary countries. Municipalities are by far the most important component of subnational expenditure (around 80%), followed by counties, and then regions.

However, the core source of municipal and county budgets is the share of income tax, and grants and subsidies. According to Swirska (2013), transfers from the state budget aspire to support those local governments that are inadequately financially equipped, to ensure the implementation of a certain minimum level of public services and to finance delegated responsibilities. The subsidy is defined as a non-earmarked transfer of funds from the state budget to local budgets that should supplement the shortfall in local units' incomes and equalize the financing situation of local governments. Municipalities receive approximately 80% from the total sum of the state subsidies to self-government units, and subsidies represent up to 30% of their revenues. For counties, subsidies represent almost 50% of revenues. The core part of this subsidy is the education subsidy (43 billion zloty in 2018) distributed among local governments in the manner set out in regulations by the minister responsible for education. To determine the value of educational subsidies, the following factors are taken into account: the type and nature of schools and educational institutions run by the local government, teachers' academic degrees, the number of students in schools and institutions and the location of schools. The basis for calculating the equalization sum of the subsidy (10.7 billion zloty in 2018) is a tax revenue ratio (revenue capacity of local self-governments). The "balancing" part of the subsidy (1.7 billion zloty in 2018) is also connected with the equalization mechanism: counties obtaining the highest tax income per inhabitant make contributions to the mechanism, and the funds are re-distributed on the basis of an algorithm involving different criteria.

The subsidy is significantly different from earmarked grants, which are also transferred from the state budget but must be used for pre-defined purposes. The structure of grants in 2018, according to data of the Ministry of Finance, was as follows: delegated responsibilities—44 billion zloty, own responsibilities—8 billion zloty, other ear-marked grants—19 billion zloty.

The structure of revenues of Polish municipal self-governments in 2018 was as follows: share of corporate income tax 7.8%, share of personal income tax 41.0%, agriculture land tax 1.2%, property tax 18.2%, forest land tax 0.2%, transport means tax 0.9%, tax card 0.1%, inheritance and gift tax 0.2%, activity tax 2.2%, wealth tax 6.2%, other own revenues 21.0%, corrections 0.8% (Ministry of Finance data).

Revenues of counties include a share (10.25%) of the income tax from private persons residing within the territory of the county, a share (1.4%) of the income tax from legal entities with registered offices within the territory of the county, profits from real estate and property and other revenues, for instance: fees, fines and penalties paid on the basis of administrative regulations; revenues obtained by autonomous county units, inheritances and donations received from residents. The personal income share is approximately 15% of total county revenues, share on company taxation is marginal (less than 1% of revenues), other own revenues are approximately 12% of total revenues. Lump sum subsidies represent approximately 45% and ear-marked grants 25% of total revenues (Ministry of Finance data).

The total municipal expenditures in 2018 were 127.1 billion zloty, with the following main expenditure categories: agriculture and hunting 3.4 billion, electricity, gas and water 0.6 billion, transport 12.4 billion, local economy 3.1 billion, administration 10.8 billion, local order and fire protection 1.3 billion, debt service 0.7 billion, education 38.5 billion, health 0.7 billion, social protection 6.3 billion, support to families 28.0 billion, environment 11.7 billion, culture and cultural heritage 4.5 billion, sports 3.3 billion (Ministry of Finance data).

The Eurostat data for all subnational government expenditure in COFOG structure are provided by Table 5.1.

Local governments are subject to relatively tight fiscal rules. Deficits for current expenditures are prohibited. From the end of 2013, a general rule applied to all subnational government units requiring that the overall debt of each local unit not exceed 60% of the revenues at the end of the year, while interest payments could not exceed 15% of revenues. From the beginning of 2014, a new rule was in force, introducing a unit-specific coefficient of debt calculated on a three-year average ratio of the sum of the current surplus and sales to total revenues.

Table 5.1 The structure of subnational expenditures in Poland: COFOG (% of GDP)

	2015	2016	2017
General administration	1.3	1.3	1.3
Defense	0	0	0
Public order and security	0.2	0.2	0.2
Economic functions	2.1	1.5	1.7
Environment	0.5	0.3	0.3
Housing	0.6	0.5	0.5
Health care	2.0	2.0	2.0
Recreation, culture, sports	0.9	0.8	0.9
Education	3.6	3.5	3.5
Social protection	1.6	2.7	2.9
Total	12.9	12.9	13.4

Source Authors, based on Eurostat data

References

Kulesza M, Sześciło D (2012) Local government in Poland. In: Moreno Á-M (ed) Local government in the member states of the European union: a comparative legal perspective. Instituto Nacional de Administración Pública, Madrid, pp 485–504

Mazur S, Możdżeń M, Oramus M (2017) Public administration characteristics in Poland. Unpublished report for EUPACK project

OECD (2016) When size matters: scaling up delivery of Czech local services. In: Lewis C (ed). Available via https://oecdecoscope.wordpress.com/2016/07/26/when-size-matters-scaling-up-delivery-of-czech-local-services/. Accessed on 10 May 2017

Radwanowicz-Wanczewska J, Dąbek D (2018) Challenges of the implementation of the European charter of local self-government in Polish legislation. Lex Localis 16(4):971–982

Swirska A (2013) General subsidy from the state as a financial support for local governments (lgu). Case of Poland. In: Kuć-Czajkowska K, Sienkiewicz MV (eds) Local government in selected Central and Eastern European countries: experiences, reforms and determinants of development. Marie Curie Sklodowska University Press, Lublin, pp 293–313

Wójcik ZK (2013) Origins of local government in the third polish republic: issues in outline. In: Kuć-Czajkowska K, Sienkiewicz MV (eds) Local government in selected Central and Eastern European countries: experiences, reforms and determinants of development. Marie Curie Sklodowska University Press, Lublin, pp 10–38

Chapter 6
The Fiscal Decentralization in Romania

Romania is democratic unitary state with a complicated history (in part because it consists of more territories). The name Romania officially appeared for the first time on February 21, 1862 during the government of Alexandru Ioan Cuza. After World War I and the disintegration of the Habsburg Monarchy, the Kingdom of Romania was established. Peace treaties with Austria, Bulgaria and Hungary delineated the new borders in 1919 and 1920 and Romania achieved its greatest territorial extent, expanding to 295,000 km². After World War II, in 1947, King Michael I was forced to abdicate and leave the country and Romania as a people's republic was established, remaining under the direct military occupation and economic control of the USSR until the late 1950s. After the 1989 revolution, democratic and free market measures changed Romania to its current politico-economic status.

Romania borders the Black Sea to the southeast, Bulgaria to the south, Ukraine to the north, Hungary to the west, Serbia to the southwest, and Moldova to the east. The area of Romania is 238,397 km². Romania is the 12th largest country and also the 7th most populous member state of the European Union, having almost 20 million inhabitants with the population density 84.4 inhabitants per km². Romania has been a member of NATO since March 29, 2004 and the European Union (EU) since January 1, 2007.

The new Constitution of Romania was approved in a national referendum on December 8, 1991 and amended in October 2003 to bring it into conformity with EU legislation. Romania is a semi-presidential republic, where executive functions are held by both government and the president. The President is elected by popular vote for a maximum of two terms of five years and appoints the Prime Minister, who in turn appoints the Council of Ministers. Deconcentrated state administration is represented especially by prefects on the regional level.

The legislative branch of the government, Parliament, consists of two chambers (Senate: 136 Senators and Chamber of Deputies: 329 deputies) whose members are elected every four years by simple plurality. The lower legislative levels are two tiers of administrative-territorial units (entities with full legal capacity, possessing their own assets). The intermediate level consists of 41 counties plus the municipality of

© Springer Nature Switzerland AG 2020

M. Plaček et al., *Fiscal Decentralization Reforms*, Public Administration, Governance and Globalization 19, https://doi.org/10.1007/978-3-030-46758-6_6

Bucharest. The basic level is comprised of 2861 municipalities or communes and 320 towns (103 towns have specific status of a municipality, which gives them greater administrative power over local affairs).

The justice system is independent of the other branches of government and is made up of a hierarchical system of courts culminating in the High Court of Cassation and Justice, which is the supreme court of Romania. There are also courts of appeal, county courts and local courts. The Constitutional Court is responsible for judging the compliance of laws and other state regulations to the Constitution (Stamule 2017).

The developments of local self-government in Romania

During the medieval period in Romania, the focus of local self-government was the villages, which were grouped into associations that constituted historic regions (counties). In the nineteenth century, Alexandru Ioan Cuza initiated the modernization of the newly created state, which included administrative reform. On the level of local administration, rural and urban communes were established as public legal persons with elected councils and budgets. Villages were obliged to regroup into larger rural communes and to pool scarce resources.

After the end of the "communist" regime in 1991, the principle of local self-government was incorporated into the Constitution and the first local government law was passed (significantly amended several times subsequently, the most important change came in 2001, was revised in 2006 and modified and completed in 2008). Three types of local self-governments were established: communes, towns, and municipalities.

The new legislation has brought real progress in terms of local self-government. The law on local self-government now includes the principles of subsidiarity and proportionality, states that local councils exercise local self-government based on the subsidiarity principle and are free to decide the tasks to be performed to meet the needs of local communities. The list of self-government competences is quite long and includes housing, town planning, environmental protection, waste management and public health, transport infrastructure, water supplies and roads, education, management of the cultural heritage, public order, and the management of parks, public gardens, and other green spaces (Tananescu 2012).

6.1   The Level of Decentralization in Romania from the Point of View of the Principles of the European Charter of Local Self-government

Romania signed the European Charter on Local Self-government on October 4, 1994, ratified it with the Law 199/1997 on November 26, 1997 (effective upon publication) with one reservation and one interpretative declaration. The reservation, which remains in effect, concerns Article 7, paragraph 2 of the Charter and the interpretative declaration explained the Romanian concept of region (counties as regions, communes, towns and municipalities as local self-governments). According to Article 11 of the Constitution, the Charter became part of the national legislation upon ratification. The inclusion of the Charter in the Romanian legal system is formal, automatic and explicit, but this does not mean that it will be directly applicable, although it is legally binding (Tananescu 2012).

The most recent monitoring report about Romania is from 2011, based on the monitoring visit of May 2010. Because this report is rather old, we try to augment the information with the results of existing academic studies, listed in this text, especially the study of Ticlau et al. (2018).

The constitutional and legal foundation for local self-government

In Romania, the principle of local self-government is recognized in the Constitution and other legal instruments. Concerning the Constitution, Article 120 declares decentralization as one of the basic principles of local public administration and Article 121 refers to local autonomy of communes and towns.

The core specific law is the law on local public administration passed in 1991, improved in 2001, 2006 and 2008 to be in full compliance with the principles defined by the Charter. Other important legal sources related to local self-government are Law No. 67/2004 on local elections, Law No. 393/2004 on the conditions of office of local elected representatives, Framework Law No. 195/2006 on decentralization (updated in February 2016), Law No. 315/2004 on regional development in Romania, Law No. 273/2006 on local public finances, Law No. 2/1968 on the administration of Romania, Law No. 350/2001 on town and country planning and Law No. 284/2010 on the unitary remuneration of personnel paid from public funds. The monitoring report does not include any negative comments concerning the implementation of Article 2 of the Charter.

The concept of local self-government

The share of competences entrusted to local government is relatively broad, this means that Romanian municipalities regulate and manage a "substantial share of public affairs." Article 38 of the local administration law allows local councils to decide, within the framework prescribed by law, on all matters of local interest, except in cases in which the law has delegated such matters to another local or central authority.

Local councils are the deliberative authority at the local level and their members are elected for a four-year term by universal, equal, direct, secret and freely expressed suffrage. The mayor is also directly elected by the local community and his term of office is four years. The monitoring report does not include any negative comments concerning the implementation of Article 2 of the Charter.

The scope of local self-government

The independence of Romanian local self-governments is high. Within the limits set by the law, they have their own budgets and assets and independently manage them. Local self-governments may issue ordinances that bind all individual or corporate bodies within their jurisdiction. Binding ordinances are submitted to the prefect for a review of their legality. In the event the council refuses to set aside decisions considered illegal by the prefect, the latter can bring the matter before the administrative courts.

As already indicated, local authorities in Romania have full discretion to exercise their initiative with regard to any matter which is not excluded from their competence nor assigned to any other authority (Article 38 of the local administration law).

According to the monitoring report, all principles of the Charter are well transposed into the respective paragraphs of the local administration law, however the report proposes to continue improving the consultation mechanisms, so that the local authorities are systematically consulted, in due time and in an appropriate manner, on all matters that concern them directly.

The protection of local authority boundaries
The protection of local authority boundaries is guaranteed in Romania—especially by Article 22 of the local administration law. The monitoring report does not include any challenges concerning this principle.

Administrative structures and resources for the tasks of local authorities
The Romanian legislation centrally determines the number of municipal council members and the election rules. The number of council members may vary between 9 and 31, according to the population of the local self-government unit. The electoral legislation provides for separate direct elections for the mayor. The mayor is the local public administration authority and acts as the executive authority according to the Law on the conditions of office of the elected local representatives. The core mayoral duties include representing the State; working with the local council; drawing up local budgets and providing public services for citizens.

Local councils have the right to adopt their own regulations for their organization and operation adapted to their specific needs. These internal regulations must be approved by two-thirds of the elected councilors. However, the staff salaries (and to some extend also the number of staff) is centrally regulated. The monitoring report does not include any negative comments concerning the implementation of Article 6 of the Charter.

Conditions under which responsibilities at the local level are exercised
Romania does not feel bound by principle 2 of Article 7, although in reality, the legislation (especially Law No. 393/2004 on the conditions of office of local elected representatives) provides for several arrangements for paying elected representatives bonuses and financial compensation in the exercise of their functions. The free exercise of local elected functions is provided for by Articles 4 and 20 of the above-mentioned law. Functions and activities that are deemed incompatible with the holding of local elective office are set out by different legislation pieces—like Part IV of Law No. 161/2003 on certain measures for guaranteeing transparency in the exercise of public activities and missions and in the business sphere, or Law No.

176/2010 on integrity in the exercise of public offices and functions. The monitoring report does not include any negative comments concerning the implementation of Article 7 of the Charter.

The administrative supervision of local authorities' activities
The core role concerning the administrative supervision of local authorities is played by the prefect. The secretary of the local self-government sends all provisions and legal decisions signed by the mayor or issues decided by the council to the prefect to review the legality of acts and decisions. If necessary, the prefect calls for the revision or revocation of the administrative act or measure considered partly or entirely illegal. If this is refused, the prefect can bring the matter before the administrative courts.

The Court of Accounts is the independent external public auditor of public finances and has the right to audit local budgets. It delivers financial control, compliance and performance audits. The Court's activities warn about existing risks, make observations and recommendations, and signal the presence of both deficiencies and successes. It contributes to the improvement of the financial management of public resources and to the promotion of transparency. The monitoring report does not include any negative comments concerning the implementation of Article 8 of the Charter.

The financial resources of local authorities and the financial transfer system
According to the legislation, local authorities in Romania have the power to determine the rate of taxes and local charges under the conditions foreseen by law—the powers and responsibilities of local self-governments with regard to the determination of taxes and tax rates are defined by the law on local public finance (however, local taxes are only marginal revenue for local authorities).

Article 9, paragraph 2, of Law No. 215/2001 on local public administration provides that the financial resources at the disposal of local public authorities should be commensurate with their powers and responsibilities. The reality is not so positive (see the latter part of this text). Local borrowing is also regulated by the state.

The monitoring report proposes that Romania allocate to the local authorities financial resources commensurate with their responsibilities, as stated in Article 9(2) of the Charter, thus enabling them fully to exercise their functions. Romania may formally comply with principles stated in Article 9 of the Charter, but this is not true for the local financial practices.

Local authorities' right to associate
In the mid-1990's, established associations of local authorities (Association of Communes, Association of Municipalities and Association of Towns) merged in a single federation of associations of local authorities to form the Federation of Associations of Local Authorities (but this Federation does not appear to be functioning well today).

The law on local public administration allows local authorities to associate through intercommunity development entities. Hundreds of joint bodies were created to pool available resources and share the burden of some of the common services. Local authorities may also sign agreements or participate, with funds, in implementing local or regional development programmes and in cross-border cooperation. The monitoring report does not include any negative comments concerning the implementation of Article 10 of the Charter.

The legal protection of local self-government

The monitoring report is relatively critical concerning the failure to guarantee the right of local administration to lodge a legal remedy in order to secure the free exercise of the right to local self-government. Local authorities can take legal action, before the ordinary courts, to demand compliance with the provisions of the Constitution and/or domestic legislation that affect them directly. Taking this into account, the report proposes to Romania to "provide the local authorities with effective judicial protection by granting them a genuine right to bring an action in the domestic courts if there has been a breach of one of the principles guaranteed by the Charter ratified by Romania."

The core challenges for fiscal decentralization in Romania

Subnational revenue in Romania represents 9.3% of GDP (OECD 2016), one of highest in the CEE region, but this figure includes the regional level and some methodological problems. According to OECD data (2016), Romania seems to have the highest percentage of transfer revenue in the local budget revenues in the EU (more than 75% of local revenues are derived from grants and transfers). This figure can be correct, if shared taxes and hospital fees are counted as transfers. According to Savov et al. (2018), municipal revenues are 28% of total revenues, but most of this money comes from hospital fees. Shared taxes and block grants are also 28% each. In any case, the powers of municipalities to generate revenues are rather restricted. According to the Court of Accounts (2015), 90% of local revenues are not under the control of local administrations, and 50% (VAT, PIT and subsidies) require political and/or administrative decisions at the state level.

Local taxes include property taxes on buildings and land from both legal entities and individuals (68% of local tax revenue and around 0.7% of GDP), tax on transportation vehicles and various taxes on stamps, transactions and the issuance of certificates and licenses. The base and reference rates for property tax are fixed by law but each local council can adopt a rate up to 50% higher or lower than the reference rates. Shared taxes (PIT, VAT) were previously considered as local government taxes, but were reclassified in Romania to the transfer category in 2014 (Oprea and Bilan 2015).

In addition, there is a horizontal equalization grant funded from the state budget, which is allocated according to a formula. Besides these transfers, local self-governments receive earmarked grants from sectoral ministries (such as support for disabled people, abandoned children, fuel subsidies, and infrastructure) as well as subsidies from the EU (Stamule 2017).

The extreme dependence of local authorities on transfers creates a lot of practical problems for local finance (Tananescu 2012). Local authorities can hardly adopt their annual budgets before the national budget is passed, because they must first know the rules established in the national budget. Annual changes in general budgetary rules are still common practice. The method of calculating PIT and VAT based—but also other—transfers is criticized in terms of lack of predictability, clarity and transparency. Delays in transferring funds from the central level still happen and may impede functioning of local authorities. The amounts of transfers depend on the economic performance of the country—for example the economic crisis caused a decrease in local budget revenues from income tax from 15.0 billion lei in 2009 to 14.5 billion lei in 2011. The impact of the crisis on local budgets was worsened by the decision to reduce the quotas broken down from personal income tax allocated to local budgets (Oprea and Bilan 2015).

According to the data from the Romanian Institute of Statistics, the structure of the municipal revenue in 2016 was as follows. The total revenue reached 59,518 million RON. The transfer based on VAT and PIT was 40,197 million RON. Different state subsidies amounted to 11,884 million RON and the property taxation revenues were 4638 mil. RON.

Table 6.1 shows the structure of subnational expenditure in Romania (counties and local self-governments combined), and Table 6.2 indicates allocation of these expenditures between municipalities and counties (the interesting fact is that the share of municipalities in subnational expenditures increases slightly).

Borrowing is regulated—local budgets, excluding loans to finance investment and debt refinancing, must be balanced (golden rule). Since 2013, each government's budget must be balanced, excluding investment projects financed by drawings on loans contracted before 2013. If local annual debt service (principal payment, interest, commissions) exceeds 30% of its own revenues, local authorities can no longer contract or guarantee loans (Oprea and Bilan 2015).

Table 6.1 The structure of local government expenditures: COFOG (% of GDP)

	2015	2016	2017
General administration	0.9	0.9	1.0
Defense	0	0	0
Public order and security	0.1	0.1	0.2
Economic functions	2.0	1.6	1.4
Environment	0.7	0.4	0.4
Housing	1.0	0.8	0.7
Health care	1.3	1.4	1.5
Recreation, culture, sports	0.7	0.6	0.5
Education	1.9	2.1	1.9
Social protection	1.1	1.2	1.3
Total	9.9	9.1	9.0

Source Authors, based on EUROSTAT data

Table 6.2 The structure of local government expenditures: share of municipalities and counties (%)

		2015	2016	2017
General administration	Counties	16	13	14
	Municipalities	84	87	86
Public order and security	Counties	7	5	4
	Municipalities	93	95	96
Economic functions	Counties	17	16	16
	Municipalities	83	84	84
Environment	Counties	40	17	10
	Municipalities	60	83	90
Housing	Counties	3	3	3
	Municipalities	97	97	97
Health care	Counties	43	32	28
	Municipalities	57	68	72
Recreation, culture, sports	Counties	22	23	23
	Municipalities	78	77	77
Education	Counties	7	7	7
	Municipalities	93	93	93
Social protection	Counties	55	52	50
	Municipalities	45	48	50
Total	Counties	17	15	15
	Municipalities	83	85	85

Source Authors based on Ministry of Finance data

References

Oprea F, Bilan I (2015) Evaluation of the economic and financial crisis's impact on local budgetary aggregates: the Romanian case. Proc Econ Financ 20:467–477

Stamule T (2017) Public administration characteristics in Romania. Unpublished report for EUPACK project

Tananescu S (2012) Local government in Romania. In: Moreno Á-M (ed) Local government in the member states of the European union: a comparative legal perspective. Instituto Nacional de Administración Pública, Madrid, pp 533–554

Ticlau TC, Moldovan BA, Hintea CM (2018) Challenges of the implementation of the european charter of local self-government in Romania's legislation. Lex Localis 16(4):873–893

Chapter 7
The Fiscal Decentralization in Slovakia

The Slovak Republic is a fully independent sovereign, democratic unitary state, established after the friendly split of Czechoslovakia on January 1, 1993. The Slovak Constitution was ratified September 1, 1992, became fully effective January 1, 1993; and was significantly changed in September 1998 to allow direct election of the president; and again in February 2001 to allow Slovakia to apply for NATO and EU membership.

The territory of the Slovak Republic is 49,034 km^2, the total length of the borders of the state is 1681.9 km. The surrounding countries are the Czech Republic, Poland, Ukraine, Hungary and Austria. The average density of population in Slovakia is 109.7 inhabitants per km^2. Slovakia has been a member of NATO since March 29, 2004, a member of the EU since May 1, 2004 and a member of the Eurozone since January 1, 2009.

With the exception of some short periods in early medieval times, Slovaks did not have their own state prior to 1918, and for more than 1000 years belonged to the Austrian and Austro-Hungarian monarchies. In 1918 the first independent Czechoslovak Republic was established, as a unitary state of two nations—Czech and Slovaks, but broke up in 1939 as the consequence of the pre-Second World War changes. The history of Czechoslovakia resumed in 1945, with an important change from a unitary to a federal state in 1968, and which ended on December 31, 1992.

The head of the executive branch is the president, elected by direct, popular vote for a five-year term. The head of government is the prime minister. The cabinet is appointed by the president on the recommendation of the prime minister. The administrative system consists of central administration bodies, district offices ("okresné úrady") and a few specialized state administration bodies on the regional or district level. Central administration consists of a Government Office, ministries, central state administration bodies and other central bodies (mainly agencies), that are of special status. Most state administration tasks at the lower level are delivered by 79 district offices, responsible for general and specialized state administration. District offices are under the Ministry of the Interior. A few other ministries still have their deconcentrated offices at lower levels (like police force, fire and rescue corps, mining office board, labor inspectorate, financial administration, monuments board,

© Springer Nature Switzerland AG 2020
M. Plaček et al., *Fiscal Decentralization Reforms*, Public Administration,
Governance and Globalization 19, https://doi.org/10.1007/978-3-030-46758-6_7

state trade inspection, veterinary and food administration). Delegated administrative services are delivered by municipalities.

The system of judicial power is represented by general courts and the Constitutional Court of the Slovak Republic. The Slovak Republic has a two-level court system. District courts are competent courts which decide on proceedings of first instance. Regional courts hear cases as appeal courts. The Supreme Court of the Slovak Republic has the function of an appellate review court. The courts decide in civil and criminal matters and they also review the lawfulness of decisions by public administration bodies. One specific body is the Specialized Criminal Court in Pezinok.

The legislative powers are connected to three levels (all three levels have legislative powers, as defined by the Constitution)—parliament (Unicameral National Council of the Slovak Republic with 150 deputies), regional self-governments, and local self-governments (Němec 2017).

The development of local self-government in Slovakia
The first reform measures after the Velvet Revolution in 1989 were oriented mostly towards the local level, based on the conceptual document, "Proposal for the reform of national committees and local state administration," discussed by the government of the Slovak Republic on June 6, 1990. The first administrative reform wave was oriented mostly towards creating real self-government institutions, to divide executive and legislative powers on all levels, change the territorial structure of Czechoslovakia, and restructure the central government and the system of control in the public sector.

The government of the Slovak Republic decided by governmental resolution on June 6, 1990 to abolish the system of national committees effective from December 31, 1990, create self-government structures in each municipality, organize direct self-government elections in November 1990, and split self-government and state administration functions on the local level. New local bodies of state administration (general and specialized bodies) were created, applying vertical superiority and subordination.

Based on these decisions, self-governing municipalities with a high level of independence were established by Law No. 369/1990 Coll. on Municipal Administration from January 1, 1991. Local self-governments became the fully-fledged policy-making decision makers at the local level, with budgets and bodies equipped with the exclusive right to take decisions independently and act in all matters pertinent to the administration of the municipality and its property where a special law does not assign such acts to the State or to another legal bodies or a natural person (Nemec and Berčík 1997). According to the Constitution and the above law, the municipal authorities are the municipal assembly and the mayor of the municipality. The municipal assembly consists of representatives of municipal representation. The municipal residents permanently residing therein elect the representatives for a four-year term. Elections of the representatives are performed on the basis of universal, equal, and direct suffrage by secret ballot. The mayor of a municipality is elected by the municipal residents permanently residing therein on the basis of a universal, equal, and direct suffrage by secret ballot for a four-year term. The municipal mayor is the executive authority of the municipality; the mayor shall perform municipal administration and shall represent the municipality externally. Reasons for and the manner of recalling a mayor before expiration of his electoral term shall be laid down by a law (Němec 2017).

The core responsibilities allocated to municipalities in 1991 were management of movable property and real estate in the ownership of the municipality, providing for public order in the municipality, local public transport in big cities, construction, maintenance and management of local roads and parking places, public space, public greens, public lights, market places, cemeteries, local water resources and wells, water supply networks, sewerage and water cleaning establishments in small municipalities, construction, maintenance and management of local cultural establishments, part of the sport, leisure and tourist establishments, infant homes, part of the ambulatory health services establishments, creation and provision of basic social services, the support of education, nature and heritage protection, culture and artistic hobbies, physical culture and sports, humanities activities, municipal police forces, and fire service (Nemec et al. 2000).

The functioning of municipalities was significantly influenced by so called decentralization reforms, realized during the 2000–2005 period. The main idea of this period was the assumption that decentralization would solve all inefficiencies in the public administration system (almost explicitly the statement of the core reform document Strategia decentralizacie a reformy verejnej spravy 1999). The start of the reform was often postponed and only massive interventions of Prime Minister Dzurinda in the beginning of 2001 pushed the processes forward. After this, in too short a time, all the expected basic legislation was approved by the parliament: Civil Service Code, Public Service Code, law on creation of territorial self-governments, law on elections of territorial self-governments, law on transfer of competencies of the state to the regional and local self-governments, amendment of the law on municipalities, amendment of the law on municipal property and the law on the property of territorial authorities, amendment of the law on budgetary rules and the law on financial control and audit (Žárska and Šebová 2005). The Act on Municipalities was substantially amended, whereby the autonomous status of municipalities was significantly strengthened (Kováčová 2010).

According to the Law on Transfer of Competencies, a really large number of competencies were transferred to self-governments (also regional self-governments) in 2001–2002. Municipalities got new responsibilities in the areas of road communications, water management, registry of citizens, social care, environmental protection, education (elementary schools and similar establishments), physical culture, theaters, health care (primary and specialized ambulatory care), regional development and tourism. Regional self-government became responsible for competencies in areas of road communications, railways, road transportation, civil protection, social care, territorial planning, education (secondary education), physical culture, theaters, museums, galleries, local culture, libraries, health care (polyclinics and local and regional hospitals), pharmacies, regional development, and tourism. A large set of these competencies was re-allocated from the direct ministerial responsibility (hospitals, education, etc.). The first phase of the decentralization reform transferred a massive set of responsibilities to local and regional self-governments but did not introduce a new fiscal decentralization mechanism; new responsibilities were financed by grants and not by incomes of self-governments. The new fiscal mechanism was introduced only from 2006 (Klimovský 2015).

7.1   The Level of Decentralization in Slovakia from the Point of View of the Principles of the European Charter of Local Self-government

Slovakia signed the European Charter of Local Self-government (Charter) in 1999, but with reservations (in accordance with Article 12 of the Charter). Slovakia declared itself to be bound by the provisions of the charter as follows: Article 2; Article 3, paragraph 2; Article 4, paragraphs 1, 2, 4, and 6; Article 5; Article 6, paragraph 1; Article 7, paragraphs 1, 2, and 3; Article 8, paragraphs 1, 2, and 3; Article 9, paragraphs 2, 3, 4 and 8; Article 10, paragraph 1; and Article 11. Later on, Slovakia accepted all principles of the charter in two steps. On July 31, 2002, Slovakia declared that it considered itself to be bound by Article 6, paragraph 2, and on May 16, 2007, Slovakia declared that it extends its obligations and considers itself bound by the remaining charter provisions: Article 3, paragraph 1; Article 4, paragraphs 3 and 5; Article 9, paragraphs 1, 5, 6 and 7; and Article 10, paragraphs 2 and 3. The charter was incorporated as an "acceptance of an international treaty," and, according to the Slovak Constitution, international treaties were to be approved by parliament and would supersede domestic laws. The most recent Council of Europe monitoring visit to Slovakia took place in 2015, and in its monitoring report, entitled "Local and Regional Democracy in the Slovak Republic" and which was approved on March 24, 2016, the council expressed satisfaction with the overall positive situation of local and regional democracy in Slovakia. The findings of this report are one of the core inputs for the following text.

The constitutional and legal foundation for local self-government
The core legal base for the existence of LSG in Slovakia is the Constitution of the Slovak Republic. Chapter 4 of the Constitution, entitled Territorial Self-administration, and including Articles 64–71, pro-vides all of the main principles for the organization of local self-govern-ment, which are almost fully in line with the principles set by the Charter. Article 65 defines a municipality as a legal person, which manages its own property and financial means independently, under the conditions laid down by a law, and expects that a municipality shall finance its needs primarily from its own revenues and from state subsidies. Article 67 states that the duties and limitations in the realization of territorial self-administration may be imposed on a municipality only by a law and on the basis of an international treaty and that the State may

intervene in the activities of a municipality only by means laid down by a law. Article 71 deals with delegated competences—the exercise of certain powers of local self-administration may be delegated to a municipality by a law (the costs of the delegated exercise of state administration shall be covered by the state).

The constitutional arrangements are framed by all the necessary legislation mentioned above. Therefore the Council of Europe monitoring visit concluded that "it can be said that the requirements of Art. 2 of the charter are satisfied by the present legal and constitutional situation of the Slovak Republic." The visit only recommended drawing up legislation which would clearly define the exclusive fields of the competencies of the regional and the local levels respectively to avoid any overlapping of responsibilities, and elaborating a legislation allowing local authorities to take initiatives when the corresponding competencies have not been expressly attributed to them and when this is not explicitly prohibited by law.

The concept of local self-government
The previous part of the text clearly demonstrates that Slovak municipalities regulate and manage a "substantial share of public affairs." The representative bodies of municipalities are composed of "deputies" elected through a process of secret, general, and direct voting. The mayor is also elected directly (and independently from the council) by the citizens for a four-year term, through a secret and general voting process. Therefore, the two key bodies of the municipalities enjoy full and direct democratic legitimacy.

Taking these facts into account, the monitoring reports states: "In the light of the precedent considerations, the Slovak Republic does fully comply with Art. 3 of the Charter."

The scope of local self-government
The independence of Slovak municipalities is high (for example Swianiewicz (2014) names Slovakia as a decentralization "hero"). Within the limits set by the law, municipalities have their own budgets and assets and manage them independently. Local governments may issue ordinances that bind all individ-ual or corporate bodies within their jurisdiction and only parliamentary acts can supersede or invalidate these ordinances. Any modification of the powers of local authorities must be decided by Parliament. Barring statutory exceptions, local authorities are independent of state supervision (the only body with "general" mandate to control/audit municipalities for all their activities is the Supreme Audit Office). All valid decisions made by municipalities and state authorities are reviewable by the courts in application of the "cassation" or repeal principle.

Taking this into account, the monitoring report states that the requirements of Article 4 of the Charter are respected in Slovakia, with one (already indicated) reservation; it states that "the Slovak system lacks a residual powers clause or a clause générale de competence (as French Law calls it) in favor of local authorities, which is common in other European countries."

Legal experts, in particular, feel that it is actually the other way around, since if a certain competency or responsibility is not expressly allocated to the municipal level of government, the power is understood to be allocated to the state administration. However, Article 4 of the Act on Municipalities states that municipalities independently decide and act in all areas related to municipal administration, except for areas directly given to the state by the Act. In any case, more explicit formulations of the "general competence" principle in Slovak legislation would help.

The protection of local authority boundaries

The general constitutional statement on the protection of boundaries of municipalities is specified in the Act on Municipalities. Paragraph 2 of the act states that changes of municipal boundaries can be made only if approved by the municipality involved: for example, the merging or splitting of several municipalities requires a positive result from a preceding referendum (in all the municipalities concerned in the case of a merger) and an agreement between the municipalities concerned. There is no case connected with the violation of this principle in practice, and the monitoring report states that "the Slovak Republic complies with Art. 5 of the Charter."

Administrative structures and resources for the tasks of local authorities

The core principles determining the structures and resources of LSGs in Slovakia are set by the Act on Municipalities, but implementation details are to a large extent left in "local hands." The only major centrally determined issue is the number of municipal council members, defined by the act as follows (Buček and Němec 2012):

- Up to 40 inhabitants: 3 councilors
- 41–500 inhabitants: 3–7 councilors
- 501–1000 inhabitants: 5–7 councilors
- 1001–3000 inhabitants: 7–9 councilors
- 3001–5000 inhabitants: 9–11 councilors
- 5001–10,000 inhabitants: 11–13 councilors
- 10,001–20,000 inhabitants: 13–19 councilors
- 20,001–50,000 inhabitants: 15–25 councilors
- 50,001–100,000 inhabitants: 19–31 councilors
- More than 100,000 inhabitants: 23–41 councilors.

The municipal assembly establishes the post of municipal auditor/comptroller and decides on the salaries of the mayor/lord mayor and the municipal auditor within the framework provided by law (minimum salaries are defined). In larger municipalities, the municipal office may be run by a "principal" appointed by the municipal council upon the proposal of the mayor. This person is responsible to the mayor. Municipal offices consist of different categories of employees (civil servants, public servants, and labour-code regulated employees) who are responsible for the administrative and organizational aspects of municipal life as well as for other activities of municipal bodies.

This means that, as a rule, Slovak local authorities are able to determine their own internal administrative structures with due respect to general legislation. Municipalities in Slovakia are quite independent in the field of human resources, and they can freely appoint and remove their own employees. The salaries of most municipal employees are pre-determined by law. The act sets the specific basic salaries for all employees with the status of civil or public servant. Apart from this main "remuneration," municipal employees may receive allowances and other types of compensation for expenses incurred in the fulfilment of their tasks. The salaries of the main municipal representatives are competitive in the light of the overall national economic situation and salaries paid in the public and private sectors.

Taking all above-mentioned facts into account, the monitoring report concludes that "the requirements of Article 6 of the Charter are met by the Slovak Republic."

Conditions under which responsibilities are exercised at the local level
The conditions of office of elected local representatives provide for the free exercise of their functions. According to the Labour Code (paragraph 136), the employer shall provide them with necessary free time to be able to perform all duties, responsibilities, and activities connected with their position (the public interest clause). All municipalities pay appropriate financial compensation for expenses incurred in the exercise of the public office in question and remuneration for specifically-ordered work that is carried out. Most big and some middle-sized municipalities also pay compensation for loss of earnings and corresponding social welfare protection. In larger municipalities, many deputies are members of municipal companies and receive benefits connected with their position.

The list of functions and activities which are deemed incompatible with the holding of local elective office is determined by law. However, the list of such limitations is rather short. A municipal councilor cannot be simultaneously a municipal employee, or the head of a municipal budgetary organization, and his position is also incompatible with a few top or specific public administrative posts (like judge, prosecutor, and ombudsman). However, the same person may sit in the municipal and regional councils as well as in Parliament.

Consequently, the monitoring report concludes that the current Slovak system complies with the requirements of Article 7 of the charter.

The administrative supervision of local authorities' activities
The administrative control of the state over local authorities is aimed solely at ensuring compliance with the law and with constitutional principles. An exclusive role in the control or oversight of municipalities is played by the General Prosecutor's Office (Prokuratúra), which is an independent body established by the Constitution (Articles 149 to 151) and governed by Act 153/2001 on Prosecution. Among other things, the office also supervises the legality of decisions, measures, and binding regulations adopted by local authorities. The office acts either on request or on its own initiative (ex officio). The control exercised by the Prosecutor's Office over local self-government bodies is only the control of legality and "ex post facto." The office cannot cancel or quash any decision by a local authority. Under no circumstance can the office order a local authority to do something or refrain from doing something. Nor can the office suspend a local body's decision. If the findings of the office show that the activity of a local body is not in conformity with the law, then the office

can issue warnings or protests addressed to the local authority. The local body has the duty to answer within thirty days, accepting or rejecting the office's concerns. If the local authority refuses to amend or modify its decision or measure, then the office may lodge an appeal in court within two months asking for the annulment of the contested decision. Such cases are very rare; local decrees and decisions are usually drafted with care from the legal point of view, and sometimes the office itself is consulted on a preliminary basis, as noted above.

As indicated above, the only Slovak body with the "general" mandate to control/audit municipalities (from 2006) is the Supreme Audit Office (NKÚ). NKÚ was given the right to audit local authorities, including in areas where these bodies have exclusive responsibility. The NKÚ delivers both compliance and performance audits on a local level. All local authorities must cooperate with the NKÚ to provide support for its activities, de-liver the necessary information or materials on time, provide explanations, and conduct "ordered" audits and inspections of all bodies within their sphere of responsibility. The NKÚ has the right to direct access to any information system used by self-government bodies.

Concerning the area of delegated responsibilities, sectoral legislation foresees the possibility to appeal a measure or a decision adopted by a local authority before the local state administration body. This happens especially in the area of construction, urban planning procedures, roads, and transportation. This form of inter-administrative control is anticipated in the Constitution (Article 71.2) and does not contradict the principles of the Charter, because in those cases the municipalities perform the delegated administrative functions financed by the state.

Consequently, the monitoring report concluded that the current Slovak system fully complies with Article 8 of the charter.

The financial resources of local authorities and the financial transfer system
The "quality" of the fiscal decentralization is the topic where some challenges can still be found. Municipal representatives and the Association of Towns and Communities (ZMOS) always claim that the total amount of disposable resources is insufficient to perform all municipal tasks; in contrast, the state argues that the financial situation of municipalities is healthy. Municipalities in general show a budget surplus or balanced budgets. The crisis in 2008–2010 did not impact their finances much; the decrease of revenues from the personal income tax was compensated by the additional transfer to the municipalities of €100 M in 2009 and €72.5 M in 2010.

ZMOS representatives argue especially that delegated competencies are only partly financed by the state, in contradiction to the constitutional requirements. For example, Balážová and Dienerová (2002) published very negative calculations (Table 7.1). However, such calculations are based only on assumptions and simplifications.

The real issue is the structure of revenues. A great part of municipal revenues still comes from the state level via the system of shared taxes. Most authors and resources accept that shared taxes are municipal revenues (and tax collection is just delegated to the state), but in the case of this tax the Charter principle "*of which they have the power to determine the rate*" is not the full reality.

Table 7.1 The level of financing selected delegated competencies by the state

Registry	39.48%
School office	14.37%
Specialized building office	25.02%
General building office	31.75%
ŠFRB (housing) agenda	12.04%
Environment	57.10%
Total	20.70%

Source Balážová and Dienerová (2002)

The last but maybe most critical issue is equalization. The formula for the redistribution of income tax back to municipalities is defined by law and includes equalization elements: namely the altitude of a location, population size, the number of pupils, and the number of retired people. Such a selection of equalization indicators is insufficient to guarantee effective horizontal and vertical redistribution (redistribution for a different revenue capacity and for different expenditure needs). Under current conditions, small municipalities allegedly receive a minimum amount of money for the functioning of their administrative apparatus (some of them spend up to 90% of revenues to cover fixed administrative costs). However, the real question is whether very small municipalities should be specifically supported or forced by financial instruments to amalgamate.

With respect to the above indicated limitations in the area of financial resources of municipalities, the monitoring report states: "In the light of the above, the Slovak Republic meets the basic standards enshrined in Art. 9 of the Charter."

Local authorities' right to associate
In Slovakia, the right of local authorities to associate is recognized directly by the Constitution, and this right is also executed without any problem. In terms of international partnerships, Slovakia has signed and ratified the European Outline Convention on Transfrontier Cooperation between Territorial Communities or Authorities as well as two o f is protocols. This provides for a robust legal and political basis for engaging in trans-border cooperation. Taking all the above into account, the monitoring report states: "Consequently, the present situation of the right of association is fully in compliance with the requirements of Art. 10 of the Charter."

The legal protection of local self-government
Slovak local authorities have the right of recourse to a judicial remedy (including litigation in the Constitutional Court) in order to secure the free exercise of their powers and respect for principles of local self-government, just like any other legal entity in Slovakia. (Administrative courts do not exist in the country.) The frequency of this type of action is very low. The monitoring report suggests that "the Slovak Republic meets the basic standards enshrined in Art. 11 of the Charter."

The core challenges for fiscal decentralization in Slovakia
As indicated above, the Slovak local self-government situation complies to a great

extent with the expectations set by the Charter principles. However, one issue that needs to be discussed in this regard is the excessive fragmentation and the limited reaction to it.

The territory of Slovakia has always been highly fragmented in terms of the number of municipalities. For instance, there were 3473 municipalities in 1921 and 3237 in 1947. The lowest total number of municipalities (2669 municipalities) in Slovakia was in 1989, but this number increased to 2891 (not counting city parts) over the following decades (Klimovský 2015). According to Thijs et al. (2017) Slovakia has the second lowest average number of inhabitants per municipality—1871 (the Czech Republic has 1690 and France 1885).

The average Slovak municipality has an area of approximately 17 km². Only two cities, Bratislava and Košice, have a population in excess of 100,000 inhabitants (approximately 430,000 in Bratislava and 250,000 in Košice). According to the last general census (2011), only seven other towns/cities have a population of over 50,000 inhabitants. Almost 70% of all Slovak municipalities have fewer than 1000 inhabitants, but they are home to only slightly more than 16% of the total population of Slovakia. Furthermore, several years ago the smallest municipality, Príkra, had only seven inhabitants, (it currently has 12); however; according to the relevant legal provisions, it has the same competencies as the largest Slovak municipalities (Klimovský et al. 2016).

Three steps relating to decentralization have been planned in Slovakia since 1989 and especially in connection with the "decentralization reform after 2000":

(1) devolution,
(2) fiscal decentralization, and
(3) territorial consolidation.

However, since the implementation of the first two steps, no central government has had any interest in continuing with these processes and all of them preferred the status quo (Klimovský 2015).

There is no doubt that some municipalities are simply too small to execute a full set of their original and delegated responsibilities. This issue is not addressed and probably will not be in the near future. Two core (political and technical ones) and many small barriers block such changes. The core political issue is a strong political opposition to amalgamation at the municipal level: the lobby of mayors is strong enough to block needed changes (Klimovský et al. 2016).

The technical—implementation—barrier is connected to the fact that comprehensive data necessary to prepare such a change in an evidence-based way are not available. First, the general optimum size of a municipality does not exist in the real world; moreover, the theoretical optimum size of a municipality is a trade-off between "democracy" and "efficiency." The existing academic research does not confirm clear patterns of economies of scale (savings thanks to a larger size) in the conditions of a fragmented post-communist country (see for example Matějová et al. 2017). Data about the real structure of municipal costs in Slovakia are not available, either—because of the use of old fashioned accounting and financial management systems (Němec 2017).

In this situation, the central government, and especially the Ministry of Finance and the Ministry of the Interior, should promote all forms of municipal cooperation to help to municipalities to deliver cost effective public and administrative services to citizen and businesses. However, not much is done in Slovakia from this point of view, except for the limited methodical support for the establishment of joint municipal offices for delegated competencies (Němec 2017). The Czech example of different categories of municipalities from the point of view of delegated responsibilities should also be utilized, to cope with rather limited human resource capacities in small fragmented settlements (responsible for the same scale of own and delegated responsibilities as large cities).

Most important data about the level of fiscal decentralization
Slovak municipalities spend approximately 7% of GDP (the central level approximately 30% of GDP). Despite a strong decentralization process in 2002, Slovakia remains a centralized country from the perspective of local government spending. The level of LSG spending is half of the OECD average for unitary countries (OECD 2016).

Financing local governments between 1990 and 2005 was based mainly on shared taxes (personal income tax, legal entities' income tax, and road tax) and transfers. Since the state budget was approved on a yearly basis, the local governments prepared their own budgets under very uncertain conditions and had to wait for approval of the state budget in order to be able to plan their own revenues. Locally determined revenues were rather marginal, and the only significant local tax was the "real estate" tax. This situation changed somewhat after 2005, when fiscal decentralization was implemented. Some fees became local taxes, whereas in terms of shared taxes, only personal income tax remained in this category. All these measures led to an improvement in the local governments' capacity to predict and determine their own revenues and in the overall enhancement of local policy making (Klimovský et al. 2016).

However, tax revenues still represent only a small share of municipal financial resources, among the lowest levels in the OECD. The share of central government transfers is one of the highest of the OECD countries, with an OECD average of 37.3% in 2013 (OECD 2016). Municipalities are able to levy seven different taxes, including a property tax and six specific local taxes on goods and services. Municipalities are free to decide whether or not to levy each tax, and to set the rates of all local taxes, and have extensive autonomy on tax bases (exemptions, rate reduction).

The largest financial source for municipalities is the (non-earmarked) share of the personal income tax (the percentage of this share oscillates near the level of 70%, and can change annually, because it not fixed at least in a middle term perspective). As indicated, this transfer is expected to serve also as an equalization instrument, as the allocation is calculated on the basis of needs, as well as population criteria (number of inhabitants, age structure, size, population density, etc.). Earmarked transfers from the central government aim at financing certain services and represent around one third of municipal budgets. The main grant is for education, allocated according to the number of pupils and covering in particular payment of teachers' salaries (Nemec 2017).

Table 7.2 Municipal
revenues (Million EUR)

Revenue	2015	2016	2017
Total tax revenues	1973.9	2191.8	2342.0
Shared personal income tax	1467.7	1669.0	1797.0
Property tax	324.1	336.4	347.9
Other local taxes	182.0	186.3	196.7
Other revenues	2606.1	21971	2252.4
Total revenues	4580.0	4388.9	4594.4

Source Authors, based on Ministry of Finance data

Municipalities may also benefit from several EU funds, as many operational pro-grammes include eligible activities in fields related to municipal life. However, these revenues are not at all stable and depend on a large series of factors, especially the design of the specific programme. The absorption capacity varies significantly, par-ticularly as smaller municipalities do not have their own capacity to draft projects and may outsource this.

Concerning expenditures, the most important expenditure item are the salaries of teachers (delegated responsibility, financed by the above-mentioned ear-marked transfer). Tables 7.2, 7.3 and 7.4 provide a statistical overview of Slovak local self-government finances for the last few years.

Municipalities are free to borrow or issue bonds, but the law does set some specific limits to prevent fiscal problems, such as: (a) loans which can only be used for capital purposes; (b) total debt stock which cannot exceed 60% of the budget of the previous year; and (c) annual debt payments which may not exceed 25% of the budget of the previous year. The indebtedess, bailouts or bankruptcy are not a hot issue at the Slovak municipal level (Němec 2017).

Table 7.3 Structure of
transfers for delegated
responsibilities (thousands of
EUR)

	2014	2015	2016
General public services	35,523	31,643	19,325
Security	3896	3200	1509
Economic functions	114, 993	292,166	55,056
Environment	72,543	107,704	26,397
Housing	54,856	53,858	94,869
Health care	734	3340	868
Recreation, culture, sports	6285	6410	5103
Education	714,35	760,683	796,447
Social protection	52,178	52,573	60,150
Total	1,055,743	1,311,577	1,059,724

Source Authors, based on Ministry of Finance data

Table 7.4 Structure of municipal expenditures: COFOG (thousands of euros)

	2015	2016	2017
General administration	977.4	989.7	985.1
Defense	1.1	0.8	0.8
Public order and security	68.6	67.8	76.4
Economic functions	476.0	369.4	438.7
Environment	364.7	283.7	291.8
Housing	471.4	328.6	346.2
Health care	9.0	5.7	6.6
Recreation, culture, sports	231.5	231.0	254.0
Education	1554.4	1,576.2	1700
Social protection	180.6	175.8	188.3
Total	4334.8	4028.7	4292.0

Source Authors, based on Ministry of Finance data

References

Balážová E, Dienerová H (2002) Financovanie prenesených kompetencií zo štátnej správy na miestnu samosprávu. Územná samospráva 8(2):18–19

Buček M, Němec J (2012) Local government in Slovakia. In: Moreno Á-M (ed) Local government in the member states of the European union: a comparative legal perspective. Instituto Nacional de Administración Pública, Madrid, pp 555–576

Klimovský D (2015) Slovakia as decentralization champion: reality or myth? Regions Magazine 298(1):14–16

Klimovský D, Mikušová Meričková B, Nemec J et al (2016) Local government in Slovakia: selected issues. In: Kuć-Czajkowska K, Sienkiewicz MV (eds) Local government in selected Central and Eastern European countries: experiences, reforms and determinants of development. Marie Curie Sklodowska University Press, Lublin, pp 90–118

Kováčová E (2010) Verejná správa na Slovensku. Úlohy a postavenie územnej samosprávy, FPVaMV UMB, Banská Bystrica

Matějová L, Nemec J, Křápek M et al (2017) Economies of scale on the municipal level: fact or fiction in the Czech Republic? NISPAcee J Publ Adm Policy 10(1):39–60

Němec J (2017) Public administration characteristics in Slovakia. Unpublished report for EUPACK project

Nemec J, Berčík P (1997) Zlučovanie obci alebo ich funkcií: efektívnosť a rovnosť. In: DelMartnino F, Versmessen E, Miháliková S et al (eds) Nové podoby verejnej správy (slovenská a flámska skúsenosť). SAV, Bratislava, pp 178–189

Nemec J, Berčík P, Kukliš P (2000) Local governments in Slovakia. In: Horvath TM (ed) Decentralisation: experiments and reforms. Open Societies Institute, Budapest, pp 297–342

OECD (2016) When size matters: scaling up delivery of Czech local services. In: Lewis C (ed) Available via https://oecdecoscope.wordpress.com/2016/07/26/when-size-matters-scaling-up-delivery-of-czech-local-services/. Accessed on 10 May 2017

Swianiewicz P (2014) An empirical typology of local government systems in Eastern Europe. Local Gov Stud 40(2):292–311

Thijs N, Hammerschmid G, Palaric E (2017) A comparative overview of public administration characteristics and performance in EU28. EU Commission, Brussels

Žárska E, Šebová M (2005) Decentralizácia verejnej správy Slovenskej republiky—otvorené otázky. Ekonomická univerzita, Bratislava

Chapter 8
Fiscal Decentralization in Slovenia

Slovenia (officially the Republic of Slovenia) is a fully independent sovereign, democratic unitary state. In June 1991, Slovenia became the first republic to secede from Yugoslavia and became an independent sovereign state. The Slovenian Constitution was approved on December 23, 1991. In 2004, Slovenia joined NATO and the European Union; in 2007 it became the first former communist country to join the Eurozone.

The territory of Slovenia covers 20,273 km^2 and has a population of 2.07 million. Slovenia is located in southern Central Europe and it is bordered by Italy to the west, Austria to the north, Hungary to the northeast, Croatia to the southeast, and the Adriatic Sea to the southwest.

With the exception of some short periods in early medieval times, Slovenes did not have their own state before 1918. Following the dissolution of the Austro-Hungarian Empire, the National Council of Slovenes, Croats and Serbs took power in Zagreb on October 6, 1918 and on October 29, 1918, independence was declared by a national gathering in Ljubljana. The State of Slovenes, Croats, and Serbs was created. On December 1, 1918, the State of Slovenes, Croats and Serbs merged with Serbia, becoming part of the new Kingdom of Serbs, Croats, and Slovenes; in 1929 it was renamed the Kingdom of Yugoslavia. Slovenia was completely annexed into Fascist Italy during World War II. In addition, the Prekmurje region in the east was annexed by Hungary, and some villages in the Lower Sava Valley were incorporated in the newly created Nazi puppet Independent State of Croatia. After the re-establishment of Yugoslavia, Slovenia became part of Federal Yugoslavia. In 1947, the Slovene Littoral and the western half of Inner Carniola, which had been annexed by Italy after World War One, were annexed by Slovenia. A socialist state was established, but because of the Tito–Stalin split in 1948, economic and personal freedoms were broader than in the Eastern Bloc countries. On December 23, 1990, more than 88% of the electorate voted for a sovereign and independent Slovenia, and on June 25, 1991, Slovenia became formally independent. On June 27, 1991, the Yugoslav People's Army attacked Slovenian territory, which led to the Ten-Day War. On July 7, 1991, the Brijuni Agreement was signed, implementing a truce and a three-month halt to the enforcement of Slovenia's independence.

© Springer Nature Switzerland AG 2020
M. Plaček et al., *Fiscal Decentralization Reforms*, Public Administration, Governance and Globalization 19, https://doi.org/10.1007/978-3-030-46758-6_8

The head of state is the President, who is elected by popular vote for a term of five years and a maximum of two consecutive terms. The executive and administrative authority in Slovenia is the Government of Slovenia, headed by the Prime Minister and the cabinet, who are elected by the Parliament. The deconcentrated state administration is represented by 58 state local-administrative units established in 1995. According to experts, for the most part, these administrative units are too small and were formed in a rather unusual way, i.e. as joint territorial branches of several ministries rather than general decentralized units of the state, such as e.g. administrative districts. Thus, even if the head of the administrative unit is appointed by the government, the administrative unit is subordinated to individual ministries. Moreover, there are parallel territorial units of departmental state executive agencies within ministries, 62 centers of work, territorial branches of the compulsory social insurance institutes, etc. (Virant and Rakar 2017).

The legislative authority is the bicameral Parliament of Slovenia. The bulk of power is concentrated in the National Assembly, which consists of ninety members. The National Council consists of forty members, appointed to represent social, economic, professional and local interest groups and has a limited advisory and control power.

Judicial powers in Slovenia are executed by judges elected by the National Assembly. Judicial power in Slovenia is implemented by courts with general responsibilities, and specialized courts. The central bodies are the Supreme Court and the Constitutional Court. The Constitutional Court is composed of nine judges, who are elected for nine-year terms.

Slovenia is a unitary state with one level of local self-government established (municipalities). A constitutional provision on a second level of local self-government has not been implemented yet (Virant and Rakar 2017).

The development of local self-government in Slovenia

The process of implementing a new constitutional design for local government began in 1991 with the adoption of a new Constitution. The Local Government Act was adopted in 1993 (since then it has been amended more than 30 times), and in 1994 the first "network" of new municipalities was established. The new local self-government system began to function in January 1995. According to the Constitution, citizens exercise local self-government rights by means of municipalities and other local government units, i.e. (future—not yet established) provinces. In 2006, several provisions of the Constitution were changed to codify the core principles of the local self-government in a constitutional way (Grad 2012).

The number of municipalities has increased over the last 20 years from 60 in 1991, to 147 in 1993 and stands at 212 today. Out of 212 municipalities, 11 are urban municipalities: Celje, Koper, Kranj, Ljubljana, Maribor, Murska Sobota, Nova Gorica, Novo Mesto, Ptuj, Slovenj Gradec and Velenje. According to law, a municipality comprises one or more settlements connected by common needs and interests of the local community and has at least 5000 inhabitants. A municipality may obtain the status of an urban municipality if a town with at least 20,000 inhabitants and 15,000 active jobs are situated in its territory, and if it is an economic, cultural and administrative center of a wider area. Urban municipalities have the same competences as municipalities. However, urban municipalities may also exercise transferred state administrative tasks, which refer to the development of the town (Vlaj 2012).

8.1 The Level of Decentralization in Slovenia from the Point of View of the Principles of the European Charter of Local Self-government

Slovenia signed the European Charter of Local Self-government on October 11, 1994, ratified it on November 15, 1996, and it entered into force on March 1, 1997, without reservations. Slovenia signed the Additional Protocol to the European Charter of Local Self-government on the right to participate in the affairs of a local authority on November 16, 2009 and ratified it on September 6, 2011. Regarding the legal status of the Charter, the Constitutional Court has the competence to declare that any law is not in conformity with the Charter (since the Charter has been ratified by Slovenia, it has superiority over domestic legislation). The Court is very active in guaranteeing the applicability and effectiveness of the Charter, as can be seen from many court decisions that interpret it extensively.

The most recent Council of Europe monitoring visit to Slovenia took place in 2018, and in its monitoring report, entitled "Local and Regional Democracy in Slovenia" and which was approved on November 6, 2018, the council expressed satisfaction with the overall positive situation of local democracy in Slovenia, but with some reservations, especially concerning municipal finance. The findings of this report are one of the core inputs for the following text.

The constitutional and legal foundation for local self-government
Article 9 of the Slovenian Constitution states that "Local self-government in Slovenia is guaranteed"—by this the principle of local self-government is constitutionally recognized. Part V of the Constitution is devoted to the basic principles of self-government and includes the following paragraphs—Articles 138–139 contains the definition of a municipality; Article 140 refers to the scope of local self-government; Article 141 defines urban municipalities; Article 142 defines municipal revenues and Article 144 covers the scope of supervision by state authorities (Article 143 deals with expected regions). Provisions related to local self-government can also be found in other Articles of the Constitution, namely Article 44, which defines public participation in public affairs; Article 146 defines financing of local municipalities; Article 147 is devoted to local taxes and Article 148 describes principles of local budgets.

The main law regulating local self-government is the Local Self-government Act (1993, last amended in 2018). Municipal property is regulated by the Physical Assets of the State and Local Government Act. Other important pieces of legislation are the Local Elections Act (1994, last amended in 2017); the Capital City of the Republic of Slovenia Act (2004, last amended in 2017); the Financing of Municipalities Act (2006, last amended in 2017; with corrigendum of one article in 2018); the Public Finance Act (1999, last amended in 2018); the Establishment of Municipalities and Municipal Boundaries Act (1994, last amended in 2018); the Act Regulating Measures Aimed at Fiscal Balance of Municipalities (2015) and the Fiscal Rules Act (2015).

In 2016, the Development Strategy for Local Self-government up to 2020 was adopted as a medium-term development strategy for local self-government. The Strategy expresses the vision of implementing a more systematic and planned approach to the future development of local self-government in Slovenia.

The conclusion of the monitoring report is obvious—Slovenia is in compliance with Article 2 of the Charter.

The concept of local self-government

Local municipalities in Slovenia have the right to independently and autonomously regulate and manage a substantial share of public affairs, as is set out by the Constitution and domestic laws. The tasks of a local unit can be broken down into three types (Vlaj 2012):

1. Local issues or issues of local importance, i.e. tasks determined by municipalities themselves in their statutes and other documents;
2. Local issues delegated to municipalities by the state via laws;
3. Transferred tasks of state administration carried out by municipalities under state supervision and financed by state resources (delegated responsibilities).

A municipality can regulate social relations in the municipality's own competence by general acts: municipal statutes, rules of procedure of the municipal council, municipal by-laws, budget, final account, physical and general development plan of the municipality, and physical implementation. The municipality regulates matters in its competence as well as public services with by-laws.

The main bodies of the municipality are a council, a mayor and a municipal administration. The municipal council is the decision-making body on all matters concerning the municipality. Municipal councilors are elected by the citizens through a process of secret, general and direct voting. The Local Elections Act provides two types of principles regarding elections of municipal councilors—the principle of majority (majority elections) and the principle of proportionality (proportional elections). Councilors are elected according to the majority principle if a municipal council has fewer than 12 members; if a municipal council has more than 12 members, then councilors are elected according to the principle of proportionality. In the case of proportionality-based elections, voters may only vote for one list of candidates and chose a candidate to whom they give preference in the election.

The municipal council is the highest decision-making body and according to the Local Self-government Act (Article 38) consists of 7 to 45 members depending on the number of residents in the respective municipality.

The mayor is the top executive authority and official representative of the municipality. Mayors are elected by direct elections for a term of four years by the citizens having permanent residence in the municipality.

A municipal administration is established in each municipality to implement local policies. A mayor is the head of the municipal administration. Everyday operation of the municipal administration is managed directly by the secretary of the municipality, who is appointed and dismissed by the mayor.

Taking all the above into account, the 2018 Council of Europe monitoring report states that the Slovenian situation is in full compliance with the Article 3 of the Charter.

The scope of local self-government
The competences of municipalities are established by the Local Self-government Act and other legal acts. Along with the general competences, municipalities cover the following policy areas: assets of the municipality; economic development of the municipality; spatial development and planning as well as building and land management; creating the conditions for housing construction; management of local public services and services of social welfare; environmental protection; management of water supply and power supply facilities; educational activities, culture, sports and recreational activities; public roads and other public areas; and other local matters of public interest.

In practice, municipalities perform mainly service delivery functions (e.g., delivery of public services), while a central government keeps regulatory and policy design functions (e.g., legal regulation). Public services are rarely provided by state or municipal bodies themselves—contracting is a common solution.

Delegated competences must be financed by the central government: The Constitution clearly states that "By law, the state may transfer to municipalities the performance of specific duties within the state competence if it also provides the financial resources to enable such." However, lack of clarity in distribution of competences of local authorities (own and delegated competences) in practice creates important implementation problems.

The issue is a growing number of legal standard-setting regulations in certain areas of local self-government tasks. Such over-regulation results in increasing bureaucracy and pressure on local municipalities in the exercise of their competences and increases the cost of services that local authorities are expected to cover from their own resources.

In the light of the above, the report concludes that "articles 4.1.–4.5. of the Charter are generally complied with in Slovenia. However, it would be advisable that the central government in consultation with local authorities undertake a review of the degree of prescription in existing legal regulations of certain tasks and responsibilities at the local level with a view of removing as many as cannot be of overriding necessity." Concerning Article 4.6., the report states: "The rapporteurs cannot conclude that the government acts in a systematic way in breach of Article 4.6. However, having regard to the concerns expressed by the local authorities and their associations, the rapporteur would recommend increasing the degree of involvement of local representatives at every stage of preparing new laws and regulations on all matters of their concern, and extending the timescale for consultations to make them more efficient."

The protection of local authority boundaries

The Constitution explicitly states that, "A municipality is established by law following a referendum by which the will of the residents in a given territory is determined. The territory of the municipality is also defined by law." A referendum is mandatory in order to establish a new local municipality, either by splitting off from a current local municipality or merging together. Taking this into account, the Slovenian situation complies with the Charter.

Administrative structures and resources for the tasks of local authorities

A municipal administration is established in each municipality and everyday operation of the municipal administration is managed directly by the secretary of the municipality, who, in turn, is appointed and dismissed by the mayor. The Local Self-government Act states that members of the municipal council, the mayor and the deputy mayor are municipal functionaries and they shall perform their functions on a non-professional basis. However, the mayor may decide to perform his/her functions on a professional basis and the deputy mayor may also decide to perform his/her functions on a professional basis if he/she obtains consent from the mayor. This means that main municipal officials have the right to a salary if performing their functions in a professional capacity, or to an allowance if performing functions in a non-professional capacity (mayors who perform their functions on a non-professional basis may receive their wages in the amount of 50% of the "professional" wages). Salaries for professional municipal officers are determined by the law regulating public sector wages as prescribed in the Public Service Salary Act. In this area, Slovenia complies with the Charter.

Conditions under which responsibilities are exercised at the local level

A member of a municipal council is entitled to an attendance fee for sessions of the municipal council or meetings of the working body of the municipal council (the amount of fees to be paid may not exceed 7.5% of the salary of the mayor). The municipal council decides on criteria for the payment of attendance fees for municipal council members, members of working bodies of the municipal council and other municipal bodies.

Conflicts of interest are comprehensively regulated—the mayor is not allowed to hold a position of deputy mayor, member of a municipal council, member of a supervisory committee or to serve as a municipal bureaucrat. Since 2011, mayors have no longer been allowed to represent their electorate in the parliament since dual mandates, that is, as a member of parliament and a mayor, are now prohibited. The report concludes that Article 7 is fully respected in Slovenia.

The administrative supervision of local authorities' activities

Administrative supervision is expected to focus entirely on the legality of the work of local municipalities, as prescribed by the Constitution: "State authorities supervise the legality of the work of local community authorities." The main governmental body responsible for the development of the local self-government system is the Ministry of Public Administration (hereafter, the Ministry) and its Local Self-government Service. Budget and finances of local municipalities are supervised by the Slovenian Court of Audit, following the Constitution: "The Court of Audit is the highest authority for supervising state accounts, the state budget, and all public spending." The National Assembly can dissolve a municipal council and dismiss a mayor on a proposal from the Government, but only under specific conditions under which the National Assembly can interfere in local affairs. In case a municipality does not follow the legal norms in the exercise of its own competences, the ministry should propose that the Government initiate proceedings before the Constitutional Court for conformity. The report concludes that Slovenia complies with the principles of Article 8.

The financial resources of local authorities and the financial transfer system

In general, the system of local government financing in Slovenia is based on its own resources, additional state funds distributed as financial equalization for economically weaker municipalities and borrowing (for more details see the last part of this subchapter). Fiscal equalization is included in the system: the financial equalization transfers are delivered to local governments as a general grant, the calculation of an equalization grant to municipalities is based on the average costs for appropriate expenditures and own revenues.

The report concludes article 9 of the Charter "is globally respected in Slovenia. However, if the cost of the provision of services those local authorities have to provide continues to rise and their revenues will not increase respectively there will be a significant risk of non-compliance with paragraphs 1, 2 and 4 of Article 9 of the Charter."

Local authorities' right to associate

The principle of voluntary municipal cooperation and the right to associate are included in the articles of the Local Self-government Act. There are three core municipal associations in Slovenia, respected as partners for the state: the Association of Municipalities and Towns of Slovenia as the largest association of municipalities comprising 175 member municipalities, the Association of Municipalities of Slovenia (ZOS) with a current membership of 115 municipalities and the Association of Urban Municipalities of Slovenia (ZMOS) consisting of the eleven largest cities and urban centers of Slovenia. Slovenia complies with the principles of Article 10.

The legal protection of local self-government
Slovenian local authorities have the right to address courts in order to defend their rights and interests. Local authorities can refer issues to the Constitutional Court and to the Administrative Court (particularly in cases of conflicts regarding central government decisions)—and the referrals to the Constitutional Court are not rare. This means that Slovenia fully meets the requirements of Article 11 of the Charter.

The core challenges for fiscal decentralization in Slovenia
Two issues could be mentioned in this part—fragmentation and "over-regulation." Concerning fragmentation, in total (2018) 111 municipalities do not meet the criteria of 5000 inhabitants, while the smallest municipality has only 362 inhabitants. There is a rather large diversity among local municipalities in Slovenia. For example, Kočevje covers the largest area, 555 km^2, while Odranci covers only 7 km^2. The monitoring report of 2001 emphasized that Slovenia should apply measures tailored to prevent further fragmentation, but, the process of establishing new local authorities continued. The last new municipality was established in 2015—the municipality of Ankaran, which is now one of the smallest municipalities by size, covering only 8 km^2. According to academic findings (such as Rakar and Klun 2016) small municipalities may have problems performing many tasks and are more dependent on the equalization under the Financing of Municipalities Act.

Currently, there has been no reform on the agenda tailored to merge municipalities and because of this, academia and advisors propose to extend the forms of inter-municipal co-operation. The creation of joint municipal administration (JMA) bodies was the option foreseen for smaller municipalities in the LSGA of 1993; it was not until 1999 that the first such organization was founded. The reason was a shortcoming of a provision in the law: it did not regulate the question of founding a joint body of this kind (Rakar and Klun 2016). As of today (2016 data) there are 48 such bodies and most of them are active in the field of administrative tasks (like inspection and local police activities).

Some authors argue that Slovenia is currently one of the most centralized countries in Europe. Local self-government operates strongly under the auspices of the state in terms of content and finances (Vlaj 2012, pp. 682) and contrary to the practice of many EU member states, the functions of central administration have not been transferred to municipal administrations, but rather remained within the structure of central administration through administrative units and territorial branches of central agencies. Local branches of central agencies correspond to a special-purpose administrative body model of organization (e.g. Police, Financial Administration, Land Survey Authority, Inspectorates, etc.). At the local level, the excessive organizational dispersion of authority generates a reactive, unstable and inefficient system of political decision-making (Virant and Rakar 2017).

Most important data about the level of fiscal decentralization
Slovenia ranks below OECD unitary countries in terms of municipal expenditure share in GDP and total public spending, which accounted for 13.4% of GDP and 29.0% of general government spending on average in 2013 (OECD 2016).

Similar to other CEE countries, the core source of local government revenues are shared taxes. According to the data of the Ministry of Finance, if shared taxes are included, the total own tax revenues in local government budgets amount to a bit more than 50% of total municipal revenue (this figure significantly fluctuates—it was 64% of total municipal revenues in 2009, in 2013 municipal tax revenues amounted to 69.45% of total municipal revenues, 58.76% in 2015, and in 2017, tax revenues accounted for 71% of total municipal revenues).

The core own sources are taxes + fees and revenues from the assets of the municipality. Up to date, the share of the personal income tax is the most important local government revenue source, with municipalities receiving 54% of this tax, according to the criteria defined by the Financing of Municipalities Act. Local taxes are property tax; vessel tax; tax on real property transactions; inheritance and gift tax; tax on winnings from conventional games of chance, and any other tax where so provided by the Act governing taxes (Grad 2012).

The system of distribution of the share of PIT is rather complicated and includes an equalization factor. As of today (2018) municipalities are entitled to 70% of 54% of personal income tax collected by the government, while 30% is allocated as the solidarity compensation. If 70% (of 54% of income tax) is less than the calculated appropriate expenditure, the municipality receives the difference (the solidarity compensation). "Reach" municipalities do not receive additional funding from the solidarity compensation. The calculation "appropriate expenditures level" is based on a mathematical formula including real costs of municipalities for four previous years, and objective criteria set by law (like the amount and the age structure of the population). The Ministry of Finance provides calculations and it is expected to send the results to municipalities before starting the preparation of the annual budget. To what extent the formula on appropriate expenditure reflects the real cost is questionable (Rakar and Klun 2016).

Municipalities are not free to set property tax rates freely. On the one hand, the property tax is set by the state while the tax rate can be changed by a municipal decision. The compensation for the use of building land is the only real municipal own tax source (the tax base, the tax rate and possible exemptions are defined by municipalities). Other own sources of financing for municipalities are self-imposed contributions, dues, fines, concession fees, and payments for local public services. For example, in 2017, municipal non-tax revenues amounted to 17.15% of total municipal revenues, where the majority comes from rents and leases (Rakar and Klun 2016).

Municipalities receive transfers from the state budget, from other institutions and the EU funds. The total level of transfer significantly depends on the success in absorption of EU finds (for example according to the Ministry of Finance data, in 2015, municipal transfers reached 24.59% out of total municipal revenues, the majority of which came from the EU funds, but in 2017 this figure dropped to 7.97%. The lump sum state grant (per capita amount required to finance the municipalities' statutory functions) is calculated according to the formula where several equalization indicators are taken into account: number of inhabitants (with permanent residence), size of municipality, length of municipal roads and public paths, ratio of inhabitants

Table 8.1 Municipal revenues (Million EUR)

Revenue	2015	2016	2017
Total tax revenues	1308.3	1358.6	1418.5
Shared income tax	1025.0	1049.5	1096.7
Property tax	235.7	255.9	273.9
Other local taxes	47.6	53.2	47.9
Other revenues	918.1	543.1	558.2
Total revenues	2226.4	1901.7	1976.7

Source Authors, based on Ministry of Finance data

under 6 years of age, ratio of inhabitants between 6 to 15 years, ratio of inhabitants older than 65, as well as ratio of inhabitants older than 75 (Rakar and Klun 2016).

Tables 8.1 and 8.2 provide elementary characteristics of the local public finance in Slovenia.

The borrowing rights of municipalities are regulated by the Financing of Municipalities Act. Municipalities are allowed to incur debts if current year debt servicing is lower than 8% of previous year budget realized revenue. In addition, the current year debt servicing can be up to 10% if incurring debts for EU investments. Indebtedness, bailouts or bankruptcy are not a hot issue at the Slovenian municipal level (Rakar and Klun 2016).

Table 8.2 Structure of municipal expenditures: COFOG (% of GDP)

	2015	2016	2017
General administration	0.9	0.9	1.0
Defense	0	0	0
Public order and security	0.1	0.1	0.1
Economic functions	0.9	0.9	0.9
Environment	0.8	0.3	0.2
Housing	0.5	0.4	0.4
Health care	1.0	1.0	1.0
Recreation, culture, sports	0.7	0.6	0.6
Education	3.1	3.2	3.1
Social protection	1.0	1.0	0.9
Total	8.9	8.2	8.2

Source Authors, based on Eurostat data

References

Grad F (2012) Local government in Slovenia. In: Moreno Á-M (ed) Local government in the member states of the European union: a comparative legal perspective. Instituto Nacional de Administración Pública, Madrid, pp 577–598

OECD (2016) When size matters: scaling up delivery of Czech local services. In: Lewis C (ed) Available via https://oecdecoscope.wordpress.com/2016/07/26/when-size-matters-scaling-up-delivery-of-czech-local-services/. Accessed on 10 May 2017

Rakar I, Klun M (2016) Local self-government reform in Slovenia—organizational and financial dimension. In: Kuć-Czajkowska K, Sienkiewicz MV (eds) Local government in selected Central and Eastern European countries: experiences, reforms and determinants of development. Marie Curie Sklodowska University Press, Lublin, pp 119–141

Virant G, Rakar I (2017) Public administration characteristics in Slovenia. Unpublished report for EUPACK project

Vlaj S (2012) The system of local self-government in Slovenia with a special emphasis on the status of the capital city Ljubljana. Croatian Comp Publ Adm 12(3):675–694

Chapter 9
Comparative Analysis of the Results of Fiscal Decentralization in Selected CEE Countries

Comparative literature (see, e.g., Lodge 2007; Sodaro 2001) points to various applications of this method. In general, the comparison method is based on comparing a particular problem that is of interest to the compared units. The comparison is based on determining the characters to compare. Comparisons can be made in various forms (e.g. scoring on a scale, comparing numerical indicators, scoring with descriptor, etc.). Based on the comparison of observed characteristics of the compared units, we will draw conclusions from the comparative analysis.

In this study, we compared local governments in seven selected CEE countries for which we collected and summarized basic data about the organization of local self-governments in Bulgaria, the Czech Republic, Hungary, Poland, Romania, Slovakia, and Slovenia. First, we made a qualitative comparative analysis and at the end we attempt quantitative research.

Local self-governments in selected CEE countries: core comparative issues
Tha data from the first part of this chapter delivers some interesting findings. The path dependence factor is connected with the fact that all the countries surveyed are linked by a common experience with a communist regime. Six of the countries surveyed (Bulgaria, the Czech Republic, Hungary, Poland, Romania, Slovakia) were among the satellite countries of the Soviet bloc. Slovenia has a somewhat different trajectory compared to the other six countries. However, all countries surveyed had the same experience of centralistic governance in which the centralist state had a strong (paternalistic) role. After the fall of communism in 1989, the task for all countries in the sample was the re-establishment of genuine local self-government.

The common feature for all countries in the early post 1989 period was very fast abolishment of the previous system of "national committees" (or similar structures), combining state administration and self-government features under one roof (see Nemec and Berčík 1997). This task was solved very quickly in the early nineties when all countries realized major reforms and created self-government structures, based on good international practice. The main navigation tool for changes has been the

© Springer Nature Switzerland AG 2020
M. Plaček et al., *Fiscal Decentralization Reforms*, Public Administration, Governance and Globalization 19, https://doi.org/10.1007/978-3-030-46758-6_9

European Charter of Local Self-government—however, the processes of acceptance of this core international treaty within our sample of countries differed, both in timing and complexity. Hungary already signed the Charter in 1992, while Slovakia, that last, did not sign it until 1999 (despite the fact that major reform changes already took place in 1990). Some countries accepted the Charter from the beginning without reservations, other countries like Slovakia decided not to be bound by several articles. Today, the only country which has still not removed all reservations is the Czech Republic.

Despite the common history and similar beginnings, the "quality of decentralization in selected countries" varies significantly today. The core differentiation factor is finance. The indicator "level of fiscal decentralization" tracked in the form of "real revenues of municipalities as % of total municipal revenues" and in the form of "percentage of transfers in municipal revenues" showed interesting results. The indicator "real revenues of municipalities" indicates a certain capacity to own "self-financing." The scale of real revenues (not shared taxes and un-conditional transfers) is limited in all countries, but extremely limited especially in Hungary today (probably a result of recentralization), but also in Bulgaria and Romania. Taking this into account, the compliance with the Charter principle that "Local authorities shall be entitled, within national economic policy, to adequate financial resources of their own, of which they may dispose freely within the framework of their powers," is problematic in all selected countries, and dramatically problematic in Bulgaria, Hungary, and Romania.

The indicator "percentage of transfers in municipal revenues" reveals the effect of induced financial dependence on the center. This is probably due to the remnants of state paternalism. This dependency is particularly evident in Bulgaria, Hungary, Romania and to an extent also in Poland. However, rigorous conclusions cannot be drawn from these different data. The differences are likely to be due largely to different costing systems. This assumption is supported by our analysis of subnational expenditures in COFOG structure as % of GDP, 2017 and in the commentary. We will work with this conclusion (hypothesis) about the strong residues of centralism in Part III. We will examine the "decentralization paradox" that applies to countries with a historical centralist evolutionary footprint: the lower the degree of fiscal federalism, the greater the expected state paternalism.

Besides finance, the core difference within the selected sample of countries is the level of fragmentation. The Czech and Slovak systems seem to have the most fragmented local self-government systems in Europe. Poland is a singular case with three levels of self-government. In the case of municipalities in the Czech Republic (the country with the greatest fragmentation of municipalities in Europe) we will examine whether the decentralization paradox is related to fragmentation. We will examine whether the size of municipalities is related to the number of political parties in the council and whether the residual of paternalism is related to fragmentation.

Local self-governments and the quality of governance (quantitative study)
As the final step, we tried to evaluate if selected indicators of the "quality of local governance" have any impact on the countries' overall public administration performance. For our comparative analysis we use the OLS regression panel with fixed effects on data obtained from the World Bank and Eurostat databases for the years 2000–2017.

There exist many indicators evaluating the quality of governance on the national level and at least also one specific indicator of local governance quality. The summary of the most important governance quality indicators is provided by Thijs et al. (2017). To evaluate the performance of public administration systems in the European Union, their report works with the following performance indicators on the national level: access to government information, transparency of government, voice and accountability, control of corruption, TI perception of corruption, Gallup perception of corruption, impartiality, professionalism, closedness, E-government users, pre-filled forms, online service completion, online services, barriers to public sector innovation, services to businesses, ease of doing business, strategic planning capacity, inter-ministerial coordination, SGI implementation capacity, QoG implementation capacity, societal consultations, use of evidence based instruments, regulatory quality, rule of law and trust in government. These indicators are collected by different organizations—Bertelsmann Stiftung (Sustainable Governance Indicators), World Bank (Worldwide Governance Indicators), Quality of Government Institute Gothenburg (Expert survey), Eurobarometer, World Economic Forum (Global Competitiveness Index), World Bank (Ease of Doing Business), European Public Sector Innovation Scoreboard, European Commission (Digital Economy and Society Index), UN E-government Index, Gallup World Poll and Transparency International (CPI index).

World Bank data also provide extra indicators. For the purposes of quantitative processing we decided to work with government efficiency. Government efficiency captures perceptions of the quality of public services, the quality of the civil service and the degree of its independence from political pressures, the quality of policy formulation and implementation, and the credibility of the government's commitment to such policies (Kaufmann et al. 2010).

Our study and other sources provide three independent variables for possible quantitative processing as follows:

(a) Local autonomy index—this variable is compiled according to Ladner and Keuffer (2018) and is described in detail in the theoretical part of the thesis.
(b) Level of fiscal decentralization—For fiscal decentralization we use Eurostat data measured as a share of GDP of individual countries. The variables are as follows:

- Total government revenue as a percentage of GDP;
- Subnational expenditure in COFOG structure % of GDP—in these expenses we include general administration, defense, public order and security, economic functions, environment, housing, health care, recreation, culture, religion, social protection;

Table 9.1 Results of OLS model of the impact of fiscal decentralization on the efficiency of governments

Variable	Coefficient	P-value
Constant	0.186829	0.0015
Public order and safety	0.927991	0.0001
Education	0.0614713	0.0065
Social protection	0.0743517	0.0503
Net lending/net borrowing	0.0796789	0.0015

Source Authors

- Net lending $(+)$/net borrowing $(-)$ as a surplus or deficit of the local government budget as % of GDP of the year;
- Fragmentation (measured by the average number of inhabitants per municipality, data taken from EUROSTAT)—calculated as population/number of municipalities.

Fragmentation is the issue in most countries of the region. There is a lot of discussion about pros and cons of small municipalities, but despite the fact that most studies did not confirm visible existence of economies of scale, the existence of excessively small municipalities is problematic from the point of capacities (Matějová et al. 2017). The most fragmented country in the sample is the Czech Republic, which is also the most fragmented country in Europe, followed closely by Slovakia.

Table 9.1 presents the results of our analysis. Only variables that are statistically significant are presented.

The model is statistically significant. LSDV R-square reaches 0.947778.

The results of the model are surprising. One might expect that there should be some relation between the level of local autonomy or the structure of LSG revenue and the country's PA performance. However, the results show that local government spending structure and the net lending/net borrowing variable primarily affect government efficiency. The most important is spending on public order and safety, education and social protection. A very surprising fact is that spending on environmental protection, housing and recreation, general public services is not statistically significant. Similarly, revenue and transfers are not significant. Statistically significant are local budget surpluses, which increase the efficiency of governance and a deficit, which reduce the efficiency of governance.

References

Kaufmann D, Kraay A, Mastruzzi M (2010) The worldwide governance indicators: methodology and analytical issues. Hague J Rule Law 3(2):220–246

Ladner A, Keuffer N (2018) Creating an index of local autonomy—theoretical, conceptual, and empirical issues. Regional & Federal Studies. https://doi.org/10.1080/13597566.2018.1464443

Lodge M (2007) Comparative public policy. In: Fisher R, Miller GJ, Sidny MS (eds) Handbook of public policy analysis: theory, politics, and methods. CRC Press, Boca Raton, pp 273–288

Matějová L, Nemec J, Křápek M et al (2017) Economies of scale on the municipal level: fact or fiction in the Czech Republic? NISPAcee J Pub Adm Policy 10(1):39–60

Nemec J, Berčík P (1997) Zlučovanie obci alebo ich funkcií: efektívnosť a rovnosť. In: DelMartnino F, Versmessen E, Miháliková S et al (eds) Nové podoby verejnej správy (slovenská a flámska skúsenosť). SAV, Bratislava, pp 178–189

Sodaro MJ (2001) Comparative politics: a global introduction. McGraw-Hill, New York

Thijs N, Hammerschmid G, Palaric E (2017) A comparative overview of public administration characteristics and performance in EU28. EU Commission, Brussels

Chapter 10
Fiscal Decentralization and Efficiency: The Empirical Case Study of Small Municipalities in the Czech Republic

In this section of the book, we will discuss the impact of fiscal decentralization on the efficiency of local governments in the Czech Republic. As was shown in the previous section, the Czech Republic is characterized by having the largest number of municipalities of all Central European countries. The second unique feature is having the largest share of municipalities with populations of 1000 inhabitants or less. This phenomenon deserves further attention in the context of fiscal decentralization. The case of the Czech Republic is interesting from two points of view. First of all, the Czech Republic is a typical country of Central and Eastern Europe, having forty years of experience with a solid centralization of public administration. The case of the Czech Republic is also interesting from a more general perspective. It is an inspiration for research in other countries characterized by the phenomenon of fragmentation. In this sense, the Czech Republic can be considered a "social laboratory" where we can examine the impact of fiscal decentralization on the efficiency of local governments and identify the factors that influence this efficiency. At the same time, it is possible to examine it on the public administration reform trajectory, and the growth in its development following strict centralism. We are looking for answers to the following main research question and sub-questions (Table 10.1).

To answer these research questions, we have used two stage DEA, a combination of data envelopment analysis and a regression model. We use them as tools to explain the effect of fiscal variables o n efficiency.

From a methodological point of view, the empirical part is organized as follows: First, we will present in more detail the functions and activities of local governments in the Czech Republic. Subsequently, we will describe the course of reforms and changes in the area of fiscal federalism, including the motivation for these changes. We will also consider the incomes, expenditures and net indebtedness of local governments in the Czech Republic in a broader comparison with the European Union countries.

The descriptive chapters of the empirical part will be followed by a section devoted to the methods and data used. In this section, we will explain the choice of input and output efficiency indicators in the context of municipalities' functions in the Czech Republic. We will also present the second stage of the efficiency model, i.e. selected

© Springer Nature Switzerland AG 2020   133
M. Plaček et al., *Fiscal Decentralization Reforms*, Public Administration,
Governance and Globalization 19, https://doi.org/10.1007/978-3-030-46758-6_10

Table 10.1 Main research question and sub-questions

	Main research question
	What is the impact of fiscal decentralization on the efficiency of municipalities in the Czech Republic?
Sub-research question number	**Sub-research questions**
1	What are the effects of fiscal decentralization on the efficiency of individual size categories of municipalities?
2	What are the effects of fiscal decentralization on the efficiency of municipalities according to the activities they perform?
3	What are the effects of fiscal decentralization on the efficiency of municipalities in the NUTS II region in which they are located?
4	What are the effects of fiscal decentralization on the efficiency of municipalities by region in which municipalities are located?
5	How has the efficiency of municipalities changed according to the above criteria over time?

fiscal and political variables for which we assume an association with the efficiency of Czech municipalities.

The chapter "Results" will present our empirical answers to the research questions and will provide different views on the data depending on the size of the municipalities, the activities they perform, the location of the municipality and, last but not least, dependence on time.

In conclusion, we will discuss possible recommendations for improving the efficiency of local governments in the Czech Republic.

10.1 Closer Look at Local Government and Fiscal Decentralization in the Czech Republic

The municipality can be defined as the basic territorial self-governing community of citizens, forming a territorial unit, which is delimited by the boundaries of the territory of the municipality. Pursuant to Act No. 128/2000 Coll. on municipalities, the municipality is a public corporation. It is therefore a non-state entity that has the following characteristics that each municipality must have by law (Table 10.2).

The Municipalities Act provides for all municipalities to carry out self-governing activities independently. In addition to this activity, municipalities may also exercise delegated powers. These are tasks which, by their content, fall primarily within the competence of state authorities. It is a practical fulfillment of the principle of subsidiarity, where public affairs should be carried out primarily by those authorities closest to the citizens.

Table 10.2 Characteristics of the municipality

Characteristics	Description of the characteristic
Own territory	The territorial basis of the municipality is formed by one or more Cadis of the municipality
Population	The municipality has citizens who are listed as permanently residing in the municipality. Every municipality must be *permanently* inhabited by humans. Self-administration provides them with statutory public services and citizens of the municipality are obliged to respect the authorities
Legal personality	A municipality is a legal entity that acts in its own name and has its own title and identification number
Assets	The municipality has its own property, which it is legally entitled to dispose of economically and efficiently
Competence	The municipality is governed by the provisions of the law. To promote the exercise of its self-governing activity, it publishes its own legislation (regulations and decrees)

The exercise of self-government is not only a right of the municipality, but also its ability, within the limits set by law, to organize and manage a substantial part of public affairs on its own responsibility and in its own interest. This right results from the constitutional legislation, the European Charter of Local Self-Government, the Act on Municipalities and the Act on the City of Prague.

Section 35 of the Municipalities Act defines autonomous competence as follows:

(1) The autonomous competence of a municipality includes matters of interest to the municipality and to the citizens of the municipality, unless they are entrusted to regions by law or the delegated powers of the municipal authorities or matters entrusted to the independent competence of the municipality by law.

(2) The autonomous competence of the municipality shall include, in particular, matters referred to in § 84, 85 and 102, with the exception of issuing municipal ordinances. The municipality in its independent jurisdiction also cares for the creation of conditions for the development of social care and for satisfying the needs of its citizens in accordance with local prerequisites and local customs. These are primarily meeting the needs of housing, the protection and development of health, transport and communications, the need for information, education and training, overall cultural development and the protection of public order.

In addition to these activities, municipalities (municipal authorities) carry out (or can carry out) the following activities: approve the municipal development program; approve the budget of the municipality, the closing account of the municipality and the financial statements; establish and abolish contributory organizations and organizational units of the municipality; decide on the establishment or dissolution of legal entities, approve their instruments of incorporation, articles of association, memorandum and articles of association and decide on participation in legal entities already established; issue generally binding ordinances of the municipality; decide to hold a

Table 10.3 Categories of municipalities by scope of delegated acts

Categories of municipalities	Characteristics (description) of the category
Municipalities of the first degree	They perform the most basic extent of government administration
Municipalities of the second degree	These are municipalities with designated municipal authorities. These municipalities are a lower link between municipalities with extended competence and other, lowest municipal authorities. There are about 380 in the Czech Republic
Municipalities of the third degree	These are municipalities with extended powers. These are usually larger cities with a large administrative district. These municipalities are an intermediary of delegated powers of self-government between regional authorities and other municipal authorities. There are about 200 of them in the Czech Republic The Czech POINT is available at municipal offices with extended powers[a]

[a]This is a project in which municipal authorities with extended powers, regional authorities, notaries and legal entities (e.g. the Czech Post) can issue citizens extracts from the Land Register, the Criminal Register or the Trade Register. Citizens can thus obtain through Czech POINT all data, copies and extracts which are kept in central registers and registers about their person, property and rights

local referendum; to propose changes to cadastral areas within the municipality, to approve agreements on changing the boundaries of the municipality and on merging municipalities; decide on the establishment and names of parts of the municipality, the names of streets and other public spaces; acquire and transfer tangible immovable property, including the release of real estate, and transfer flats and non-residential premises from community property; provide in-kind gifts worth over CZK 20,000; provide subsidies and repayable financial assistance over CZK 50,000; enter into credit and loan agreements; regulate real estate; issue municipal bonds; establish educational organizations (Provazníková 2011).

Municipalities may also exercise delegated powers. Delegated competence means the performance of state administration, which the state has transferred to munici-palities. Delegated powers are delegated to municipalities by the Municipalities Act, but also by a large number of other special laws and regulations (Ochrana et al. 2015). The scope of delegated powers is determined by law. A municipality, in dele-gated competence, issues a municipal regulation and an administrative decision. It is always governed by government resolutions or regulations of central administrative bodies and measures of regional authorities. The basic scope of delegated powers also includes other activities, such as registration of citizens, issuance of building permits, issuance of identity cards and passports. In terms of the scope of delegated powers, the Municipalities Act distinguishes three basic types (categories) of municipalities, as shown in the figure (Table 10.3).

In the Czech Republic, there are three types of municipalities according to the scope of delegated state administration, which are categorized according to the scope of delegated powers. The largest scope of competence is carried out by municipalities of the third degree. Besides municipalities performing delegated powers in the Czech

Table 10.4 Structure of municipalities in the Czech Republic by population

Municipality	Number of municipalities	Population	Percentage of total population
Up to 199 residents	1449	180,093	1.7
From 200 to 499 residents	1997	651,475	6.2
From 500 to 999 residents	1378	973,247	9.2
From 1000 to 1999 residents	745	1,042,569	9.9
From 2000 to 4999 residents	417	1,262,911	12.0
From 5000 to 9999 residents	141	964,031	9.1
From 10,000 to 19,999 residents	69	970,075	9.2
From 20,000 to 49,999 residents	44	1,324,522	12.6
From 50,000 to 99,999 residents	12	874,462	8.3
Over 100,000 residents	6	2,310,458	21.9

Source ČSÚ (2016)

Republic, there are approximately 1200 municipalities with a registry office and approximately 600 municipalities with a building office.

In the Czech Republic, the phenomenon of new municipalities is still current. New municipalities can be formed by the separation of part of an existing municipality. The part of the municipality that wants to separate must have a separate cadastral territory adjacent to at least two municipalities or one municipality and a foreign state and forming a coherent territorial unit. After separation, the new municipality must have at least 1000 citizens. The decision to separate the municipality is decided by a local referendum in the given part of the municipality. On the basis of the result of the local referendum and on the proposal of the municipality, the regional authority decides on the separation of the municipality. A new municipality may also be formed by changing or canceling a military area.

In the above context, it is certainly interesting to present the current structure of municipalities in the Czech Republic by population (Table 10.4).

From the table it is clear that in terms of the number of municipalities and the proportion of the population, municipalities up to 10,000 inhabitants play an essential role. This phenomenon is the result of decentralization in the 1990s.

According to the latest OECD Study (OECD 2016) a high number of municipalities in the Czech Republic, more than 1/4, have fewer than 200 inhabitants; 2/3 of municipalities have fewer than 1000 inhabitants. This causes significant losses in efficiency in the provision of public goods and services. As an example, administrative costs per capita in municipalities between 100 and 200 inhabitants were 50% higher than administrative costs in municipalities with between 1000 and 2000 inhabitants.

Small municipalities are also faced with lower school occupancy (60% of primary schools have fewer than 200 pupils) and also face procedural problems in areas such as administration and public procurement.

The highest authority of the municipality is the directly elected council. Depending on the size category of the municipality, the council has between 5 and 55 councilors. The council decides on all matters falling within the independent competence of the municipality. The municipal council prepares proposals for municipal council meetings and also ensures the fulfillment of resolutions adopted by the municipal council. If stipulated by law, the municipal council may also decide on delegated powers. The municipal council consists of the mayor, deputy mayor and other members of the council, whose number must be odd and is at least five and at most eleven members. The Council also decides on matters of reserved competences, which are described in more detail in the Act on Municipalities. The municipality is represented externally by the mayor, who is elected by the local council from among its members. The mayor convenes and manages the council meetings. Support for political authorities is provided by the municipal authority, which is also an executive body of self-government.

Municipalities may cooperate in the exercise of their independent powers. Cooperation of municipalities can affect the efficiency of local governments. This cooperation can take the form of a public contract concluded to fulfill a specific task, or a public contract to create a voluntary union of municipalities. Municipalities may also establish legal entities under a special law.

10.1.1   Introduction into Fiscal Decentralization in the Czech Republic

Theory distinguishes three basic models of fiscal federalism (Musgrave and Musgrave 1989)—a centralist, decentralized, and combined model. These models differ in the role of governments and the position public budgets have in them. The centralist model was typical of the Soviet bloc countries, where the centrally controlled economic system was headed by the Communist Party with its leading role in society. The state and the budget of the central government played a dominant role in this model. The role of self-government was suppressed. After the fall of the communist regimes, these countries started on a path to reform. This included the transition to a combined model of fiscal federalism. This is also typical of the Czech Republic.

The current model of fiscal federalism in the Czech Republic can be illustrated as follows.

As Fig. 10.1 shows, the model of fiscal federalism in the Czech Republic has three basic levels—state (central), regional, and municipal. The state level is represented by central state bodies with a central state budget, respectively state parafiscal funds. The regional level consists of regions with their regional budgets. The lowest is the municipal level. This is represented by individual municipalities with municipal budgets.

Each public budget has its own public revenue and public expenditure. At the same time, there are financial flows from higher budget levels to lower budgets levels, (e.g.

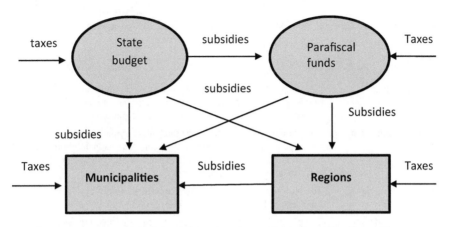

Fig. 10.1 The current model of fiscal federalism in the Czech Republic. *Source* Transparency International (2008)

in the form of subsidies, transfers, or taxes entrusted and shared). Thus, the budgetary system of the Czech Republic consists of several levels of interconnected budgets.

The public budget fulfills important roles and functions in relation to self-government. The budget is a financial plan, a planning document, management monitoring, a control document and a means of political communication (see figure below) (Table 10.5).

Public budgets take the form of a so-called budget system. The budget system consists of the state budget, budgets of municipalities, regions and voluntary unions of municipalities, budgets of contributory organizations established by territorial self-governing units, health insurance companies, state funds, and regional councils of cohesion regions. The budget system also includes rules and regulations that define how individual budgets can earn revenue and how they can spend public money. This includes, for example, Act No. 243/2000 Coll. on the budgetary determination of taxes, Act No. 218/2000 on budgetary rules, Act No. 250/2000 Coll. on budgetary rules of the TSU, Act No. 320/2000 Coll. on financial control, Act No. 134/2016 Coll. on public procurement, Act No. 23/2000 Coll. on the rules on budgetary responsibility. This also includes institutions that control the spending of funds.

From our point of view, the budgets of territorial self-governing units, i.e. regions and municipalities, and their connection to the state budget are important. The budget of the region can be simply represented as a balance of income and expenditure (Table 10.6).

Table 10.5 Characteristics, functions and roles of the budget of the self-governing organs

Characteristics and functions of the budget. Budget as	Comments
Financial plan	The budget shall include the planned flow of public revenues and public expenditures for the financial year. The plan takes the form of a balance between financial revenues and expenditure[a]
Planning document	The municipalities are based on the budgetary perspective of revenue and expenditure for a period of 2–5 years. The budget determines the projected volume of revenue and expenditure and shows the investment plan of the municipality
Control document	The budget sets out the objectives of budgetary policy, and allows the financing of local government policy
Monitoring document	The planned activities and objectives are monitored retrospectively. Monitoring allows the identification of the effectiveness and efficiency of public policies
Control tool	A programmatic or target-compiled budget allows you to control local government. This is done on the basis of monitoring the achievement of the objectives of public policies and budgetary objectives, as well as the effects of the public policy objectives and the efficiency of the allocated budgetary resources
A means of political communication	The budget is also a means of political communication—it informs about the objectives and priorities of politicians

In the Czech Republic, most municipalities strive for a balance between income and expenditures. However, the law allows municipalities to draw up a deficit budget or a surplus budget

10.1.2   The Course of Fiscal Decentralization in the Czech Republic

Reforms between 1948 and 1989

Until 1948, most municipal expenses in Czechoslovakia were covered by property income. In 1948, a communist coup took place in Czechoslovakia and the state fell under central control. This also involved the management of municipalities. Municipalities as public corporations (i.e. legal entities) were abolished, and their property was nationalized. The elected representatives of the municipalities were replaced by the appointed "representatives of the people" (proposed and approved by the Communist Party), who chaired the "national committees." If this part of history can be called a reform, then in terms of municipal financing it was a reform towards total centralism—the budgets of national committees were part of the state budget, which was centrally managed. The national committees were in fact funded by special-purpose subsidies from the state. Municipal property was devastated on the one hand, and the necessary infrastructure was built in cities and selected municipalities (factories, prefabricated houses, schools, libraries, etc.) on the other. The key prerequisites for managing national committees (replacing municipalities) were

Table 10.6 Budget of the local governments by types of revenue and expenditure

Revenue	Expenditure
1. Capital	1. Capital expenditures
(a) Revenues from the sale of fixed assets	(a) Investment expenditure-investment purchases, purchase of shares and equity shares
(b) Revenue from the sale of shares and equity shares	(b) Investment transfers—investment transfers to businesses and general interest companies, investment transfers and other payments to budgets, investment transfers abroad
	(c) Investment loans—Investment loans to companies and general benefit companies, investment loans and certain other payments to budgets, investment loans to the population
2. Current tax	2. Current expenditure
(a) Income, profit and capital income taxes	(a) Non-investment purchases—payments for work done, employer-paid premiums, purchases of goods and services, interest, advances and expenses related to non-investment purchases
(b) Taxes and fees on selected activities	(b) Non-investment transfers—non-investment transfers to companies and general contributory organizations, non-investment transfers and other payments to budgets, non-investment transfers of own funds, non-investment transfers to the population, non-investment transfers abroad
(c) Property taxes	(c) Non-investment loans—non-investment loans to businesses and general-interest companies, non-investment loans and certain other payments to budgets, non-investment loans abroad
(d) Other tax revenues	
3. Current non-tax	
(a) Revenues from own activities, contributions from established organizations	
(b) Income from renting of property	
(c) Dividends and interest	
(d) Penalties received	
(c) Loan installments received	
4. Transfers	
(a) Current	
(b) Capital	
Revenue > Expenditure = Surplus	Revenue < Expenditure = Deficit

Source Authors, Peterová (2012), Provazníková (2011)

working class origins, communist party membership, and loyalty to the party. Educated and qualified people for the management of municipalities often ended up as
factory workers, boiler workers or other blue-collar professions (unless they joined
the Communist Party). This had a very negative impact on municipal management.

In the second half of the 1960s, efforts to reform the socialist regime in Czechoslovakia (also related to municipalities) ended in 1968 with "fraternal assistance" from
five armies of friendly communist countries headed by the Soviet Union (except
Poland, Hungary, and Bulgaria). The army of the German Democratic Republic[1] also
participated in the occupation of Czechoslovakia with a small number of specialists
(Romania refused to participate in the occupation of Czechoslovakia). The reform
efforts were crushed under the tracks of tanks, and the occupation of Czechoslovakia
began. As mentioned above, in the 1970s and 1980s the communist regime worked
out a rural reform—the creation of a central system of municipalities, which led to
the violent merger of municipalities, the development of centrally designated "center
municipalities" and the decline of abolished (affiliated) municipalities. This actually
happened until 1989, i.e. until the fall of the communist regime in Czechoslovakia.

Reforms of Fiscal Federalism After 1989
In the Municipalities Act (No. 367/1990) of 1990, municipalities were given a relatively wide scope and it was clear that the state would have to provide funding.
According to the law, each municipality was obliged to ensure economic, social and
cultural development, security and creation of a healthy environment on its territory.
Furthermore, the Act also specified the competence of the municipality in the field of
education (especially kindergartens and primary schools), social care, health care and
culture; local public order matters and the establishment of municipal (city) police,
with the exception of decisions on crimes (this power was subsequently acquired by
municipalities); furthermore, the administration, maintenance and operation of facilities serving the satisfaction of citizens' needs (these were facilities owned by the
municipality); cleaning and cleanliness of the municipality, collection of household
waste and its disposal; water supply, drainage and waste water treatment. Municipalities also took over the related infrastructure from the state—such as the buildings
and land of kindergartens and primary schools, libraries, buildings of social care
facilities, etc. It was clear that municipalities could not finance this extensive list
of powers from the return of their own (historical or otherwise acquired) property.
Therefore, the method of financing municipalities was laid down in 1990 by Act
No. 576/1990 on the rules for the management of budgetary resources of the Czech
Republic and municipalities (budgetary rules).

Pursuant to this Act, the income of municipalities (1) was the entire income tax
on real estate (in the territory of the municipality), (2) the entire income tax on

---

[1] This, in particular in the Czech borderlands (former Sudetenland), which in 1938 was occupied by
Hitler's Germany, triggered an extremely negative reaction, especially among the witnesses of the
German occupation. German troops were withdrawn within a few days. In the end, only the troops
of the Soviet Army remained in Czechoslovakia. The presence of Soviet troops was legalized by an
intergovernmental treaty between the Czechoslovak government and the Soviet government signed
in October 1968. The Soviet army left Czechoslovakia in June 1991.

personal income (hereinafter referred to as DPFO), (3) the entire tax on business and other self-employment (hereinafter DPPO) paid by municipalities, (4) 40% of the county income tax on personal income from employment and on emoluments (i.e. employees' salaries).

Between 1993 and 1996, the rules for allocating taxes to municipalities changed—the revenue from employment taxes increased (at the expense of district authorities) to 60% in 1995. Representatives of municipalities have repeatedly criticized the state because municipal incomes are insufficient and mayors are unable to ensure the development of municipalities.

The partial reform took place following a lively political debate in 1996 (see Act No. 154 of 1995 amending the budgetary rules). According to this Act, municipalities had 20% of the business income tax revenue, which was distributed to individual municipalities on the basis of the number of inhabitants. However, in the framework of political agreements, this was made possible by an "exchange" for a reduction in the share of personal income tax from employment; at the same time the method of distribution of this income was changed, namely (1) 10% according to the numbers of taxpayers in the municipalities; a 20% share of the revenue of this tax was distributed in the district on the basis of the municipalities' share of the total population of the district.

In 2000, the new Act No. 128 on municipalities was passed. The Act defines the powers of municipalities similarly to the previous one, inter alia stating that a municipality takes care of the all-round development of its territory and the needs of its citizens. In terms of citizens' needs, these include environmental issues (including public spaces, parks, greenery, etc.), health and social affairs, housing, local transport (both in terms of local roads, parking and transport services), education and training. education (nursery, primary education, children's and youth houses, libraries, etc.), culture and sports, cleanliness in the city, waste, water and sewerage, public order protection, etc. Since 2001, municipalities and regions have also assumed, in the spirit of public administration reform, extensive powers delegated by the state administration. This exercise of delegated powers is paid for by municipalities and regions via funds from the state, but municipalities and regions are convinced that these are insufficient. Negotiations between the representatives of the state and local governments in this matter have been repeated since 2001 and the rules for calculating the remuneration of the transferred performance of state administration have been gradually modified.

Act No. 243 of 2000 (Act on budgetary determination of taxes) can be taken as a reform; this form of financing municipalities is still at work in the Czech Republic. Changes in the tax revenue rules of municipalities (reforms of fiscal federalism) for the years 1993–1995, 1996–2000, and a comparison with 2001, are presented in Table 10.7.

Act No. 243 of 2000 (the Act on Budgetary Determination of Taxes) changed the distribution of shared tax revenues, and thus the tax revenues of municipalities, into a form that has been used in the Czech Republic with partial changes to this day. The subject of the complicated political discussion was therefore mainly three areas of concern: (1) The revenue of which shared taxes should be generated by the emerging

Table 10.7 Changes in municipal tax revenue rules (reforms of fiscal federalism)—years 1993 to 2001

1993–1995	1996–2000	2001
100% Real estate tax		
100% DPPO paid by municipalities		
×	20% DPPO (by population)	20.59% DPPO
100% DPFO from business and other self-employment income (by domicile)		30% DPFO from self-employment income (by domicile)
40% (50% 1994; 60% 1995) DPFO's regional revenue from employment	30% of DPFO from employment tax	20.59% DPFO (employment tax)
×	×	20.59% VAT
Criteria for distribution among municipalities		
By population	20% by population and 10% by the payer	Size category, the actual population of the municipality.

Abbreviations: *DPPO* corporate tax, *DPFO* personal income tax, *VAT* value added tax
Source Authors, According to tax laws and documents of the Ministry of Finance

self-governing regions (14 regions were created in the Czech Republic including the capital Prague) in order to ensure fulfillment of these new duties including regional roads, a network of regional hospitals, a network of regional social facilities, secondary schools in the region, museums and other regional cultural facilities, etc.? (2) How should the state, regions and municipalities divide the shared taxes? (3) Under what criteria should shared taxes be shared among municipalities?

Since 2001, it has been mandated that a municipality receives 100% of the property tax collected in the municipality (the amount of this tax can be set by each municipality in its territory) and that municipalities receive 100% rebates of the corporate income tax they pay (as they are legal entities which must pay these taxes). However, the big change was that municipalities began to participate in the national value-added tax revenue system (20.59% share). This was a key result of many years of effort by mayors. Municipalities also received a share of the income tax of employed residents (employment tax, share of 20.59%), corporate income tax not including the tax paid by municipalities (share of 20.59%), personal income tax from self-employment (30%, depending on the permanent residence of the entrepreneur). Tax revenues were divided among municipalities according to two criteria, namely (1) classification of the municipality into the size category (14 of them were determined) and (2) population of the municipality. Size categories favored larger municipalities—the higher the size category, the higher the amount per citizen (see Table 10.8).

The criterion of the size category of municipalities was introduced, among other things, in order to motivate municipalities to merge. Right from its introduction, it has been the subject of heated discussions among politicians, many of whom (especially representatives of smaller municipalities) considered them unacceptable

Table 10.8 Municipal size categories

Category number	Municipal populations	Coefficient of the municipality size category
1	Up to 100	0.4213
2	101–200	0.5370
3	201–300	0.5630
4	301–1500	0.5881
5	1501–5000	0.5977
6	5001–10,000	0.6150
7	10,001–20,000	0.7016
8	20,001–30,000	0.7102
9	30,001–40,000	0.7449
10	40,001–50,000	0.8142
11	50,001–100,000	0.8487
12	100,001–150,000	1.0393
13	From 150,001	1.6715
14	Capital District of Prague	2.7611

Source Kruntorádová (2015)

and discriminatory. The problem was, among other things, that in the Chamber of Deputies there were many mayors (who were also deputies), who were mostly from cities, with few of them being from smaller municipalities.

For the years 2002–2007, the amended rules applied (according to Act No. 483 of 2001). This was when municipalities also began to participate in the national income tax on the self-employed (20.59%, 60% of the state) and on personal income tax from employment (a share of 1.5% according to the number of employees in the municipality). During these years, there was a difficult discussion about the injustice of distribution of funds among municipalities by size categories. Many politicians considered them discriminatory. For example, two small municipalities (Suchá Loz and Vysoké Pole) lodged a complaint with the European Court of Human Rights in Strasbourg. These municipalities argued in the complaint that they considered it unfair that the four largest cities in the Czech Republic (in which about 20% of the population live) received half of all the money intended for all municipalities and cities in the Czech Republic. In 2006, 28 senators filed a complaint with the Constitutional Court in this matter, requesting that the part of the law relating to size categories be abolished. Non-profit organizations and associations who opposed such discrimination were, for example, the Rural Renewal Society. In June 2007, the Treaty of Municipalities against Tax Discrimination was published. It was signed in a relatively short time by 1500 municipalities. After more than a year of investigation, the Constitutional Court did not comply with this request, i.e. it did not consider the size categories of municipalities discriminatory. However, these and similar activities ultimately led to a partial adjustment of the allocation criteria in

2008. After a very tense discussion, the state refrained from motivating municipalities to merge using the criterion for sharing taxes. However, some municipalities continued to fight against 'tax discrimination.' On the basis of these activities, a new association of municipalities, called the Association of Local Authorities, was established. The "Mayors and Independents" political movement was also formed, which received nine mandates (seats) in the Chamber of Deputies in the 2010 elections on the joint ticket with the TOP 09 party (including Mayor of Suchá Loz, Mr. Petr Gazdík and the Deputy Mayor of Vysoké Pole Mr. Stanislav Polčák, who were behind the above-mentioned complaint of discrimination at the Strasbourg Court).

In 2007, the global economic crisis also began, which subsequently led to a decrease in taxes collected in the Czech Republic and thus also to a decrease in the tax revenues of municipalities.

Since 2008, the share municipalities receive in shared taxes has increased from 20.59 to 21.4% and, in particular, the criteria for allocating shared taxes between municipalities have been adjusted (Act No. 377 of 2007). In terms of distribution criteria, the number of size categories has been reduced from 14 to 4, and the coefficient progression has also been reduced (step transitions between size categories have been replaced by successive transitions). This ended the state's motivation to merge municipalities to achieve higher tax revenues. Other criteria for distribution were also approved, namely the municipality area criterion, the simple population criterion, and the adjusted recalculated population criterion. There is a special adjustment of the criteria for the four largest cities in the Czech Republic (Prague, Brno, Ostrava and Pilsen).

In 2013, small municipalities celebrated another victory in their fight against what they call "tax discrimination." According to the amendment to the Act on budgetary determination of taxes (Act No. 295 of 2012), there was an increase in tax revenues on shared taxes. A new criterion for the distribution of shared taxes among municipalities was also approved, which concerned the number of children and pupils attending schools established by the municipality. Further increases in tax revenues were made according to the rules for 2017 (increase of share to 21.4% of value added tax) and 2018 (share increased to 23.58%). The changes are summarized in Table 10.9.

The following figure shows the result of the reforms, i.e. the distribution of shared taxes in the Czech Republic among regions, municipalities and the state budget as of January 1, 2018. Value added tax (VAT), personal income tax (withholding), 60% of the income from personal income tax from self-employment, and corporate income tax (excluding taxes paid by regions and municipalities) were divided according to the following percentages: 8.92% for regions, 23.52% for municipalities, and 67.5% for the state budget (66% in total from the employment tax). As regards to the personal income tax from employment, municipalities still have a share of 1.5% according to the converted number of employees in the municipality (the state thus has only 66%). Municipalities and regions also receive a full refund of the corporate income tax they themselves pay. Municipalities keep 100% of the income from real estate taxes.

Table 10.9 Changes in municipal tax revenues (reforms of fiscal federalism)—years 2002–2018

2002–2007	2008–2012	2013–2016	2017	2018
100% Real estate tax				
100% DPPO paid by municipalities				
20.59% DPPO	21.4% DPPO	23.58% DPPO		
20.59% Self-employed DPFO from 60% of the state's share in that tax	21.4% Self-employed DPFO from 60% of the state's share in that tax	23.58% Self-employed DPFO from 60% of the state's share in that tax		
30% DPFO from self-employment (by domicile)			×	×
20.59% DPFO (employment, withholding)	21.4% DPFO (employment, withholding)	22.87% DPFO in the years 2013—2015 and 23.58% from 2016 (employment, withholding)		
1.5% DPFO (employment) According to the number of employees in the municipality				
20.59% VAT	21.4% VAT	20.83% VAT	21.4% VAT	23.58% VAT
Criteria for distribution among municipalities				
Size category, the actual population of the municipality.	Size coefficients, area of the municipality, simple population, recalculated population+since 2013 another criterion: the number of children and pupils attending schools established by the municipality. Specific criteria for the four largest cities.			

Abbreviations: *DPPO* corporate income tax, DPFO personal income tax, VAT value added tax
Source Authors, according to tax laws and documents of the Ministry of Finance

10.1.3 Key Facts and Related Issues

- The key factors which have influenced the debate on reform since 1989:
- A fragmented settlement structure in the Czech Republic and thus a large number of municipalities for the population as well as an increase in the number of municipalities (from approximately 4100 municipalities in 1990–6258 municipalities in 2016); especially in the 1990s, more than 2000 municipalities were re-established—these were mainly ones that had been forcibly merged with towns or incorporated into "center" municipalities in the 1970s and 1980s. In this case, there is considerable influence of path dependence, both in terms of settlement structure (similar settlement structure is also seen in Slovakia and other former countries of Austria–Hungary), and in terms of resistance to the merger of municipalities.
- The reform of public administration in the Czech Republic, i.e. the creation of a system of self-governing regions, the abolition of district offices (in 2001) and the transfer of extensive state administration to established regions and municipalities. It was necessary to ensure the financing of the self-governing regions established since 2001. This significantly influenced the discussion on the financing of municipalities. There were also repeated discussions on the financing of devolved state administration to municipalities and regions. This was paid for by the state, but municipalities and regions considered this reimbursement insufficient.

- From 2007, the global financial crisis resulted in a decline in tax revenues, including in municipalities. This situation forced the public administration to save, but given the large amount of mandatory expenditures (education, street cleaning, garbage collection, snow clearing, etc.), the municipal budgets did not have much room for savings.

Table 10.10 summarizes the validity of the laws on municipal tax revenues and comments on the implemented reforms.

The state's efforts to motivate municipalities to merge by means of the criteria for sharing shared taxes (since 2001) were unsuccessful. Thus, the state failed to motivate municipalities to merge with economic arguments. The state's efforts were perceived by representatives of small municipalities as undemocratic and discriminatory. This was significantly influenced by path dependence (forceful merging of municipalities in the 1970s and 1980s by the communist regime). Discussions of the criteria for sharing taxes between municipalities led in 2006 and beyond to a constitutional complaint (not complied with), a complaint by small municipalities to the Strasbourg Court, the formation of new associations of municipalities and the formulation of the "Mayor and Independent" movement. The result of the political discussion was a change in these criteria and a higher share of shared taxes for municipalities.

10.2   Materials and Methods for Two Stage Efficiency Analysis of Czech Municipalities

10.2.1   Efficiency Estimation of Czech Municipalities

For examining the efficiency of Czech municipalities, we used the data envelopment analysis (DEA) method. According to Hugeunin (2015) the expansion of DEA in the public sector is related to the easy availability of free software as well as manuals for the use of DEA. Therefore, this tool has become widely available. Another positive aspect is the existence of pre-built models that can benefit policy makers who don't possess a deeper knowledge of operational research and quantitative methods. This process is called the democratization of DEA (Hugeunin 2015). On the other hand, it is also necessary to draw attention to the fact that the use of pre-built models having different parameters can produce divergent results and lead to ineffective decision-making.

The DEA method is applicable for examining efficiency in the public sector. The use of DEA within the context of performance management in the public sector in the spirit of New Public Management is mentioned by Schubert (2009). DEA is perceived as a tool that helps to empirically measure the results of government policies. The same view is also held by Tankersley (2000). They argue that DEA provides an interesting starting point for the comparative analysis of organizational performance.

Table 10.10 Review of laws in relation to municipal incomes (reforms of fiscal federalism)

Validity	Law as a bearer of reform or partial adjustment	Commentary in relation to reforms
1993–1995	Act ČNR No. 576/1990, on rules on the management of budgetary resources of the Czech Republic and municipalities in the Czech Republic (budgetary rules)	These are partial amendments to the original law
1996–2000	Act No. 154/1995 amending and supplementing NrNR Act No. 576/1990, budgetary rules	
2001	Act No. 243/2000, on budgetary determination of the proceeds of certain taxes to local authorities and certain state funds (Tax budget determination act)	This is a comprehensive change (reform) to the distribution of tax revenues based on extensive political debates, especially between 1996 and 2000. It has been agreed that municipalities will participate in value added tax (VAT) revenues. In 2001, public administration reform was also underway—district offices were abolished and their competencies were taken over by municipalities and established self-governing regions. The size categories and population of the municipality served for the distribution of income among municipalities. The size categories were set up so that municipalities were motivated to merge (the higher the category, the higher the per capita income). The global economic crisis also began in 2007, which led to a decrease in tax revenues in the Czech Republic and thus to a decrease in tax revenues of municipalities
2002–2007	Act No. 483/2001 amending Law No. 243/2000 on budgetary determination of taxes	
2008–2012	Act No. 377/2007 amending Law No. 243/2001 on budgetary determination of taxes	The criteria for distributing tax revenues between municipalities were considered discriminatory by smaller municipalities. After major discussions, new distribution criteria have been introduced since 2008: Adjusted size coefficients (instead of the original 14 only 4—tax revenues no longer motivate municipalities to merge), municipal area, simple population, recalculated population. Specific criteria have also been introduced for the four largest cities. Since 2013, another criterion has been added, namely the number of children and pupils attending schools established by the municipality
2013–2016	Act No. 295/2012 amending Law No. 243/2001 on the budgetary determination of taxes	
2017	Act No. 391/2015 amending Law No. 243/2001 on budgetary determination of taxes	

Source Authors, according to the mentioned law

Chalos and Cherian (1995) add that such metrics improve internal control and external accountability. More detailed instructions on the use of DEA in the public sector are provided by the publication Public Sector Efficiency Measurements: Applications of Data Envelopment Analysis by Ganley and Cubbin (1992). An overview of the modification of DEA models is given e.g. by Jablonský and Dlouhý (2004). The mentioned authors characterize DEA as a tool for evaluating the efficiency of production units.

In our study, we examine the prison service as a specific system ("production unit") which can also be evaluated in terms of efficiency, provided that the inputs and outputs are known. We reduced our approach to the public value perspective and focus on cost-efficiency, with the ratio of outcomes to inputs defined as cost-effectiveness.

> This method is suitable for evaluating the efficiency, performance, or productivity of homogeneous production units - i.e., units that produce identical or equivalent effects, which are referred to as outputs of this unit. Outputs are by their nature maximizing, their higher value results in higher performance of the tracking unit. To produce effects, the production unit consumes inputs that are minimized by their nature, the lower value of these inputs leads to higher performance of the monitored unit (Borůvková and Kuncová 2012, p. 75)." "The DEA method estimates the so-called production units whose input/output combinations lie at the efficiency boundary are efficient units, because it is not expected that a unit that achieves the same outputs with lower inputs or higher outputs with the same inputs. (Borůvková and Kuncová 2012, p. 75) When using the DEA method, we can use a constant returns to scale model or a model with variable returns to scale.

The first model calculates constant returns to scale, the so-called Charnes Cooper and Rhodes Model (CCR). This model was first introduced in 1978. With this model, it is possible to determine the amount of inputs needed to make the inefficient unit efficient. The technical efficiency factor is defined as the ratio of weighted sums of outputs and weighted sums of inputs. The scales must be determined so that the technical efficiency factor is from 1:0. A unit with a technical efficiency ratio equal to 1 is efficient, a coefficient less than 1 is an inefficient unit and shows the amount of input reduction required to ensure unit efficiency. For simple cases, the CCR can be represented graphically. The CCR model sets the input and output weights for each unit so that the unit maximizes its technical efficiency factor and meets the conditions. The balance must not be negative. When using this set of weights, no technical efficiency factor may be greater than one.

The intuition of this model is as follows:

$$\text{to maximize } z = \sum_{i=1}^{r} u_1 y_{iq} \tag{10.1}$$

$$\text{for the condition } \sum_{i=1}^{r} u_1 y_{ik} \leq \sum_{j=1}^{m} v_j x_{jk}, \quad k = 1, 2, \ldots, n \tag{10.2}$$

$$\sum_{j=1}^{m} v_j x_{jg} = 1$$

$$u_1 \geq 0, i = 1, 2, \ldots, m,$$
$$v_j \geq 0, j = 1, 2, \ldots, r.$$

where g represents the unit being evaluated, y_{ig} are the unit outputs, q, x_{jq} are the unit inputs, q, $u_i a v_j$ are the weights of the individual inputs and outputs.

The second model calculates variable returns to scale. This model is called the Banker Charnes and Cooper Model (BCC). The model was first introduced in 1984. Its intuition is as follows:

$$\text{to maximize } z = \sum_{i=1}^{r} u_i y_{iq} + \mu \tag{10.3}$$

$$\text{for the condition } \sum_{i=1}^{r} u_i y_{ik} + \mu \leq \sum_{j=1}^{m} v_j x_{jk}, k = 1, 2, \ldots, n \tag{10.4}$$

$$\sum_{j=1}^{m} v_j x_{jq} = 1 \tag{10.5}$$

$$u_i \geq 0, i = 1, 2, \ldots, m,$$
$$v_j \geq 0, j = 1, 2, \ldots, r,$$
$$\mu \text{ arbitrary}$$

The double bootstrap by Simar and Wilson was utilized. The bootstrap is one easy way to analyze the sensitivity of efficiency scores relative to the sampling variations of the estimated frontier. In order to validate the bootstrap, the main point is to define a reasonable data-generating process in this complex framework and to propose a reasonable estimator of it (Simar and Wilson 1998). The basic bootstrapping parameters were: L1 = 500, L2 = 5,000 and alfa = 0.05.

Our study uses also the Malmquist Index (MI), which evaluates changes in productivity of DMU (decisive unit) between two periods of time. MI has the capacity to distinguish between the impacts of technical efficiency (TE) improvements and technical (technological) change (TC). When interpreting the Malmquist total factor productivity, we consider all of its components greater than one as indicating improvement or progression whereas values less than one refer to the deterioration of regression.

DEA inputs and outputs

This area is critical to achieving unbiased results and there is currently a big debate about what variables should figure in inputs and outputs. Da Cruz and Marques (2014), Lo Storto (2016) and Drew et al. (2017) state that input variables may be similar for all countries, but inputs must be country specific. Moreover, Nunamaker's rule sets an upper limit on the number of outputs that can be accommodated in DEA (the maximum sum of inputs and outputs is given to be one third of the number of DMU (McQuestin et al. 2018).

In the case of inputs (Narbón-Perpiñá and De Witte 2017b), the following are the most frequent examples of inputs: total expenditures, current expenditures, capital expenditures, personnel expenditures, other expenditures. Financial expenditures are the most frequently reported cases of inputs.

In the case of the Czech Republic, there is a limit due to the availability of data, but this is gradually improving. The Ministry of Finance has launched the State Treasury Monitor portal where it is possible to find financial data for all municipalities in the Czech Republic since 2010. Searching is very difficult, so it is necessary to use datamining techniques. From the financial data, all cash expenditures are allocated to the budget structure according to the Ministry of Finance decree. This approach allows one to look at public revenue and spending from different angles. In this case, revenue and expenditure breakdown by items were selected, which demonstrate on what public money is spent.

For this case, current expenditures were chosen for the input variable, this variable being described in a number of studies (Narbón-Perpiñà et al. 2019; Plaček et al. 2019a, b; McQuestin et al. 2018; Aiello et al. 2017). In the Czech Republic, there is a justification for applying the 3E principles as this is often associated with cost-effectiveness. In the case of the Czech Republic, current expenditures are the largest part of the total expenditures of all municipalities. This area has the greatest savings potential. In public spending, we include expenditures for the salaries of municipal office staff, expenditures on the operation of the city office (energy, repairs, etc.), street cleaning costs, municipal waste treatment and disposal, public lighting, operating grants for primary school and nursery schools, social services, cultural expenditures, expenditures on building repairs, communications, etc., operating contributions founded by municipalities which provide public goods and services, and expenditures on municipal police.

In this case, a decision was made to abstain from examining investment costs, as their effects will only be reflected in the longer term. Furthermore, the Czech accounting regime does not allow for a correct assessment of the value of investment property and, paradoxically, the investment activity would reduce the cost effectiveness of the municipality.

In the case of defining outputs, the situation is more difficult. Šťastná and Gregor (2015), and Walker et al. (2018) point to the problem of the great complexity of local government activities. In the research of Narbón-Perpiñá and De Witte (2017a), the following are the most common outputs: the global output indicator (compiled as an index containing the public services provided by the municipalities), total population of the municipality, followed by the area of the municipality and the built-up area. The following are the number of issued permits or processed documents, which express the administrative tasks that the municipality must perform. According to Narbón-Perpiñá and DeWitte (2017a), outputs can also be defined by type of services provided by municipalities including the following: the number of street lighting points, the length of roads, the amount of processed municipal waste, the number of sports facilities, the number of cultural facilities, the number of recreational facilities, parks, and green areas. Great emphasis is placed on public services in the field of education and provision of social services, such as the number of children attending nursery and elementary schools, the number of elderly, the number of facilities providing social services to the elderly (Narbón-Perpiñá and De Witte 2017a).

Criticism of this approach comes from Lo Storto (2016), who states that the inclusion of multiple inputs into the analysis can lead to inconsistent results. First, it is very difficult to assign a given input to a particular output. Second, the measurements of indicators used as outputs can be affected by a number of factors which cannot be managed and controlled by the municipal government. The entire relationship is also affected by socio-demographic conditions, etc. (Lo Storto 2016).

McQuestin et al. (2018), and Lo Storto (2016) suggest the use of proxy variables; these variables make it possible to reduce the complexity while respecting Nunamaker's rule. Proxies are not precise measures of service output—although they are probably a good reflection of the minimum service need. Lo Storto (2016) argues that proxy variables could be used as indirect approximations of the demand for public services delivered to citizens. A suitable proxy variable is the population of the municipality, the size of the municipality, the number of economic subjects. The great advantage of this approach lies in the possibility to obtain data from databases of statistical offices in a given country. On the other hand, this approach also has its shortcomings. Drew et al. (2017) argue that using the population as a proxy variable overestimates outputs. If one also works with a number of economic subjects variable, it is clear that two groups may consume the same public services and, as a result, distort the results (Drew et al. 2017).

On the basis of previous knowledge, the decision was made to proceed as follows: (1) to carry out a legal analysis and, on the basis of it, determine which services the municipality must implement by law and which it implements on the basis of its own policies. The following documents were analyzed in the framework of this activity: Act on Municipalities 182/200 Coll., Purpose and Legal Analysis of Self-Governing Competences of Municipalities in the Field of Development and Implementation of Development Activities, Catalog of Activities Performed by Municipalities in Individual Categories. (2) To submit the result of the previous section to the Multidisciplinary Delphi Panel, which identifies the appropriate variables that can serve as outputs for nonparametric analysis. The composition of the multidisciplinary team is as follows (Table 10.11).

The meeting of the Delphi panel took place on October 23, 2018. The meeting had a moderate brainstorming format and lasted three hours. All documents were available to participants a week in advance. The result is the design of variables for individual public services and the design of proxy variables.

The results are presented in the following diagrams. The analysis of the regulatory environment revealed that Czech municipalities have to provide a large number of public services. For this reason, we divided the resulting scheme into three parts. The first diagram shows Delphi results for the following services: technical infrastructure, safety, sport and culture. The second diagram shows Delphi results for the following municipality services: transport, business, environment, municipal administration. The third diagram shows Delphi results for the following municipality services:

Table 10.11 Composition of a multidisciplinary team

Team member	Position and focus	Education
No. 1	Chief audit officer of a selected municipality	Tertiary education in economics
No. 2	Head of Structural Funds Implementation Department Ministry of Industry and Trade	Tertiary education in economics
No. 3	Head of the Public Administration Modernization Project Ministry of the Interior	Higher education—law
No. 4	Academic economist	Tertiary education in economics
No. 5	Academic economist	Tertiary education in economics
No. 6	Computer scientist	Tertiary Computer Science
No. 7	Computer scientist	Tertiary Computer Science
No. 8	Computer scientist	Tertiary Computer Science

Source Authors

education, health and social care, exercise of state delegated tasks (Figs. 10.2, 10.3 and 10.4).

The expert Delphi panel also included an evaluation of variables in terms of data availability. From this point of view, the Treasury Monitor database of the Ministry of Finance and the database of the Czech Statistical Office were examined. Based on the linking of these two databases, it was not possible to obtain data for all variables describing individual services provided by the municipality. For this reason, we have chosen to use a set of proxy variables.

10.2.2 Second Stage of Efficiency Estimation

In the second stage of DEA, we use a panel OLS regression model and a Tobit model to analyze the impact of fiscal and political variables on the efficiency of the municipality. The dependent variable is technical efficiency with constant and variable returns to scale.

We denote y_{it} the value of the explanatory variable for the i-th observation at time t. We denote the corresponding vector to the explanatory variables by x_{it}.

When using the fixed effect model, we assume that each observation has its own, invariant effect over time. Therefore, we use a model where α_i denotes effects independent of the observed variables in the i-th observation, β_j determines the regression coefficient of the explanatory variable j, and u_{it} are the individual error components of the estimate.

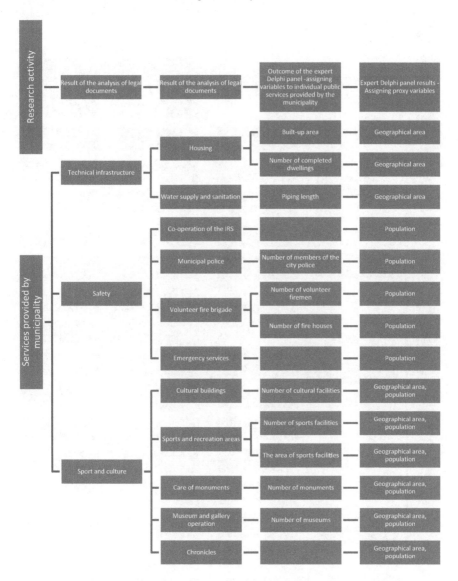

Fig. 10.2 The Delphi results for the following municipality services: technical infrastructure, safety, sport and culture

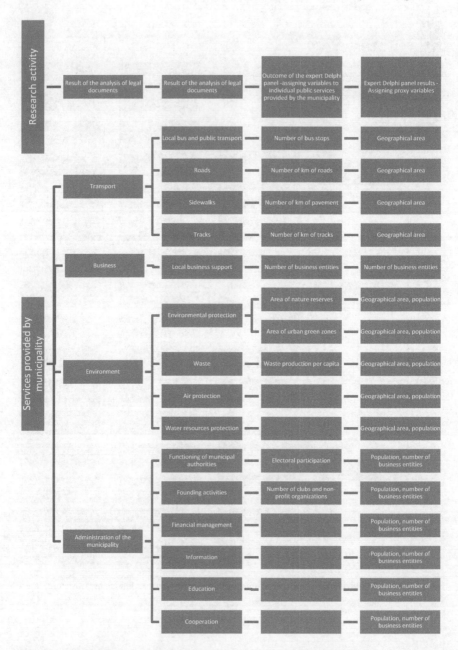

Fig. 10.3 The Delphi results for following municipality services: transport, business, environment, municipal administration

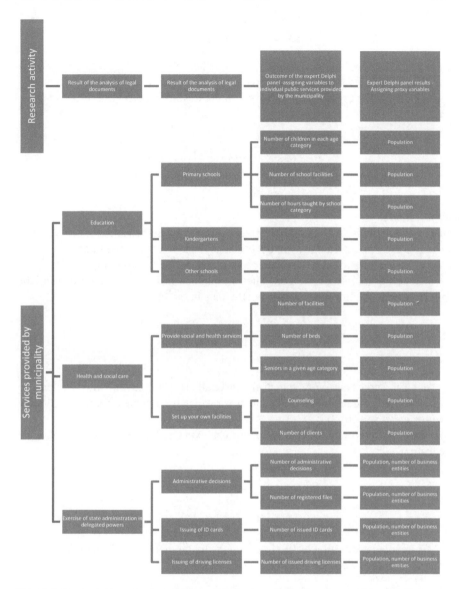

Fig. 10.4   The Delphi results for following municipal services: education, health and social care, exercise of state delegation. *Source* Authors

$$y_{it} = \mu + \sum_{j=1}^{k} \beta_j x_{it} + \alpha_i + u_{it}$$

When using the random effect model, we extend the model by the coefficient γ_t, which affects the explanatory variable in individual time units. The resulting model is:

$$y_{it} = \mu + \sum_{j=1}^{k} \beta_j x_{it} + \alpha_i + \gamma_t + u_{it}$$

Tobit model

The tobit model is a variant of linear regression in which the values of the explained variable are limited. In our case, the efficiency is a number in the interval (0,1) and therefore we have to limit the explained variable by the values 0 and 1.

Therefore, we introduce a new (latent) explained variable y* and for this variable we determine the linear regression coefficients in the form

$$y_i^* = \mu + \sum_{j=1}^{k} \beta_j x_i + u_i$$

where μ is a constant coefficient, β_j are the coefficients of the individual explanatory variables and u_i are the error components for which we assume a normal distribution with a mean value of 0.

Then we determine the real variable to be explained according to the following equation

$$y_i = \begin{cases} 0 & for \; y_i^* < 0 \\ y_i^* & for \; 0 \le y_i^* \le 1 \\ 1 & for \; 1 < y_i^* \end{cases}$$

The explanatory variables are based on the literature review given in Table 10.11. The explanatory variables are as follows:

Log. own income per capita This variable includes local fees, property tax, but also income from rental properties, own activities and business community. In the context of the Czech Republic, we assume that "*the greater this income, the greater the tendency of the municipality to be ineffective.*" This assumption is the result of a soft budget constraint. Management of a municipality that has a sufficient amount of its own income is not motivated to behave economically. In the Czech environment, this situation is exacerbated by lower accountability and fiscal illusion. The problem of fiscal illusion in this case lies in separating the process of deciding on public expenditure from securing the financing of such expenditures.

Log. shared taxes per capita this indicator includes revenue from nationally collected taxes, such as VAT, personal and corporate income tax, which are redistributed among municipalities in the Czech Republic under the Budgetary Taxation Act. These funds are used to ensure the operation of the municipality and to ensure activities within the independent competence of the municipality, including investment projects. We assume that *"the higher the volume of these funds, the higher the tendency of the municipality to be inefficient."* The main cause is fiscal illusion. Due to the payment of taxes to the central government and the subsequent redistribution of this money among the different levels of government, citizens are unable to determine the real cost of public goods and services provided by local governments, thus reducing the pressure on politicians and bureaucrats for accountability.

Log. transfers per capita This variable includes all investment and non-investment transfers from higher levels of government, i.e. central government and regions. Transfers from the European Union are also included. We assume that *the well-known "flypaper effect" will work for transfers, i.e. higher transfers will be associated with higher inefficiencies.* However, the Czech Republic belongs to a group of countries that still face the problem of corruption (Transparency International 2019) and the media discourse is filled with cases of misuse of subsidies. There is also a debate on the effectiveness of these funds compared to other countries.

Log. deficit per capita the deficit represents the difference between total revenue and total expenditure in a given year. In the case of the Czech Republic, we assume that the deficit will be associated with greater efficiency. From an international comparison, it is clear that Czech municipalities enjoy a very good financial condition and behave fiscally conservatively. We assume that if the management of a municipality promotes deficit management, it will face great criticism from the opposition and the public, which will be able to accept the deficit only if the money will be used for capital expenditure and not for operation. This will put more pressure on the municipality for efficiency.

Log. indebtedness per capita means the sum of all long-term liabilities of the municipality; we include liabilities with maturities longer than one year, especially bank loans and issued municipal bonds. We assume that higher indebtedness of the municipality will be associated with higher efficiency. In our conception, the effect of fiscal stress and financial vulnerability play a dominant role here. Indebted municipalities are forced to reduce their spending, the money previously earmarked for operating expenses, such as wages and purchases of consumables, is now used for debt repayments. Indebted municipalities are also restricted in their access to additional loans, as they are a riskier partner for banks, and they have to pay a premium for risk in the form of a higher interest rate. Municipalities therefore do not have access to available loans and are forced to reduce operating expenses and increase their efficiency.

Concentration of parties in the council value is expressed using the Herfindahl–Hirschman index, which expresses the share of representatives of a given political party in the total number of representatives. This index describes the concentration or fragmentation of the council. We assume that a higher index value will be associated with lower efficiency. This assumption may be surprising in a way, since if the council is not fragmented and few entities share power, more efficient and faster decision-making can occur. There is also no logrolling, which is trading in the votes of the councilors, which results in inefficient projects being supported. On the other hand, if the power in the municipal council is concentrated among only a few subjects, there may be a decrease in the capacity of the city management. Management is not controlled and confronted by the opposition as much, and for this reason resources are inefficiently used. We assume that given the historical legacy of the Czech Republic, this factor will have a stronger effect than other factors.

Political orientation of the winning party in our model we distinguish between left-wing political orientation, right-wing political orientation, and an indifference between right and left. The orientation on the left was determined for the parties operating at the national level, where we can determine the orientation according to their program documents. Municipal elections are unique in that a large number of local entities run, whose ideology is not dominant and mainly deals with local issues. The ideology of these subjects was identified as indifferent. We assume that left-wing ideology of the winning party will be associated with lower efficiency. In the Czech Republic, left-wing parties are associated with large public spending programs, promoting benefits for public sector employees, etc. In the case of right-wing ideology, we assume a higher association with efficiency. Right-wing parties focus on reducing the public sector and reducing the tax burden. The trend towards higher efficiency was also confirmed by the study (Šťastná and Gregor 2015). For ideologically indifferent parties, we do not assume a concrete association with efficiency or inefficiency.

Views on data

The resulting econometric models are sorted according to the following criteria:

- Size category of municipality
- The functions that the municipality performs
- Location of the municipality.

For the size categories of municipalities, we use the classification of the Czech Statistical Office, which classifies municipalities in the Czech Republic into 10 size categories. In our approach, because of the low number of municipalities in the last two highest size categories, we decided to merge these two categories. Table 10.12 shows the division of municipalities.

This approach will allow us to monitor the impact of fiscal and political variables separately for both large and small municipalities, which make up a significant proportion of municipalities in the Czech Republic.

Another view that we want to present is a look at the differences in the effectiveness of municipalities according to the activities that municipalities are obliged to

Table 10.12 Categorization of econometric model by size of municipalities

Municipality size	Number of municipalities	Total population	Share of population in %
Up to 199 inhabitants	1449	180,093	1.7
From 200 to 499 inhabitants	1997	651,475	6.2
From 500 to 999 inhabitants	1378	973,247	9.2
From 1000 to 1999 inhabitants	745	1,042,569	9.9
From 2000 to 4999 inhabitants	417	1,262,911	12.0
From 5000 to 9999 inhabitants	141	964,031	9.1
From 10,000 to 19,999 inhabitants	69	970,075	9.2
Over 20,000 inhabitants	62	2,198,984	42.8

Source Authors

perform. We distinguish municipalities according to the extent of state administration as follows:

- Municipalities with the basic scope of delegated powers—this is performed by all 6254 municipalities in the Czech Republic. We reduced the number of these municipalities by the municipalities that carry out public administration to a higher than basic extent (593 municipalities), so we will include 5661 municipalities into this category.
- Municipalities with authorized municipal office—performs a wider area of state administration than municipalities with the basic scope of delegated powers, we have included a total of 388 municipalities in this category.
- Municipalities with extended powers—these municipalities carry out the largest extent of state administration; for their citizens, but usually also for citizens of other municipalities, i.e. for citizens of municipalities within their administrative district. A total of 205 municipalities have been included in this category.

Another view that we want to provide is the classification according to membership in a higher territorial administrative unit. In the Czech Republic, the higher territorial administrative units are regions. Table 10.13 shows the breakdown of municipalities by region. Prague is also considered a region. We will exclude it from our comparison in our analysis.

Another view is the division of efficiency according to the NUTS classification (Nomenclature of Units for Territorial Statistics). Due to considerable differences in the size of regions, another level of territorial division was created, NUTS 2. This stage is called the cohesion region and flows from EU development funds. The capital Prague is also excluded from this division (Table 10.14).

Table 10.13   Distribution of municipalities by region

Region	Population (in thousands)
Central Bohemian Region	1144
South Bohemian Region	624
Plzen Region	501
Karlovy Vary Region	134
Ústí nad Labem Region	354
Liberec Region	215
Hradec Kralove Region	448
Pardubice Region	451
Vysočina Region	704
South Moravian Region	673
Olomouc Region	402
Zlín Region	307
Moravian-Silesian Region	300

Source Czech Statistical Office (2019b)

Table 10.14   Division of municipalities by jurisdiction according to NUTS 2

NUTS 2	Region	Number of municipalities
Central Bohemia	Central Bohemian Region	1144
Southwest	South Bohemian, Plzen Region	1125
Northwest	Karlovy Vary, Usti nad Labem Region	488
Northeast	Liberec, Hradec Kralove, Pardubice Region	1114
Southeast	Vysocina, South Moravian Region	1377
Central Moravia	Olomouc, Zlín Region	709
Moravian-Silesia	Moravian-Silesian Region	300

Source Czech Statistical Office (2019a)

10.3   Results of Empirical Analysis of Fiscal Decentralization and Efficiency for the Czech Republic

In the following section we present answers to partial research questions.

RQ1: What are the impacts of fiscal decentralization on the efficiency of individual size categories of municipalities?
Before presenting the results of the econometric model, it is advisable to first perform a graphical inspection of the technical efficiency values according to the size category of municipalities. The efficiency comparison is presented in Fig. 10.5.

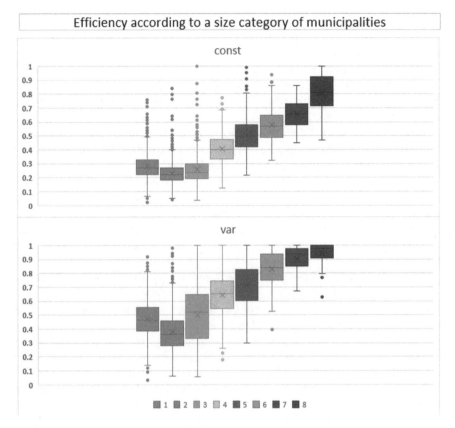

Fig. 10.5 Average technical efficiency (cons, var) in years by size category of municipalities. *Key* 1 = up to 199 inhabitants, 2 = 200–499, 3 = 500–999, 4 = 1000–1999, 5 = 2000–4999, 6 = 5000–9999 obyv., 7 = 10,000–19,999, 8 = Over 20,000 inhabitants

If we look at the average efficiency values by category of municipalities using the constant and variable DEA model, we find that small municipalities achieve the lowest efficiency values. Municipalities up to 199 inhabitants achieve average efficiency values (const. 0.284116289, var. 0.4747), municipalities from 200 to 499 inhabitants. (const. 0.232491041, var. 0.379728), municipalities from 500 inhabitants to 999 inhabitants (const. 0.258675315, var. 0.496804), municipalities from 1000 inhabitants up to 1999 inhabitants (const. 0.405768653, var. 0.643441), municipalities from 2000 inhabitants to 4999 inhabitants (const. 0.508983124, var. 0.712653), municipalities from 5000 inhabitants to 9999 inhabitants (const. 0.578598592, var. 0.830084), municipalities from 10,0000 inhabitants to 19,999 (const. 0.657073583, var. 0.903591), municipalities from 20,000 inhabitants (const. 0.805313103, var. 0.940817).

It can be stated that the average values of efficiency in municipalities are very low and especially the category of municipalities with a smaller population shows much room for efficiency improvement.

It can also be inferred from the average efficiency chart that in the case of the Czech municipality, the U curve assumption may not apply to their size categories, i.e. that from a certain size of the municipality the effect of scale revenues is reduced by the cost of coordinating activities.

Table 10.15 presents the results of a two stage DEA analysis and the impact of fiscal and political variables by size category of municipalities. For the second level of efficiency analysis, a panel OLS regression has been used.

This model uses panel data and therefore considers changes in efficiency in individual years. All models for each city size category are statistically significant and reach relatively high adjusted R-square coefficient values. The model shows that fiscal variables are statistically significant for most size categories. Political variables are significant only for the largest size category of cities over 20,000 thousand residents.

The variable indebtedness per capita is statistically significant in half of the size categories of municipalities. It has the biggest impact in the category from 20,000 inhabitants, where it decreases the efficiency of the municipality, which is the opposite result from what we had expected.

The variable describing the impact of own income on the population is statistically significant for all size categories of municipalities. Compared to other variables, it achieves the highest coefficients in all cases. Its association with efficiency is negative in line with our expectations. The coefficients of this variable have the highest value in the two largest size categories of municipalities. On the other hand, the lowest were for the smallest size categories of municipalities.

The variable tax income per capita is statistically significant for all categories of municipalities. This was true in most size categories with the exception of municipalities with 1000–1999 inhabitants and 2000–4999, which was contrary to our expectations. However, due to the magnitude of the coefficients, the effect of this variable is minimal.

The variable describing the effect of transfers per capita on efficiency is statistically significant for all size categories of cities. According to theoretical assumptions, even in our case, transfers are negatively associated with efficiency. It is very interesting that beta transfer coefficients are very small in small municipalities and in the largest cities, while beta coefficients have the highest values in size categories of municipalities with between 5000 and 9999 inhabitants.

The variables describing the effect of the deficit on efficiency are statistically significant for all size categories of cities. In accordance with our assumptions, this variable is positively associated with efficiency. Due to this variable, or the size of beta coefficients, there are no significant differences between the size categories of municipalities.

Table 10.15 Results of econometric analysis by size categories of municipalities OLS model (DEA constant returns to scale)

Variable	Up to 199 inhabitants	200–499 inhabitants	500–999 inhabitants	1000–1,999 inhabitants	2000–4999 inhabitants	5000–9999 inhabitants	10,000–19,999 inhabitants	Over 20,000 inhabitants
Log (indebtedness per capita)	−0.00204	−0.00229**	−5.8E−05	−0.00262**	−0.00309**	−0.00171	−0.00186	−0.00746***
Log (own income per capita)	−0.12772***	−0.09254***	−0.12128***	−0.17768***	−0.25116***	−0.26983***	−0.37024***	−0.30531***
Tax income per capita	2.31E−06***	3.3E−06***	3.33E−06***	−5.3E−07***	−4.2E−06***	3.56E−06***	9.43E−06***	7.84E−06***
Log (transfers per capita)	−0.09612***	−0.07688***	−0.09865***	−0.15168***	−0.20416***	−0.28291***	−0.27349***	−0.09994***
Log (deficit per capita)	0.018325***	0.014911***	0.014618***	0.021224***	0.021421***	0.016353***	0.013439***	0.013642***
Left-wing orientation	0.007101	−0.0019	0.001284	0.00268	0.010061	0.004655	−0.00508	−0.03618***
Right-wing orientation	0.001036	0.002226	−0.00415	−0.01705***	0.002974	0.007322	0.003234	0.015047***
Herfindahl index	0.000606	−0.00433	−0.00929	0.001964	0.021307	−0.05825*	−0.01287	0.085115***
Adj. R Square	0.387085	0.373742	0.413804	0.567202	0.601366	0.649746	0.616145	0.308938
P value	0	0	0	0	0	0	0	0

Signif. codes: 0 '***' 0.05 '**' 0.1 '*'

Political variables are not statistically significant for most city size categories, except for the largest size category. For large cities, in accordance with our assumptions, the left-wing orientation of the victorious party in the council reduces efficiency, while a victorious right-wing party increases efficiency. A higher Herfindal index value is also associated with greater efficiency, this result being the opposite of what we expected.

Table 10.16 shows the model results when using the variable returns to scale DEA variant.

The model of variable returns to scale considers the size of the municipality and the ability to achieve increasing or decreasing returns to scale in the provision of public goods and services. All presented models are statistically significant and achieve acceptable R-square values except for a model that describes the behavior of fiscal variables in the largest cities. Its R square value of 0.058243 can be considered very low.

The variable describing the impact of indebtedness on the population is statistically significant for almost all cities except for the smallest municipalities and the size category of municipalities with from 2000 to 4999 inhabitants. As in the previous model, this variable is associated with lower efficiency. This result is contrary to our expectations.

The variable describing own income per capita is statistically significant for all models. It is negatively associated with efficiency, which confirms our initial theoretical assumptions. The beta coefficient is the highest compared to other variables. We can also observe the differences between large and small cities, since beta values are highest in cities with more than 5000 inhabitants.

The variable per capita tax income is statistically significant for all size categories of cities except for the category with from 5000 to 9999 inhabitants. In smaller towns, their association with efficiency is mostly negative whereas in larger towns, on the other hand, this is positive. However, we have to say that beta coefficient values are very low and therefore the effect is very small.

The variable transfers per capita is statistically significant for all size categories of municipalities and its influence is negatively associated with efficiency. The size of the beta coefficients for transfers is high compared to other variables, so transfers have a higher impact than other fiscal variables, except for own income. The effect of transfers is higher for the categories of towns with population from 2000 to 9999 inhabitants. Transfers in the largest city category of 20,000 inhabitants have the lowest impact.

The variable deficit per capita is statistically significant in all size categories of municipalities. The results of this variable are in line with our assumptions, the deficit is positively associated with efficiency. The impact of the deficit is again the lowest in the category of municipalities with the largest population.

As in the previous model, the political variables are statistically insignificant, with the exception of the left-wing orientation of the winning party in municipalities of the size category from 5000 to 9999, which is positively associated with efficiency. The right-wing orientation of the winning party in municipalities from 10,000 to

Table 10.16 Results of econometric analysis by size categories of municipalities OLS model (DEA variable returns to scale)

Variable	Up to 199 inhabitants	200–499 inhabitants	500–999 inhabitants	1,000–1,999 inhabitants	2,000–4,999 inhabitants	5,000–9,999 inhabitants	10,000–19,999 inhabitants	Over 20,000 inhabitants
Log (indebtedness per capita)	−0.00343	−0.00353**	−0.00404**	−0.00515**	−0.00288	−0.0045**	−0.00559***	−0.00858***
Log (own income per capita)	−0.20601***	−0.14977***	−0.24588***	−0.24049***	−0.32416***	−0.28974***	−0.46956***	−0.28589***
Tax income per capita	−8.4E−07***	2.9E−06***	−2.4E−06***	−7.6E−06***	−3.1E−06***	9.98E−07	4.25E−06***	4.23E−06***
Log (transfers per capita)	−0.17023***	−0.12407***	−0.17165***	−0.22896***	−0.25432***	−0.2652***	−0.18072***	−0.03652***
Log (deficit per capita)	0.029387***	0.023605***	0.025867***	0.029754***	0.025628***	0.016486***	0.013076***	0.007112***
Left-wing orientation	0.025577	−0.00965	−0.02211	0.004414	−0.01002	0.025848***	−0.00085	−0.03055
Right-wing orientation	−0.003	0.002122	−0.01296	0.004417	−0.00769	0.00314	0.009307*	−0.00449
Herfindahl index	0.007593	−0.01471	−0.00193	−0.03389	−0.00601	−0.01037	−0.02518	0.035382***
Adjusted R-square	0.42893	0.37319	0.386995	0.572539	0.492715	0.388548	0.29938	0.058243
P value	0	0	0	0	0	0	0	1.9E−122

Signif. codes: 0 '***' 0.05 '**' 0.1 '*'

19,999 inhabitants is also positively associated with efficiency; the same association is recorded in the Herfindal Index for the largest category of municipalities.

These results are also verified using the Tobit model, which does not take data as a panel but as a cross-section. Table 10.17 shows the results of applying the Tobit model using DEA with a constant returns to scale.

All presented models are statistically significant. Compared to previous OLS models, we find a statistically significant variable, indebtedness per capita, which is negatively associated with efficiency in all categories of municipalities except the category of the largest municipalities. However, beta coefficient values are very low compared to other variables.

In the case of the variable "own income per capita," the results of previous OLS models are confirmed, as this variable is negatively associated with efficiency in all size categories of municipalities. This effect is again greater in the categories of municipalities with a larger population.

The variable tax income per capita is statistically significant for all size categories of municipalities. The effects of this variable, with the exception of cities between 2000 and 4999 inhabitants, have the same direction as the variable presented in OLS models.

We also considered the variable "per capita transfers," which is negatively associated with efficiency in all size categories of municipalities, to be significant. Again, the results of previous OLS models and our theoretical assumptions are confirmed. In contrast to the other variables, the beta coefficients are also higher.

The last fiscal variable, "per capita deficit," is also statistically significant in all size categories of municipalities. This variable is positively associated with efficiency. This result is in line with our theoretical assumptions and the results of previous OLS models.

Political variables produced very inconsistent results. The variable describing the left-wing orientation of the winning party is significant in the size category of 200–499 inhabitants, where it is positively associated with efficiency as well as in the largest size category, where the result was the opposite. The right-wing ideology of the winning party is significant only in the size category of 1000–1999 inhabitants and in the category of 5000–9999 inhabitants, where it is positively associated with efficiency. The degree of concentration of political parties in the council as measured by the Herfindal Index is statistically significant for all size categories of municipalities, with the exception of municipalities from 200 to 499 inhabitants and from 10,000 to 19,999 inhabitants. In the smallest and largest size categories of municipalities, a higher concentration of parties is positively associated with efficiency. For the other size categories, the Herfindal index is negatively associated with efficiency.

Table 10.18 shows the results of applying the Tobit model to the variable returns to scale DEA variant.

The model of variable returns to scale considers the size of the municipality and the ability to achieve increasing or decreasing returns to scale in the provision of public goods and services. If we look at the variable indebtedness per capita, we find that this variable is statistically significant for almost all municipalities except for the size category from 5000 to 9999 inhabitants. For the largest municipalities, this

Table 10.17 Results of the econometric analysis by size categories of Tobit model municipalities (DEA constant returns to scale)

Variable	Up to 199 inhabitants	200–499 inhabitants	500–999 inhabitants	1000–1999 inhabitants	2000–4999 inhabitants	5000–9999 inhabitants	10,000–19,999 inhabitants	Over 20,000 inhabitants
constant	0.988834***	8.35E−01***	9.36E−01***	1.47E+00***	2.18E+00***	2.98E+00***	3.12E+00***	3.47E+00***
Log (indebtedness per capita)	−0.00961***	−4.05E−03***	−3.42E−03***	−2.18E−03**	−5.81E−03***	−1.90E−03***	−9.70E−03***	1.57E−02***
Log (own income per capita)	−0.13635***	−1.09E−01***	−1.11E−01***	−1.65E−01***	−2.71E−01***	−4.00E−01***	−3.85E−01***	−6.49E−01***
Tax income per capita	4.17E−06***	4.50E−06***	5.36E−06***	1.18E−06*	−1.18E−06***	5.73E−06***	7.11E−06***	2.44E−05***
Log (transfers per capita)	−0.08364***	−8.17E−02***	−1.01E−01***	−1.45E−01***	−1.91E−01***	−2.68E−01***	−2.96E−01***	−1.74E−01***
Log (deficit per capita)	0.019597***	1.53E−02***	1.45E−02***	2.17E−02***	2.21E−02***	1.71E−02***	1.39E−02***	1.52E−02***
Left-wing orientation	−0.02418	1.74E−02***	−3.48E−04	−2.30E−03	2.40E−03	−2.13E−03	−1.15E−02	−1.40E−02***
Right-wing orientation	−0.01955	−2.68E−03	9.78E−03	1.12E−02***	6.35E−03	1.59E−02***	−9.90E−04	6.48E−03
Herfindahl index	0.01392***	−5.49E−03	−2.10E−02***	−3.75E−02***	−7.10E−02***	−5.95E−02***	1.01E−03	1.32E−01***
Log Likelihood	3576.525	4399.074	3381.549	3548.493	3063.226	4663.986	4978.784	2548.091

Signif. codes: 0 '***' 0.05 '**' 0.1 '*'

Table 10.18 Results of the econometric analysis by size categories of Tobit model municipalities (DEA variable returns to scale)

Variable	Up to 199 inhabitants	200–499 inhabitants	500–999 inhabitants	1000–1999 inhabitants	2000–4999 inhabitants	5000–9999 inhabitants	10,000–19,999 inhabitants	Over 20,000 inhabitants
constant	1.72E+00***	1.37E+00***	1.78E+00***	2.26E+00***	2.79E+00***	3.77E+00***	4.04E+00***	4.00E+00***
Log (indebtedness per capita)	−1.09E−02***	−7.07E−03***	−6.65E−03***	−2.62E−03*	−6.67E−03***	−4.10E−05	−1.00E−02***	1.13E−02***
Log (own income per capita)	−2.11E−01***	−1.78E−01***	−1.96E−01***	−2.37E−01***	−3.26E−01***	−5.03E−01***	−5.27E−01***	−7.65E−01***
Tax income per capita	2.43E−06***	5.48E−06***	3.19E−06**	−3.61E−06***	1.12E−06	7.83E−06***	−1.59E−07	2.73E−05***
Log (transfers per capita)	−1.61E−01***	−1.30E−01***	−1.76E−01***	−2.22E−01***	−2.44E−01***	−2.94E−01***	−3.00E−01***	−1.40E−01***
Log (deficit per capita)	3.14E−02***	2.47E−02***	2.60E−02***	3.29E−02***	2.99E−02***	2.23E−02***	2.14E−02***	1.92E−02***
Left-wing orientation	−2.62E−02*	2.42E−02**	−1.56E−02	7.39E−03	−9.08E−03	−2.83E−02***	−1.17E−02	6.45E−03
Right-wing orientation	−1.77E−02	−1.42E−02	2.22E−02*	1.39E−02*	2.46E−03	3.07E−02***	2.75E−02*	1.11E−02
Herfindahl index	1.00E−02	−1.07E−02	−9.13E−02***	−2.91E−02**	−1.43E−01***	−1.79E−01***	8.65E−03***	1.00E−01***
Log likelihood	1751.6695	1905.343	−105.29	927.6731	228.9306	−164.211	140.3992	−389.713

Signif. codes: 0 '***' 0.05 '**' 0.1 '*'

variable is positively associated with efficiency. However, for other size categories of municipalities the result is the opposite.

The variable describing own incomes per capita is statistically significant for all size categories of municipalities and, as in previous models, is negatively associated with efficiency.

The variable per capita tax income is statistically significant for most size categories of municipalities, with the exception of categories from 2000 to 4999 inhabitants and 10,000 to 19,999 inhabitants. The effect of this variable is positively associated with efficiency in almost all size categories of municipalities except for the size category of municipalities from 1000 to 1999 inhabitants.

Transfers per capita yield the same result as in previous models, with transfers being negatively associated with efficiency in all size categories of municipalities.

In the case of deficit per capita, the results are the same as in previous approaches, i.e. they are positively associated with efficiency.

The application of political variables brings inconsistent results. The left-wing orientation of the winning party is statistically significant only in cities of the size category up to 199 inhabitants, from 200 to 499 inhabitants and from 5000 to 9999 inhabitants. With the exception of the category of 200–499 inhabitants, it is negatively associated with efficiency. In contrast, right-wing orientation is statistically significant in size categories of municipalities from 500 to 999 inhabitants, from 1000 to 1999 inhabitants, from 5000 to 9999 inhabitants, and from 10,000 to 19,999 inhabitants. In all these categories, it is positively associated with efficiency. The Herfindahl index i s statistically significant for cities in the size category over 500 inhabitants, in the two largest city categories the concentration rate is positively associated with efficiency, in the others the direction of action is negative.

RQ2: What are the impacts of fiscal decentralization on the effectiveness of municipalities according to the activities they perform?
First, we will perform a graphical inspection of the results of the efficiency of models with constant and variable returns to scale according to the extent of the performance of state administration functions that individual categories of municipalities perform. Figure 10.6 gives us a comparison of efficiency according to the extent of the performance of state administration.

It is clear from the figure that the highest average efficiency is achieved by municipalities that perform the highest extent of state administration functions (const. 0.634546, var. 0.859629). This is followed by towns with an authorized municipal office (const. 0.520765, var. 0.747008). The lowest average efficiency is achieved by municipalities that perform only the basic scope of state administration functions (const. 0.289296, var. 0.859629). This figure corresponds to the previous analysis of municipalities' efficiency by size category, since the smallest municipalities perform the basic functions. In contrast, the largest extent of state administration is carried out by the largest municipalities. The size of the municipality is also reflected in the efficiency of the delegated powers. Nevertheless, all categories of municipalities show a lot of room for improvement in technical efficiency in terms of the performance of state administration.

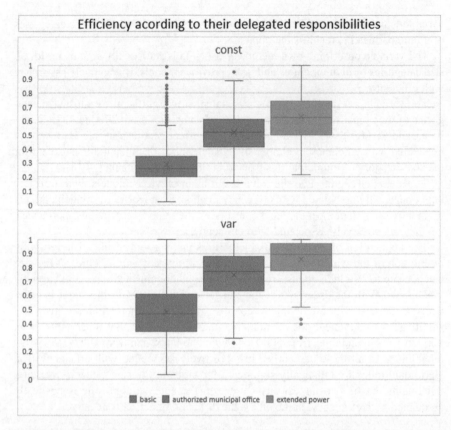

Fig. 10.6 Average technical efficiency in 2010–2018 according to the extent of performance of state administration by municipalities. *Source* authors

Table 10.19 presents the results of a two-stage DEA analysis and the impact of fiscal and political variables according to the extent of government that municipalities are required to perform. For the second level of efficiency analysis panel OLS regression is used (Table 10.19).

All models presented are statistically significant and bring relatively high R-Square values. The first DEA model provides an insight into the effect of fiscal and political variables under the assumption of constant returns to scale, while the second model assumes the possibility of achieving returns from a range. Both models consider changes in efficiency over time.

Indebtedness per capita is statistically significant, especially for the group of cities that are in charge of the largest extent of state administration. In this category, it is negatively associated with efficiency. This contradicts our theoretical assumptions.

The variable describing the effect of own incomes per capita is statistically significant for all categories of government performance. Its influence is negatively associated with efficiency, which is in line with our theoretical assumptions. Beta

Table 10.19 Results of the econometric analysis according to the extent of the state administration municipalities are obliged to carry out, OLS model (DEA constant and variable returns to scale)

	Basic scope		Designated municipal office		Extended scope	
	CCR	VCR	CCR	VCR	CCR	VCR
Log (indebtedness per capita)	−0.00145	−0.00323*	−0.00284**	−0.00247	−0.00367**	−0.00686***
Log (own income per capita)	−0.11727***	−0.1935***	−0.25295***	−0.28548***	−0.31352***	−0.43111***
Tax income per capita	2.28E−06***	−8.3E−07	−1.9E−06***	−1.7E−06**	7.54E−06***	4.75E−06***
Log (transfers per capita)	−0.09848***	−0.16151***	−0.22103***	−0.26447***	−0.24906***	−0.21266***
Log (deficit per capita)	0.01701***	0.026655***	0.017746***	0.020492***	0.012592***	0.012579***
Left-wing orientation	0.001747	−0.0078	0.014054***	−0.0059	−0.01656***	−0.00195
Right-wing orientation	−0.00135	0.001259	0.002836	−0.01307**	0.014387***	0.023127***
Herfindahl index	−0.00235	−0.00395	0.014504	0.007763	0.045964***	0.021293
Adjusted R square	0.410518	0.412689	0.581271	0.416887	0.553704	0.277167
P value model	0	0	0	0	0	0

Signif. codes: 0 '***' 0.05 '**' 0. 1 '*'

coefficients for this variable are significantly higher than for other fiscal and political variables. This variable has the highest influence in the category of municipalities performing the largest extent of state administration. On the other hand, it has the least influence in the group of municipalities that perform the smallest extent of state administration.

Tax revenues per capita have different effects depending on the extent of state administration performance. For municipalities that perform the smallest extent of state administration, their activity is positively associated with efficiency. In the case of municipalities with an authorized authority, the association of this variable is negative. For municipalities that perform the largest extent of state administration, the effect of this variable is positively associated with efficiency. We must also point out that beta coefficients are very low and therefore the effect on efficiency is small. Our theoretical assumption was therefore not confirmed.

The variable transfers per capita is statistically significant in all categories of municipalities according to the performance of state administration. It is also associated with lower efficiency in all categories. Beta coefficients are also high compared to other variables. The effect of transfers is higher for categories of municipalities performing a larger scope of state administration. Our theoretical background is confirmed in the case of transfers.

The deficit per capita is positively associated with efficiency in all categories of municipalities according to the performance of state administration, which confirms our theoretical assumptions.

Again, there are inconsistent results for political variables. Left-wing orientation only affects models with constant returns to scale. In municipalities with extended powers its influence is negative, in municipalities with authorized municipal office its influence is positive. Right-wing orientation only affects municipalities with extended powers, where it is positively associated with efficiency. The Herfindal index is statistically significant only in the model with constant returns; in municipalities with extended powers, the influence of this index is positively associated with efficiency.

Table 10.20 shows the verification of previous models using the Tobit model, which perceives the data as cross-section. Again, both DEA variants are presented as both constant and variable range returns.

All presented models are statistically significant. The variable describing the indebtedness per capita is statistically significant for all groups of cities according to the extent of the performance of state administration. In the case of municipalities performing basic competence and extended competence, it is positively associated with efficiency. In the case of municipalities with a designated municipal office, this association is negative. For all categories, beta coefficients are of very low value. The results are also different from the previous models.

In the case of the variable describing the impact of own income on the population, we have the same results as in the previous models. For all categories of municipalities, this variable is associated with lower efficiency. Beta coefficients have a higher value than other variables.

Table 10.20 Results of econometric analysis by size categories of municipalities Tobit model (DEA constant and variable returns from the range)

	Basic scope		Designated municipal office		Extended scope	
	CCR	VCR	CCR	VCR	CCR	VCR
constant	1.02E+00***	1.71E+00***	2.92E+00***	3.75E+00***	3.82E+00***	4.99E+00***
Log (indebtedness per capita)	2.52E−03**	3.90E−03**	−5.42E−03***	−6.64E−03***	7.58E−03***	2.87E−03
Log (own income per capita)	−1.32E−01***	−2.10E−01***	−3.52E−01***	−4.24E−01***	−5.57E−01***	−7.13E−01***
Tax income per capita	4.46E−06***	3.56E−06***	−7.86E−07	1.24E−06	1.91E−05***	1.34E−05***
Log (transfers per capita)	−9.24E−02***	−1.54E−01***	−2.91E−01***	−3.71E−01***	−3.75E−01***	−4.31E−01***
Log (deficit per capita)	1.76E−02***	2.83E−02***	1.72E−02***	2.46E−02***	1.20E−02***	1.68E−02***
Left-wing orientation	3.81E−02***	4.41E−02***	2.42E−02***	1.37E−02	4.51E−02***	2.87E−02***
Right-wing orientation	7.29E−02***	9.65E−02***	1.95E−02***	2.85E−02***	3.83E−02***	4.21E−02***
Herfindahl index	−4.38E−02***	−6.79E−02***	−1.71E−01***	−2.76E−01***	1.12E−01***	6.96E−02**
Log likelihood	2666.286	349.93	3014.489	−226.816	2924.474	−257.598

Signif. codes: 0 '***' 0.05 '**' 0. 1 '*'

Tax incomes per capita are statistically significant only for municipalities performing basic state administration and state administration in delegated powers. As in previous models, tax revenues are associated with higher efficiency.

Transfers per capita are statistically significant in all categories of municipalities according to the performance of state administration and are also negatively associated with efficiency. This result is confirmed by the results of previous models. Beta coefficients are also higher than for other fiscal and political variables.

The deficit per capita is statistically significant in all categories of municipalities according to the performance of state administration and, as in previous models, it is associated with higher efficiency.

The results regarding political variables were interesting. Compared to previous models, all political variables in all DEA variants are statistically significant. The left and right orientation of the winning party is statistically significant for all categories of municipalities according to the performance of state administration. Both variables are associated with higher efficiency. The level of concentration of political parties in the council expressed by the Herfindal index is also statistically significant for all the monitored categories. In the case of municipalities with the basic scope of public administration and municipalities with an authorized municipal office, it is negatively associated with efficiency, in municipalities with the largest extent of state administration the result is the opposite.

RQ3: What are the impacts of fiscal decentralization on the efficiency of municipalities in the NUTS II region in which they are located?

First, we perform a graphical inspection of the results of DEA technical efficiency in a variant of constant and variable returns of scale. The results of the average efficiency for the period 2010–2018 by NUTS II cohesion regions are shown in Fig. 10.7.

We excluded a region called CZ01, which consists of the capital city of Prague, from the analysis, The DEA models deliver the following average efficiency values: CZ 02 (const. 0.320039, var. 0.520278), CZ03 (const. 0.302427, var. 0.496518), CZ04 (const. 0.327755, var. 0.501344), CZ05 (const. 0.303803, var. 0.512006), CZ06 (const. 0.286469, var. 0.47873), CZ07 (const. 0.299548, var. 0.488076), CZ08 (const. 0.374084, var. 0.570001).

First of all, in a constant or variable return model, all regions achieve very low average efficiency values. The highest efficiency values are achieved in the CZ08 (const. 0.374084, var. 0.570001) and CZ06 (const. 0.286469, var. 0.47873) regions. There is therefore much room for improvement within the cohesion of regions. On the other hand, it is interesting that there are not such significant efficiency differences between regions as those visible in previous approaches.

If we look at the maturity of individual regions as measured by GDP in EUR per capita as a percentage of the EU 27 average, the regions in the reporting period have the following average values: CZ 02 (54), CZ03 (52), CZ04 (44), CZ05 (49), CZ06 (55), CZ07 (48), CZ08 (50). We will find that the richest region achieves the lowest average efficiency values among the monitored regions.

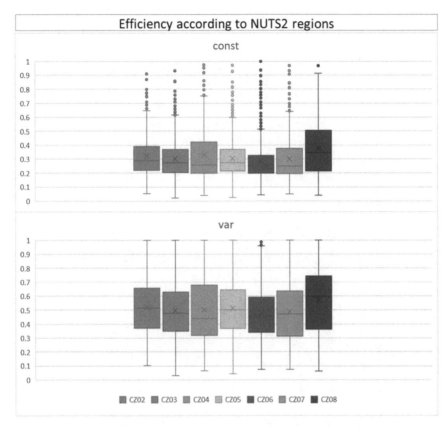

Fig. 10.7 The results of the average efficiency for the period 2010–2018 by NUTS II cohesion regions. CZ02 = Central Bohemia, CZ03 = Southwest, CZ04 = Northwest, CZ05 = Northeast, CZ06 = Southeast, CZ07 = Central Moravia, CZ08 = Moravian-Silesian region

Table 10.21 presents the results of a two stage DEA analysis and the impact of fiscal and political variables according to NUTS 2 municipalities. For the second level o f dfficiency analysis, a panel OLS regression is used.

All presented models are statistically significant, and R-square reaches a reasonable value. The model takes into account changes in variables over time.

The variable describing indebtedness per capita is statistically significant only in two regions where it is associated negatively with efficiency.

Much stronger results are provided by the variable describing own income per capita. This variable is statistically significant in all cohesion regions. Compared to other fiscal and political variables, it achieves very high beta values. In accordance with our theoretical assumptions, it is negatively associated with efficiency. This variable has the smallest effect on efficiency in the Central Moravian (CZ07) cohesion region and the largest in the Central Bohemian (CZ02) region.

Table 10.21 Results of econometric analysis according to NUTS 2 cohesion regions OLS model (DEA constant returns from scale)

	Central Bohemia	Southwest	Northwest	Northeast	Southeast	Central Moravia	Moravian-Silesian
Log (indebtedness per capita)	4.76E−05	−0.00194	−0.004032***	−0.00205	−0.00075	−0.00184*	−0.00514***
Log (own income per capita)	−0.13846***	−0.12142***	−0.11912***	−0.12068***	−0.10276***	−0.09703***	−0.13614***
Tax income per capita	4.41E−06***	1.16E−06**	4.99E−07	3.44E−06***	1.76E−06***	2.07E−06***	1.85E−06***
Log (transfers per capita)	−0.09433***	−0.10231***	−0.107112***	−0.0986***	−0.09873***	−0.10422***	−0.13299***
Log (deficit per capita)	0.019067***	0.017334***	0.0150092***	0.017052***	0.016364***	0.01538***	0.018451***
Left-wing orientation	0.003455	0.000782	0.002858	0.009885	0.006913	0.001281	−0.00405
Right-wing orientation	−0.00275	0.002348	0.004256	−0.00963	−0.00522	0.000985	0.002619
Herfindahl index	−0.00745	−0.00165	−0.00219	0.011641	−0.00327	−0.01644*	−0.00839
Adjusted R-square	0.443506	0.372387	0.308583	0.407655	0.433365	0.472634	0.469759
P value	0	0	0	0	0	0	0

Signif. codes: 0 '***' 0.05 '**' 0. 1 '*'

The variable tax per capita income is significant in all regions except the Northwest (CZ04). Contrary to our theoretical assumptions, it is positively associated with efficiency, but the beta coefficients in each model are very small.

As in previous models, transfers seem to be a very important variable. This variable is statistically significant for all regions. In accordance with our theoretical assumptions, it is negatively associated with efficiency. Compared to other fiscal policy variables, the beta coefficients for transfers are very high. Transfers have the greatest influence in the Moravian-Silesian Region (CZ08) and the lowest in Central Bohemia (CZ02).

The per capita deficit is also statistically significant for all regions. Its effect is positively associated with efficiency in accordance with theoretical assumptions. There are very small differences in the effects of this variable between regions.

The political part of the explanatory variables is not statistically significant in the vast majority of cases.

Another model presents results of application of OLS regression to efficiency measured by DEA with variable returns of scale (Table 10.22).

The variable returns model takes into account the possibility of generating returns of scale. All presented models are statistically significant and bring relatively high R square values.

In contrast to the previous variant, the debt-related variable is statistically significant for almost all cohesion regions except for Central Bohemia (CZ02). Contrary to our theoretical assumptions, this variable is negatively associated with efficiency.

The variable describing the effect of own income on efficiency is in all cases statistically significant and is negatively associated with efficiency. Compared to other variables, the beta coefficient values for this variable are very high. As with the constant returns of scale model, the effect of this variable is highest in Central Bohemia (CZ02) and lowest in Central Moravia (CZ07).

The variable describing tax revenues per capita is statistically significant only in the cohesion regions Southeast (CZ06) and Central Moravia (CZ07) and, unlike the previous model, is negatively associated with efficiency. In this case it would be a confirmation of the initial theoretical assumptions.

The variable describing transfers per capita is statistically significant in all cohesion regions. Beta coefficients reach high levels and are associated with lower efficiency in accordance with theoretical assumptions. Transfers in the Moravian-Silesian Region (CZ08) have the biggest influence and the smallest in Central Bohemia (CZ02).

The variable describing the deficit per capita is statistically significant in all cohesion regions and, in line with our assumptions, is positively associated with efficiency.

The variable describing political factors is statistically insignificant in the vast majority of the regions.

We verify the results of OLS models using the Tobit model, which uses data as a cross-section. The results of the constant return to scale DEA model are shown in Table 10.23.

Table 10.22 Results of the econometric analysis according to NUTS 2 cohesion regions OLS model (DEA variable return to scale)

	Central Bohemia	Southwest	Northwest	Northeast	Southeast	Central Moravia	Moravia-Silesia
Log (indebtedness per capita)	−0.00189	−0.00433**	−0.00409**	−0.00393*	−0.00316*	−0.00376**	−0.00761***
Log (own income per capita)	−0.21732***	−0.19383***	−0.18558***	−0.19635***	−0.1898***	−0.16734***	−0.16921***
Tax income per capita	−1.3E−06	1.01E−06	8.22E−07	−1.1E−06	−2.2E−06***	−2.3E−06***	1.07E−08
Log (transfers per capita)	−0.15392***	−0.1656***	−0.15633***	−0.16037***	−0.16144***	−0.1683***	−0.18627***
Log (deficit per capita)	0.029302***	0.026342***	0.020572***	0.026982***	0.026739***	0.022714***	0.024272***
Left-wing orientation	−0.00989	0.007001	−0.00091	−0.00793	−2.5E−05	−0.00971	0.020041*
Right-wing orientation	−0.00675	0.020923	0.006392	0.002781	−0.00964	0.002374	0.009285
Herfindahl index	−0.00749	0.004078	−0.02366	0.0131	−0.00988	−0.02901**	0.013812
Adjusted R-square	0.44831	0.374751	0.297002	0.395586	0.429661	0.430033	0.404012
P value	0	0	0	0	0	0	0

Signif. codes: 0 '***' 0.05 '**' 0. 1 '*'

Table 10.23 Results of the econometric analysis according to NUTS 2 cohesion regions Tobit model (DEA constant returns to scale)

	Central Bohemia	Southwest	Northwest	Northeast	Southeast	Central Moravia	Moravia-Silesia
constant	1.03E+00***	1.00E+00***	1.28E+00***	9.85E−01***	9.03E−01***	8.35E−01***	1.29E+00***
Log (indebtedness per capita)	6.61E−03***	1.88E−03	6.04E−03***	1.15E−02***	6.37E−03***	8.05E−03***	1.53E−02***
Log (own income per capita)	−1.45E−01***	−1.23E−01***	−1.80E−01***	−1.36E−01***	−1.08E−01***	−6.45E−02***	−1.43E−01***
Tax income per capita	5.82E−06***	5.36E−06***	7.03E−06***	4.19E−06***	4.16E−06***	7.04E−06***	6.25E−06***
Log (transfers per capita)	−7.51E−02***	−8.92E−02***	−8.20E−02***	−7.62E−02***	−8.24E−02***	−9.27E−02***	−1.20E−01***
Log (deficit per capita)	1.92E−02***	1.74E−02***	1.56E−02***	1.73E−02***	1.74E−02***	1.58E−02***	1.93E−02***
Left-wing orientation	3.53E−02***	7.97E−02***	1.05E−01***	1.36E−01***	7.59E−02***	1.06E−01***	1.71E−01***
Right-wing orientation	1.02E−01***	1.06E−01***	8.26E−02***	1.45E−01***	8.70E−02***	1.02E−01***	8.31E−02***
Herfindahl index	−8.14E−02***	−5.73E−02***	−2.37E−01***	−7.39E−02***	−6.49E−02***	−2.02E−01***	−2.75E−01***
Log likelihood	2072.647	2239.44	960.7918	2464.483	2518.562	2283.12	1407.396

Signif. codes: 0 '***' 0.05 '**' 0. 1 '*'

All models are statistically significant. If we focus on fiscal variables, we find that the model confirms the results of previous models.

The per capita indebtedness variable is statistically significant in all cohesion regions, with the exception of the Southwest cohesion region. According to the theory, it is associated with higher efficiency.

The variable describing own income is statistically significant in all regions and is negatively associated with efficiency. This again confirms the results of the previous models.

The tax revenue variable is statistically significant in all regions and is associated with higher efficiency. This result is confirmed by the results of the previous analysis.

Again, the transfer variable operates in all cohesion regions and is negatively associated with efficiency. This again confirms the theoretical assumptions.

The last fiscal variable describing the effect of the deficit on efficiency is statistically significant in all cases and is positively associated with efficiency.

The results of the political variables are interesting. Unlike all previous models, political variables are statistically significant in all regions.

Left-wing orientation is positively associated with efficiency in all cohesion regions. This result is the opposite of our theoretical assumptions.

The right-wing orientation of the winning political party is also important in all regions and is positively associated with efficiency, which is in line with our expectations.

The Herfindahl index is also statistically significant in all cohesion regions. A higher degree of concentration of parties in the council is negatively associated with efficiency. This result confirms our theoretical assumptions.

The following model introduces the Tobit model, which is applied to variable-return to scale DEA results (Table 10.24).

All presented models are statistically significant. Like the previous model, it confirms the general conclusions of previous analyses. In the field of political variables, the results are very similar to the previous model.

The variable per capita debt is positively associated with efficiency, which is in line with theoretical assumptions. The variable describing municipal income is also statistically significant in all regions and is negatively associated with efficiency, which is in line with theoretical assumptions. In statistically significant cases, the variable per capita income tax is positively associated with efficiency. In contrast, transfers are negatively associated with efficiency, in line with theory. The per capita deficit is also statistically significant in all regions and is positively associated with efficiency.

Political variables work in the same direction as the previous model. The left and right orientation of the winning party is positively associated with efficiency. The degree of concentration of parties in the council expressed by the Herfindahl index is negatively associated with efficiency.

Table 10.24 Results of the econometric analysis according to NUTS 2 cohesion regions Tobit model (DEA variable return to scale)

	Central Bohemia	Southwest	Northwest	Northeast	Southeast	Central Moravia	Moravia-Silesia
constant	1.72E+00***	1.62E+00***	1.98E+00***	1.73E+00***	1.52E+00***	1.60E+00***	1.99E+00***
Log (indebtedness per capita)	6.82E−03***	2.57E−03	4.87E−03***	1.31E−02***	1.04E−02***	1.14E−02***	1.97E−02***
Log (own income per capita)	−2.22E−01***	−1.89E−01***	−2.73E−01***	−2.24E−01***	−1.65E−01***	−1.45E−01***	−2.16E−01***
Tax income per capita	3.24E−06**	6.36E−06***	9.88E−06***	1.61E−06	1.06E−06	5.27E−06***	4.84E−06***
Log (transfers per capita)	−1.25E−01***	−1.44E−01***	−1.33E−01***	−1.35E−01***	−1.40E−01***	−1.63E−01***	−1.82E−01***
Log (deficit per capita)	3.10E−02***	2.75E−02***	2.31E−02***	2.79E−02***	2.89E−02***	2.43E−02***	2.77E−02***
Left-wing orientation	3.78E−02**	1.18E−01***	1.17E−01***	1.57E−01***	1.03E−01***	1.28E−01***	1.89E−01***
Right-wing orientation	1.34E−01***	1.75E−01***	9.76E−02**	1.99E−01***	1.17E−01***	1.33E−01***	7.76E−02***
Herfindahl index	−1.33E−01***	−8.68E−02***	−2.93E−01***	−1.04E−01***	−9.86E−02***	−2.91E−01***	−3.11E−01***
Log likelihood	−261.932	−14.891	−752.25	20.11068	349.0153	60.92802	−558.385

Signif. codes: 0 '***' 0.05 '**' 0. 1 '*'

RQ4: What are the impacts of fiscal decentralization on the efficiency of municipalities according to the region in which the municipalities are located?
First of all, we will perform a graphical inspection of the average efficiency of municipalities for the years 2010–2018 according to individual regions calculated using the DEA method with constant and variable returns to scale. Figure 10.8 shows the results of the comparison.

Individual regions achieve the following average efficiency: Central Bohemian Region (const. 0.320039, var. 0.520278), South Bohemian Region (const. 0.300757, var. 0.495075), Pilsen Region (const. 0.304515, var. 0.498321), Karlovy Vary Region (const. 0.375434, var. 0.555204), Ústí nad Labem Region (const. 0.310467, var. 0.481814), Liberec Region (const. 0.318135, var. 0.535476), Hradec Kralove Region (const. 0.312961, var. 0.52499), Pardubice Region (const. 0.287823, var.

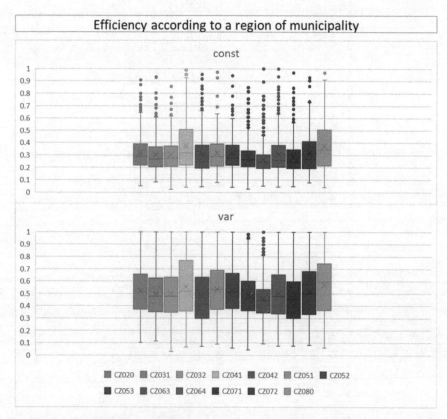

Fig. 10.8 Average efficiency of municipalities in the period 2010–2018 by regions by the DEA method with variable and constant returns to scale. *Key* CZ020 = Central Bohemian Region, CZ031 = South Bohemian Region, CZ032 = Plzen Region, CZ041 = Karlovy Vary Region, CZ042 = Ústí nad Labem Region, CZ051 = Liberec Region, CZ052 = Hradec Kralove Region, CZ053 = Pardubice Region, CZ063 = Vysočina Region, CZ064 = South Moravian Region, CZ071 = Olomouc Region, CZ072 = Zlín Region, CZ080 = Moravian-Silesian Region

0.487842), Vysočina Region (const. 0.266601, var. 0.455872), South Moravian Region (const. 0.307288, var. 0.502681), Olomouc Region (const. 0.285923, var. 0.467335), Zlín Region (const. 0.317518, var. 0.515431), Moravian-Silesian Region (const. 0.374084, var. 0.570001).

It is clear from the results that in the case of the analysis of municipalities' efficiency according to regions in the Czech Republic, there is much room for improvement in all regions. The technical efficiency values achieved are very low. The most efficient municipalities are in the Moravian-Silesian Region and the least efficient are in the Vysočina Region. It should also be noted that the differences in the efficiency of municipalities are very low among regions.

Table 10.25 presents the results of a two stage DEA analysis and the impact of fiscal and political variables according to NUTS 2 municipalities. For the second level of efficiency analysis, a panel OLS regression is used, which considers the changes in efficiency over time.

Central Bohemian Region = 1, South Bohemian Region = 2, Plzen Region = 3, Karlovy Vary Region = 4, Ústí nad Labem Region = 5, Liberec Region = 6, Hradec Kralove Region = 7, Pardubice Region = 8, Vysočina Region = 9, South Moravian Region = 10, Olomouc Region = 11, Zlín Region = 12, Moravian-Silesian Region = 13.

All models for individual regions are statistically significant and the R-square can be considered sufficiently high.

The variable describing indebtedness is statistically significant only in the South Bohemian Region, the Karlovy Vary Region, the Ústí nad Labem Region, the Hradec Králové Region, the Olomouc Region, the Zlín Region and the Moravian-Silesian Region. In all these regions, it is negatively associated with efficiency, which is contrary to our theoretical assumptions. On the other hand, this result was confirmed by previous models.

The municipalities' own incomes are statistically significant in in all regions. Beta coefficients for this variable are the highest of all the fiscal and political variables analyzed. In accordance with our assumptions, the effect of this variable is associated with lower efficiency. This variable reaches the highest values of beta coefficients in the Moravian-Silesian Region and the lowest in the Vysočina Region.

The tax revenues of municipalities are statistically significant in all regions. With the exception of the Karlovy Vary Region, they are positively associated with efficiency, which is contrary to our theoretical assumptions. It should be noted that the beta coefficients of this explanatory variable are very low in all regions.

The effect of transfers is also statistically significant in all regions. According to our assumptions, transfers are negatively associated with efficiency and beta coefficients are high compared to other variables. Transfers have the highest influence in the Moravian-Silesian Region and the lowest in the Plzen Region.

The variable per capita deficit is also statistically significant in each region. In accordance with our expectations, it is positively associated with efficiency. The differences in beta coefficients are very low for all regions, with the highest values in the Central Bohemian Region and the lowest in the Liberec Region.

Table 10.25 Results of econometric analysis by regions in the Czech Republic OLS model (DEA constant returns to scale)

Variable	1	2	3	4	5	6	7
Log (indebtedness per capita)	4.76E–05	−0.00232*	−0.00151	−0.00639***	−0.0029***	−0.00095	−0.00309***
Log (own income per capita)	−0.13846***	−0.10678***	−0.13967***	−0.10365***	−0.11895***	−0.13972***	−0.12024***
Tax income per capita	4.41E–06***	2.19E–06***	3.14E–07***	−5.9E–07***	1.04E–06***	5.64E–06***	2.92E–06***
Log (transfers per capita)	−0.09433***	−0.11425***	−0.08442***	−0.11963***	−0.10364***	−0.10543***	−0.09684***
Log (deficit per capita)	0.019067***	0.016978***	0.017568***	0.016981***	0.014272***	0.014184***	0.018189***
Left-wing orientation	0.003455	−0.01066	0.005001	0.023469***	−0.00366	0.029079***	−0.00113
Right-wing orientation	−0.00275	0.000849	0.002554	0.010158	0.001487	0.004566	−0.01367
Herfindahl index	−0.00745	−0.00297	0.001525	−0.01473	0.002641	−0.005	0.018858***
Adjusted R-square	0.443506	0.405931	0.332004	0.285059	0.329876	0.426568	0.404659
P value	0	0	0	0	0	0	0

Variable	8	9	10	11	12	13
Log (indebtedness per capita)	−0.00034	−0.00153	0.000126	−0.00163*	−0.00182*	−0.00514***
Log (own income per capita)	−0.11452***	−0.09564***	−0.11225***	−0.10276***	−0.08733***	−0.13614***
Tax income per capita	2.75E–06***	1.77E–06***	1.51E–06***	1.52E–06***	2.68E–06***	1.85E–06***
Log (transfers per capita)	−0.09796***	−0.09205***	−0.10407***	−0.10396***	−0.10348***	−0.13299***
Log (deficit per capita)	0.017341***	0.015911***	0.01686***	0.015006***	0.015671***	0.018451***
Left-wing orientation	0.005803	0.012806	0.000363	−0.00335	0.001667	−0.00405
Right-wing orientation	−0.01467	0.010096	−0.0119*	−0.00452	0.006505	0.002619
Herfindahl index	0.009701	−0.00569	−0.00101	−0.01301	−0.01827***	−0.00839
Adjusted R-square	0.420897	0.415664	0.447599	0.483696	0.463455	0.469759
P value	0	0	0	0	0	0

Signif. codes: 0 '***' 0.05 '**' 0. 1 '*'

There are inconclusive results for political variables. The left-wing orientation of the winning political party is statistically significant only in the Karlovy Vary and Liberec regions and, contrary to our theoretical assumptions, is positively associated with efficiency. The Herfindahl index is statistically significant only in the Hradec Králové Region, where it is positively associated with efficiency, and in the Zlín Region, where the result is the opposite.

Table 10.26 presents the results using the DEA model with variable returns to scale that reflect the size of the municipality and the ability to achieve returns to scale.

Central Bohemian Region = 1, South Bohemian Region = 2, Plzen Region = 3, Karlovy Vary Region = 4, Ústí nad Labem Region = 5, Liberec Region = 6, Hradec Kralove Region = 7, Pardubice Region = 8, Vysočina Region = 9, South Moravian Region = 10, Olomouc Region = 11, Zlín Region = 12, Moravian-Silesian Region = 13.

All presented models are statistically significant and achieve satisfactory R-square coefficients. The results are very similar to the previous model.

The indebtedness of municipalities is statistically significant only in some regions, namely the South Bohemian Region, the Ústí nad Labem Region, the Vysočina Region, the Olomouc Region, the Zlín Region and the Moravian-Silesian Region. As in previous cases, indebtedness is negatively associated with efficiency.

Municipal income is a very important variable. This variable is statistically significant in all regions and beta coefficients are the highest of all fiscal and political variables. As in previous cases, it has a negative effect on efficiency. Compared to the previous model, it has the largest influence in the Pilsen Region and the lowest influence in the South Bohemia Region.

Tax revenues per capita are statistically significant in the South Bohemian Region, the Pardubice Region, the South Moravian Region, the Olomouc Region and the Zlín Region. In all cases, they are positively associated with efficiency.

A very important variable is again transfers, which are statistically significant in all regions. They are negatively associated with efficiency. However, there are very small differences in their activities between the individual regions; they operate most strongly in the South Bohemian Region and have the least effect in the Plzeň Region.

As in previous cases, the latest fiscal variable, per capita deficit, is statistically significant in all regions and, in line with theory, is positively associated with efficiency. It has the greatest effect in the Central Bohemia Region and the least effect in the Ústí Region.

If we look at political variables, we have to say that their impact is significantly lower than fiscal variables. The left-wing political orientation of the winning party is statistically significant only in the Vysočina Region, the South Moravian Region and the Moravian-Silesian Region. In the South Moravian Region, it is positively associated with efficiency. The right-wing political orientation of the winning party is statistically significant only in the South Moravian Region and is negatively associated with efficiency. The Herfindahl index is statistically significant in the Karlovy Vary, Hradec Králové, Olomouc and Zlín regions. Only in the Hradec Kralove region is the Herfindahl index positively associated with efficiency.

Table 10.26 Results of econometric analysis by regions in the Czech Republic OLS model (DEA variable returns to scale)

Variable	1	2	3	4	5	6	7
Log (indebtedness per capita)	−0.00189	−0.00693***	−0.00059	0.002206	−0.00596***	−0.00273	−0.0026
Log (own income per capita)	−0.21732***	−0.1582***	−0.24029***	−0.1762***	−0.18053***	−0.23076***	−0.18942***
Tax income per capita	−1.3E−06	2.5E−06***	−4.7E−07	5.06E−07	9.69E−07	7.98E−07	−1.2E−06
Log (transfers per capita)	−0.15392***	−0.18815***	−0.13185***	−0.17235***	−0.15279***	−0.18227***	−0.15625***
Log (deficit per capita)	0.029302***	0.025781***	0.026849***	0.022723***	0.019875***	0.021174***	0.028773***
Left-wing orientation	−0.00989	−0.0223	0.021084	0.016026	−0.00686	−0.00853	−0.01567
Right-wing orientation	−0.00675	0.019425	0.019001	0.007951	0.005408	0.0054	0.012259
Herfindahl index	−0.00749	−0.00045	0.007773	−0.04622***	−0.01589	−0.02211	0.030133***
Adjusted R-square	0.44833	0.41351	0.328818	0.295183	0.304575	0.37291	0.403591
P value	0	0	0	0	0	0	0

Variable	8	9	10	11	12	13
Log (indebtedness per capita)	−0.00311	−0.00366***	−0.00226	−0.00367***	−0.0034***	−0.00761***
Log (own income per capita)	−0.18591***	−0.18546***	−0.19758***	−0.16835***	−0.16505***	−0.16921***
Tax income per capita	−2.2E−06***	−1.2E−06	−3.4E−06***	−2E−06***	−2.9E−06***	1.07E−08
Log (transfers per capita)	−0.15694***	−0.15202***	−0.16799***	−0.16782***	−0.16993***	−0.18627***
Log (deficit per capita)	0.027937***	0.026331***	0.026912***	0.022547***	0.02284***	0.024272***
Left-wing orientation	−0.00753	0.033975*	−0.02583**	−0.01352	−0.01367	0.020041*
Right-wing orientation	−0.00602	0.024807	−0.02573***	0.005382	0.002164	0.009285
Herfindahl index	0.008226	−0.00222	−0.01926	−0.03259***	−0.02511*	0.013812
Adjusted R-square	0.410323	0.402744	0.455077	0.440694	0.417823	0.404012
P value	0	0	0	0	0	0

Signif. codes: 0 '***' 0.05 '**' 0. 1 '*'

Table 10.27 represent verification of previous results using the Tobit model, which perceives data as a cross-section. The first table shows the DEA model with constant returns to scale.

Central Bohemian Region = 1, South Bohemian Region = 2, Plzen Region = 3, Karlovy Vary Region = 4, Ústí nad Labem Region = 5, Liberec Region = 6, Hradec Kralove Region = 7, Pardubice Region = 8, Vysočina Region = 9, South Moravian Region = 10, Olomouc Region = 11, Zlín Region = 12, Moravian-Silesian Region = 13.

All models presented are statistically significant and have a sufficiently high informative ability.

In the case of the variable of the indebtedness of the municipality, we get contrary results. In this model, indebtedness is associated with higher efficiency, which is in line with our original assumptions. It should be added that beta coefficients are very low, so this variable has no major effect. Moreover, it is not statistically significant in the Plzen Region and the Vysočina Region.

Regarding municipal incomes, we get the same results as in all previous models. This variable is statistically significant in all regions and is negatively associated with efficiency.

The results of the variable per capita income tax confirm previous analyses. They are statistically significant in all regions and positively associated with efficiency.

In the case of transfers, our previous results were again confirmed. This variable is statistically significant in all regions and is associated with lower efficiency.

The per capita deficit is also in line with previous results. It is statistically significant in all regions and is positively associated with efficiency.

The last table presents results using the Tobit model and DEA with variable returns to scale. This approach considers the size of the municipality and the ability to achieve returns to scale (Table 10.28).

Central Bohemian Region = 1, South Bohemian Region = 2, Plzen Region = 3, Karlovy Vary Region = 4, Ústí nad Labem Region = 5, Liberec Region = 6, Hradec Kralove Region = 7, Pardubice Region = 8, Vysočina Region = 9, South Moravian Region = 10, Olomouc Region = 11, Zlín Region = 12, Moravian-Silesian Region = 13.

All models are statistically significant. In contrast to to previous models, this Tobit model also confirms the statistical significance of municipal debt. Indebtedness is statistically significant in all regions. In accordance with our theoretical assumptions, it is positively associated with efficiency.

For municipalities' own incomes, the variables move in the same direction as in all previous models. This variable is statistically significant in all regions and is negatively associated with efficiency.

The variable describing tax per capita income is not statistically significant in all regions. Tax revenues do not affect efficiency in the Liberec Region, Hradec Králové Region, Pardubice Region and Vysočina Region. This variable is positively associated with efficiency, but beta coefficients are very small.

Table 10.27 Results of econometric analysis by regions in the Czech Republic Tobit model (DEA constant returns to scale)

Variable	1	2	3	4	5	6	7
constant	1.03E+00***	1.08E+00***	9.14E-01***	1.10E+00***	1.34E+00***	1.21E+00***	9.75E-01***
Log (indebtedness per capita)	6.61E--03***	2.42E-03***	1.62E-03	9.35E-03***	3.53E-03***	2.79E-02***	6.71E-03***
Log (own income per capita)	-1.45E-01***	-1.35E-01***	-1.23E-01***	-1.19E-01***	-1.96E-01***	-1.80E-01***	-1.40E-01***
Tax income per capita	5.82E-06***	6.52E-06***	4.72E-06***	4.84E-06***	6.60E-06***	5.27E-06***	4.55E-06***
Log (transfers per capita)	-7.51E-02***	-1.04E-01***	-6.27E-02***	-7.79E-02***	-8.30E-02***	-9.28E-02***	-7.04E-02***
Log (deficit per capita)	1.92E-02***	1.71E-02***	1.80E-02***	1.83E-02***	1.48E-02***	1.41E-02***	1.98E-02***
Left-wing orientation	3.53E-02***	1.13E-01***	4.56E-02***	1.05E-01***	9.71E-02***	1.34E-01***	2.17E-01***
Right-wing orientation	1.02E-01***	8.96E-02***	1.31E-01***	9.65E-02***	7.33E-02***	1.42E-01***	1.58E-01***
Herfindahl index	-8.14E-02***	-5.83E-02***	-5.65E-02***	-2.28E-01***	-2.37E-01***	-9.71E-02***	-5.77E-02***
Log-likelihood	2072.647	2300.737	2236.456	202.8101	1350.271	2302.68	2381.348

Variable	8	9	10	11	12	13
constant	9.44E-01***	8.16E-01***	1.00E+00***	7.12E-01***	9.44E-01***	1.29E+00***
Log (indebtedness per capita)	1.01E-02***	2.55E-04	1.07E-02***	9.63E-03***	5.38E-03***	1.53E-02***
Log (own income per capita)	-1.31E-01***	-1.12E-01***	-1.10E-01***	-4.52E-02***	-7.55E-02***	-1.43E-01***
Tax income per capita	3.14E-06***	3.90E-06***	5.48E-06***	7.02E-06***	6.34E-06***	6.25E-06***
Log (transfers per capita)	-7.06E-02***	-6.03E-02***	-9.73E-02***	-8.70E-02***	-1.00E-01***	-1.20E-01***
Log (deficit per capita)	1.68E-02***	1.65E-02***	1.79E-02***	1.57E-02***	1.53E-02***	1.93E-02***
Left-wing orientation	1.21E-01***	7.95E-02***	5.83E-02***	1.01E-01***	1.29E-01***	1.71E-01***
Right-wing orientation	1.12E-01***	1.04E-01***	6.68E-02***	8.88E-02***	1.19E-01***	8.31E-02***
Herfindahl index	-7.05E-02***	-2.00E-02***	-1.51E-01***	-1.62E-01***	-2.44E-01***	-2.75E-01***
Log-likelihood	2839.015	2936.3	2153.519	2435.209	2210.795	1407.396

Signif. codes: 0 '***' 0.05 '**' 0.1 '*'

Table 10.28 Results of econometric analysis by regions in the Czech Republic Tobit model (DEA constant returns to scale)

Variable	1	2	3	4	5	6	7
constant	1.72E+00***	1.71E+00***	1.51E+00***	1.81E+00***	2.01E+00***	2.12E+00***	1.65E+00***
Log (indebtedness per capita)	6.82E−03***	3.58E−03**	2.07E−03	2.07E−02***	−1.84E−03	3.62E−02***	6.91E−03***
Log (own income per capita)	−2.22E−01***	−2.00E−01***	−1.94E−01***	−2.33E−01***	−2.79E−01***	−2.90E−01***	−2.15E−01***
Tax income per capita	3.24E−06***	8.78E−06***	4.79E−06***	8.15E−06***	8.75E−06***	7.50E−07	2.24E−06
Log (transfers per capita)	−1.25E−01***	−1.67E−01***	−1.06E−01***	−1.16E−01***	−1.37E−01***	−1.66E−01***	−1.26E−01***
Log (deficit per capita)	3.10E−02***	2.69E−02***	2.84E−02***	2.65E−02***	2.23E−02***	2.30E−02***	3.17E−02***
Left-wing orientation	3.78E−02***	1.47E−01***	8.82E−02***	1.27E−01***	1.09E−01***	1.11E−01***	2.56E−01***
Right-wing orientation	1.34E−01***	1.56E−01***	1.95E−01***	8.88E−02***	9.46E−02***	1.53E−01***	2.41E−01***
Herfindahl index	−1.33E−01***	−8.93E−02***	−8.06E−02***	−2.82E−01***	−2.88E−01***	−1.33E−01***	−7.06E−02***
Log likelihood	−261.932	−11.6641	31.63777	−1199.97	−528.64	135.6575	−199.437

Variable	8	9	10	11	12	13
constant	1.71E+00***	1.46E+00***	1.62E+00***	1.37E+00***	1.82E+00***	1.99E+00***
Log (indebtedness per capita)	1.05E−02***	1.01E−03***	1.85E−02***	1.36E−02***	8.17E−03***	1.97E−02***
Log (own income per capita)	−2.31E−01***	−1.85E−01*	−1.56E−01***	−1.13E−01***	−1.64E−01***	−2.16E−01***
Tax income per capita	9.04E−07	2.19E−06***	8.81E−07	6.49E−06***	1.94E−06***	4.84E−06***
Log (transfers per capita)	−1.27E−01***	−1.15E−01***	−1.60E−01***	−1.50E−01***	−1.81E−01***	−1.82E−01***
Log (deficit per capita)	2.71E−02***	2.74E−02***	2.95E−02***	2.47E−02***	2.34E−02***	2.77E−02***
Left-wing orientation	1.65E−01***	1.09E−01***	7.71E−02***	1.19E−01***	1.58E−01***	1.89E−01***
Right-wing orientation	1.63E−01***	1.53E−01***	8.31E−02***	1.28E−01***	1.40E−01***	7.76E−02***
Herfindahl index	−1.09E−01***	−3.30E−02***	−2.17E−01***	−2.29E−01***	−3.65E−01***	−3.11E−01***
Log likelihood	354.9576	824.3022	−49.0649	239.8504	−66.74	−558.385

Signif. codes: 0 '***' 0.05 '**' 0. 1 '*'

In the case of transfers, we see the same results as in all previous models, with transfers being statistically significant in all regions and negatively associated with efficiency.

Deficits are also statistically significant and positively associated with efficiency, which is in line with our assumptions.

In contrast to other models, all political variables are statistically significant in this model. The right-wing and left-wing orientation of the winning political party is statistically significant in all regions, and both of these variables are positively associated with efficiency. In the case of left-wing parties, this result contradicts our theoretical assumptions. The variable describing the degree of concentration of political parties in the council is also statistically significant and, in accordance with our theoretical assumptions, is associated with a lower degree of efficiency.

RQ5: How has the efficiency of municipalities changed according to the above criteria over time?

In this part of the book, we will introduce an analysis of changes in the efficiency of municipalities over time. The basic tool is the Malmquist index. To calculate the Malmquist index, we use the input-oriented DEA model with constant returns to scale. The Malmquist productivity index has components which are used in performance measurement; these are changes in technical efficiency (Effch), change in technological change (Techch), change in pure technical efficiency (pech), and change in scale efficiency (sech) as well as change in total factor productivity (**Tfpch**). This approach allows us to compare productivity changes in municipalities but also within individual groups of municipalities. Total factor productivity represents a change of all factors affecting productivity. It consists of a change in technical efficiency (getting closer to the production frontier over time) and technological change (whether the production frontier is moving outwards over time). Pure technical efficiency is a change over the course of time caused by cost management. Scale efficiency indicates whether municipalities operate to the optimum extent. Table 10.29 presents the Malmquist index values by size category of municipalities. Interpreting the index is simple, a value greater than 1 means improvement. Values less than 1 indicate deterioration.

The table shows that all categories of municipalities recorded improvements in all productivity factors (TPFch). However, there are significant differences between individual categories of municipalities. The greatest improvement over time was recorded in municipalities up to 199 inhabitants and in municipalities from 200 to 499 inhabitants. In contrast, the category of municipalities from 5000 to 9999 inhabitants and municipalities over 20,000 inhabitants showed the least improvement. The main cause of the positive change was changes in technical efficiency, i.e. the municipality moving closer to the production frontier over time. On the other hand, the municipality worsened in terms of technological efficiency. In the case of

Table 10.29 Average change in productivity for the period 2010–2018 according to size category of municipalities

	Malmquist index				
	Effch	Techch	Pech	Sech	Tfpch
To 199 inhabitants	1.299591914	0.995861405	1.268777775	1.022873445	1.224946054
200–499 inhabitants	1.296894935	0.991809989	1.286937608	1.013554511	1.161502317
500–999 inhabitants	1.268121759	0.989362831	1.225823302	1.029659262	1.110688929
1000–1999 inhabitants	1.251419958	0.988746547	1.120747481	1.093854816	1.081712014
2000–4999 inhabitants	1.190057319	0.987067369	1.072658715	1.113341767	1.039381824
– 9999 inhabitants	1.168908373	0.982152672	1.061966682	1.092659214	1.019977534
10,000–19,999 inhabitants	1.178422553	0.979243488	1.050001501	1.109428045	1.031565363
Over 20,000 inhabitants	1.16172879	0.975570243	1.018034724	1.135540882	1.021969186

Source Authors

small municipalities, we can see improvements in pure technical efficiency, i.e. cost management. The improvement in scale efficiency was very small in the category of small municipalities. In contrast, if we look at larger municipalities, we can see a slight improvement in pure technical efficiency, but this result is offset by a more significant improvement in scale efficiency. Small municipalities are therefore more dominant in resource use, while large municipalities are improving by operating at optimum size.

The following table presents the average change in the productivity of municipalities in terms of the extent of state administration performance.

Table 10.30 presents the Malmquist index values by performance of state administration tasks.

Municipalities, depending on the extent of state administration performance, recorded an improvement in overall productivity. The most significant improvement is in municipalities that perform the basic scope of state administration. This category of municipalities consists mainly of the smallest municipalities. On the contrary, the category of municipalities with an authorized municipal office recorded the smallest improvement. Technical efficiency improvements have been achieved in all categories of government performance; in contrast, technological efficiency has deteriorated. Again, the greatest improvement in the category of municipalities with the basic scope of state administration was achieved in the field of pure technical efficiency, i.e. by simply operating. On the contrary, municipalities with a larger scope of state administration achieved improvements in scale efficiency mainly by operating at the optimum scale.

Table 10.30 Malmquist index values by performance of state administration tasks

| | Malmquist index | | | | |
	Effch	Techch	Pech	Sech	Tfpch
Basic scope	1.279575896	0.991654654	1.236184215	1.034969587	1.148923005
Designated municipal office	1.170322997	0.986103445	1.053105072	1.104020009	1.017526441
Extended scope	1.180160482	0.976997838	1.054109674	1.112222194	1.03483196

Source Authors

Another view is the division of municipalities into cohesion regions according to their jurisdiction.

Table 10.31 presents the Malmquist index values according to the NUTS 2 cohesion regions.

All NUTS 2 regions experienced an improvement in average productivity. The greatest improvement was recorded in the Northwest, Southwest and Central Moravia regions. The region of Central Bohemia showed the smallest improvement. Improving overall productivity was mainly due to improvements in technical efficiency, while conversely, technological efficiency worsened in all regions. The regions have achieved the greatest improvement thanks to better resource management, i.e. in pure technical efficiency. The only exception is the region of Central Bohemia, where there was no improvement in pure technical efficiency. This region has, however, seen improvements in scale efficiency.

The final table presents the breakdown of productivity development over time by region (Table 10.32).

Through the lens of the development of the productivity of municipalities based on their membership in individual regions in the Czech Republic, we can state that

Table 10.31 Average changes in municipal productivity by cohesion regions NUTS 2

| | Nuts2 | Malmquist index | | | | |
		Effch	Techch	Pech	Sech	Tfpch
Central Bohemia	CZ01	1.103465421	0.942519597	1	1.103465421	1.012891396
Southwest	CZ02	1.306288972	0.982213398	1.26576946	1.032511943	1.164392412
Northwest	CZ03	1.291222854	0.991374016	1.255668642	1.038379633	1.197211945
Northeast	CZ04	1.230323585	0.991131239	1.180768616	1.051568543	1.105139627
Southeast	CZ05	1.248813477	0.986139489	1.203900783	1.035727239	1.113873411
Central Moravia	CZ06	1.27361022	0.99730076	1.225819548	1.035463037	1.139818016
Moravia-Silesia	CZ07	1.270082783	0.99652736	1.201012637	1.04609472	1.105395895

Source Authors

Table 10.32 Average change in the productivity of municipalities by region

		Malmquist index				
		Effch	Techch	Pech	Sech	Tfpch
Central Bohemian Region	CZ010	1.103465421	0.942519597	1	1.103465421	1.012891396
South Bohemian Region	CZ020	1.306288972	0.982213398	1.26576946	1.032511943	1.164392412
Plzen Region	CZ031	1.355633298	0.989002063	1.325270617	1.036019508	1.258454509
Karlovy Vary Region	CZ032	1.210709798	0.994338958	1.168666174	1.04132979	1.120658739
Ústí nad Labem Region	CZ041	1.190050489	0.989885781	1.132700273	1.060371687	1.080054035
Liberec Region	CZ042	1.24492686	0.991582849	1.198198497	1.048376468	1.114235819
Hradec Kralove Region	CZ051	1.194169674	0.977887561	1.15370187	1.03904736	1.072442834
Pardubice Region	CZ052	1.261394419	0.982872562	1.224598583	1.032325299	1.128443416
Vysočina Region	CZ053	1.262454317	0.993343233	1.207332521	1.037524212	1.119207
South Moravian Region	CZ063	1.246877017	0.999902384	1.209807918	1.02677699	1.140928639
Olomouc Region	CZ064	1.301622141	0.994574694	1.242597056	1.04456456	1.13865427
Zlín Region	CZ071	1.293904413	1.002021538	1.220161643	1.044961477	1.123269864
Moravia-Silesia	CZ072	1.238663557	0.989280886	1.175756306	1.047589397	1.081821258

Source Authors

the overall factor of productivity improved in all regions. However, there are considerable differences between regions. The greatest improvement was recorded in the Plzen Region, the values of total productivity growth in municipalities in this region are significantly higher than in all other regions. On the other hand, the lowest productivity growth was recorded in the Central Bohemia Region. Improvements in overall productivity are driven mainly by improvements in technical efficiency, which was relatively significant in all regions. On the other hand, all regions, with the exception of the Zlin region, saw their technological efficiency fall. The regions improved mainly thanks to better resource management. In the area of scale efficiency, which is where the Central Bohemian Region performed best, their improvement was very small.

References

Aiello F, Bonanno G, Capristo L (2017) Explaining differences in efficiency: the case of local government literature. Working paper no. 04-2017, Università Della Calabria, Rende. Available via http://www.ecostat.unical.it/RePEc/WorkingPapers/WP04_2017.pdf

Borůvková J, Kuncová M (2012) Porovnání očních oddělení kraje Vysočina pomocí DEA modelů. Acta Oeconomica Pragensia 20(5):75–84

Český statistický úřad (2016) Malý lexikon obcí České republiky. Available via https://www.czso.cz/csu/czso/maly-lexikon-obci-ceske-republiky-2016. Accessed 15 June 2017

Český statistický úřad (2019a) Rozdělení obcí podle příslušnosti k NUTS 2. Available via https://www.czso.cz/csu/czso/cz-nuts2. Acessed 28 Oct 2019

Český statistický úřad (2019b) Rozdělení obcí podle příslušnosti ke krajům. Available via https://www.czso.cz. Acessed 28 Oct 2019

Chalos P, Cherian J (1995) An application of data envelopment analysis to public sector performance measurement and accountability. J Account Public Pol 14(2):143–160

da Cruz NF, Marques RC (2014) Revisiting the determinants of local government performance. Omega-Int J Manage Sci 44:91–103

Drew J, Kortt MA, Dollery B (2017) No Aladdin's cave in New South Wales? Local government amalgamation, scale economies, and data envelopment analysis specification. Admin Soc 49(10):1450–1470

Ganley AJ, Cubbin JS (1992) Public sector efficiency measurement: application of data envelopment analysis. Elsevier, Amsterdam

Hugeunin J-M (2015) Adjusting for the environment in DEA: a comparison of alternative models based on empirical data. Socio-Econ Plan Sci 52:41–54

Jablonský J, Dlouhý M (2004) Modely hodnocení efektivnosti produkčních jednotek. Professional Publishing, Praha

Kruntorádová I (2015) Politické aspekty financování českých měst. Karolinum, Praha

lo Storto C (2016) The trade-off between cost efficiency and public service quality: a non-parametric frontier analysis of Italian major municipalities. Cities 51:52–63

McQuestin D, Drew J, Dollery B (2018) Do municipal mergers improve technical efficiency? An empirical analysis of the 2008 Queensland municipal merger program. Aust J Publ Admin 77(3):442–455

Musgrave RA, Musgrave PB (1989) Public finance in theory and practice. McGraw-Hill Education, Maidenhead

Narbón-Perpiñá I, De Witte K (2017a) Local governments' efficiency: a systematic literature review—part I. Int T Oper Res 25(2):431–468

Narbón-Perpiñá I, De Witte K (2017b) Local governments' efficiency: a systematic literature review—part II. Int T Oper Res 25(4):1107–1136

Narbón-Perpiñá I, Balaguer-Coll M, Tortosa-Ausina E (2019) Evaluating local government performance in times of crisis. Local Gov Stud 45(1):64–100

Ochrana F, Půček MJ, Špaček D (2015) Veřejná správa. Masarykova Univerzita, Brno

OECD (2016) When size matters: scaling up delivery of Czech local services. In: Lewis C (ed) Available via https://oecdecoscope.wordpress.com/2016/07/26/when-size-matters-scaling-up-delivery-of-czech-local-services/. Accessed on 10 May 2017

Peterová H (2012) Finanční hospodaření územních samosprávných celků. Institut pro veřejnou správu, Praha

Plaček M, Špaček M, Ochrana F et al (2019a) Does excellence matter? National quality awards and performance of Czech municipalities. J East Eur Manag Stud 24(4):589–613

Plaček M, Půček M, Ochrana F (2019b) Identifying corruption risk: a comparison of Bulgaria and the Czech Republic. J Comp Policy Anal 21(4):366–384

Provazníková R (2011) Financování měst, obcí a regionů teorie a praxe, 2. aktualizované a rozšířené vydání. Grada Publishing, Prague

Schubert T (2009) Empirical observations on New Public Management to increase efficiency in public research—boon or bane? Res Policy 38(8):1225–1234

Simar LL, Wilson WP (1998) Sensitivity analysis of efficiency scores: how to bootstrap in nonparametric frontiers models. Manage Sci 44(1):49–61

Šťastná L, Gregor M (2015) Public sector efficiency in transition and beyond: evidence from Czech local governments. Appl Econ 47(7):680–699

Tankersley W (2000) The impact of external control arrangements on organizational performance. Admin Soc 32(3):282–304

Transparency International (2008) Průvodce komunálními rozpočty: aneb jak může informovaný občan střežit obecní pokladnu. Transparency International. Praha. Available via https://www.transparency.cz/wp-content/uploads/kr_pruvodce2008.pdf. Accessed 10 May 2017

Transparency International (2019) Corruption perception index. Available via https://www.transparency.org/research/cpi/overview. Accessed 10 May 2017

Walker RM, Lee MJ, James O et al (2018) Analyzing the complexity of performance information use: experiments with stakeholders to disaggregate dimensions of performance, data sources, and data types. Public Admin Rev 78(6):852–863

Chapter 11
Conclusion and Public Policy Recommendation: Efficiency Improvement Through Managerial Approach and Accountability Mechanisms

Our results confirmed the previous research by Šťastná and Gregor (2015) which stated that there are significant performance differences between large and small municipalities. The impact of the size category of the municipality was confirmed by t-tests and correlation analysis, which we performed to verify our results. The average efficiency values of the DEA models show a large space for efficiency improvement in all size categories of municipalities, but the largest space is in the category of the smallest municipalities.

If we focus on the impact of fiscal and political variables on the efficiency of municipalities according to size categories, the extent of state administration performance, and from the perspective of NUTS2 cohesion regions and individual regions in the Czech Republic, we can state that our models have proved the fiscal variables.

The most important fiscal variables are those describing the fiscal capacity of the municipality and transfers. In our case, we expressed fiscal capacity as a log of the municipality's own income per capita. We assumed that the higher the municipality's own income, the lower the efficiency. The own income pillow does not force municipal management to spend public funds efficiently. Moreover, in the Czech Republic, this problem is supported by fiscal illusion and a lower public interest in the economy. In the Czech Republic, it is already a standard that most municipalities have their own budget, and there is also a central website managed by the Ministry of Finance, where you can also get all the information on the management of municipalities. It is also surprising that own income adversely affects efficiency in all size categories of municipalities. The negative impact of this variable is surprising in small municipalities, where we would assume greater pressure on the accountability of public politicians, as small municipalities are expected to be closer to citizens via their elected politicians. Larger beta coefficients for large municipalities are in line with the assumption that from a certain size of municipality it is more difficult for citizens to control the use of public funds. Our results are consistent with previous evidence (Balaguer-Coll et al. 2010; Boetti et al. 2012; Agasisti et al. 2015; Peréz-Lopéz et al. 2015; Borge et al. 2008; Balaguer-Coll and Prior 2009; Porcelli 2014; Šťastná and Gregor 2015).

M. Plaček et al., *Fiscal Decentralization Reforms*, Public Administration, Governance and Globalization 19, https://doi.org/10.1007/978-3-030-46758-6_11

In the case of grants, we can confirm the effect of the flypaper effect, i.e. that grants are negatively associated with efficiency. This phenomenon is apparent in all size categories of municipalities and also in the breakdown by NUTS 2 regions and official regions. Again, we are encountering a problem with accountability and control. According to beta coefficients, grants have less influence in small municipalities. This can be explained by the budget level of small municipalities, where the grants received are more visible and thus more publicly controlled. Public procurement studies highlight statistically significant overpricing of public procurement when funded by EU subsidy programs (Plaček et al. 2016), while other studies (Plaček et al. 2019a, b) show that one of the problems of using subsidies is the focus on the formal checking of formalities rather than the checking of real results. Our results are consistent with previous results (De Borger and Kerstens 1996a; Balaguer-Coll et al. 2010; Geys et al. 2009; Boetti et al. 2012; Pacheco et al. 2014; Yusfany 2015; Peréz-Lopéz et al. 2015; Balaguer-Coll and Prior 2009; Porcelli, 2014; Štastná and Gregor 2015; Doumpos and Cohen 2014; Grossman et al. 1999).

Another variable that has been shown to be statistically significant is per capita tax income, which consists mainly of shared taxes, i.e. taxes that are levied by the state and then redistributed among budget levels. Contrary to theoretical assumptions, this variable is positively associated with efficiency, which is reflected in all areas examined. Theory would assume that this variable would have the same effect as transfers, but the allocation of these funds is at the discretion of the municipality and there is no control by the central government. These funds constitute the main revenue source of the Czech municipal budget. However, it should be added that the effect of this variable on efficiency is very small. Our results are consistent (Borger and Kerstens 1996a, b).

The results of variables describing the budget deficit of a given year and long-term debt were interesting. Deficit management is positively associated with efficiency in all views of data; on the other hand, long-term debt is not always statistically significant and, if significant, is negatively associated with efficiency. We can view this situation as a time trade off of accountability. This means that the effect of the deficit is stronger only in a given period of time, when the local government has to defend it against the opposition and the public exerts pressure for efficiency under this mechanism, since the deficit is acceptable if the funds go to investment and repair and not operating expenses. In the case of long-term indebtedness, the responsibility of a particular local government is lost and the accountability decreases. Czech municipalities being in a very good financial condition when comparing EU countries while their indebtedness is low (Eurostat 2019) is another important factor, so debt is not perceived by the public as a fundamental problem. In the case of the effect of the deficit on efficiency, our results are in opposition to most literature, according to which the deficit is associated with lower efficiency e.g. (Balaguer-Coll et al. 2010; Agasisti et al. 2015; Peréz-Lopéz et al. 2015). The same is true in the context of long-term debt, which in the literature is more positively related to efficiency e.g. (Balaguer-Coll et al. 2010; Balaguer-Coll and Prior 2009; Bönisch et al. 2011; Benito et al. 2010).

There are no clear results for political variables. In most cases, the winning party's political orientation is not statistically significant as is the unequivocal direction of previous fiscal variables. In our opinion, this problem is one of methodology. In our case, we were able to determine right-wing vs. left-wing orientation only for nationally active parties. In local elections, a large number of local entities run that deal with topics at the local level and which are not typically characterized by a uniform ideology. These subjects are often referred to as impartialities. This trend is very significant, especially in the smallest municipalities, where the decisive factors are the personalities of the candidate and the personal experience of the voters with the candidates. The Herfindahl index is statistically significant only when using the Tobit cross-sectional model and looking at data from the perspective of NUTS 2 regions and official regions. In most cases, the concentration of political parties is negatively associated with efficiency. This phenomenon can be explained by the fact that, in spite of the benefits of simpler decision making and the absence of complicated bargaining, there is a loss of accountability and political control resulting in lower efficiency, which is in line with the assumptions (Geys et al. 2009).

In terms of productivity development over time, the conclusions of the analysis of average efficiencies by size categories of municipalities are confirmed. Although all categories of municipalities recorded productivity improvements and, paradoxically, the smallest categories of municipalities improved the most, we find considerable differences in the causes of this improvement. For large cities, the improvement in productivity is mainly due to the fact that they operate at the optimum scale, in small municipalities the main driver of productivity growth is better management of resources, with the improvement in the area of optimal scale being marginal. This phenomenon is quite logical, because if small municipalities do not have the space to achieve economies of scale, they must focus on better resource manage-ment. However, this also confirms the fact that Czech municipalities do not have the optimum size in terms of achieving efficiency. Another significant finding is that the main driver of efficiency improvement in all categories of municipalities is technical change, while in the area of technological change, all categories of municipalities are getting worse.

In view of the previous sections of our book, we can conclude that efficiency is hampered by the fact that municipalities do not operate on an optimal scale. There is also the problem of the accountability of politicians and bureaucrats.

In the area of achieving the optimal scale, it seems logical to propose a policy that would mean merging municipalities. Merging municipalities brings implications in the areas of economic efficiency and cost savings, management, and democracy (Tavares 2018). Economic efficiency lies mainly in the possibility of spreading fixed costs among more inhabitants, but this assumption does not apply if we focus on services. In the area of management, the positive aspect is greater professionalism and the possibility of specialization. In the area of democracy, this means greater bargaining power for local governments. Tavares (2018) synthesized empirical arti-cles published over the last 20 years. The results, of course, vary from country to country, but according to the author, several recurring features of the process can be traced. If we focus on economic efficiency and cost savings, we conclude that the merged municipalities often exceed the optimum size and economies of scale are often outweighed by the costs of general administration. Empirical studies provide a very mixed picture of the effects of better service quality. On the other hand, these studies confirm the risk of local democracy deteriorating (Tavares 2018), bringing this problem to the beginning of the original tradeoff between efficiency and democracy. (Drew et al. 2015) offers an innovative way of DEA application for scale-based amalgamation analysis, which can estimate the outcome of merging municipalities in the area of economies of scale. The results of the authors differ from the assumptions of the proposed government policies, especially in that the municipalities in most cases exceed the optimum size after the proposed merger. Drew et al. (2015) also point to the problem of government policies and analyses that are based on general assumptions rather than on specific analyses.

If we focus this topic on the Czech Republic, we can say that there are enough studies describing the problem of economies of scale. The problem, however, is at a political level, because the Constitution of the Czech Republic ensures the right of municipalities to self-government and the solution in the form of merging municipalities is politically and socially unacceptable. We can say that, given the past of the Czech Republic, public discourse tends to favor local democracy in the above-mentioned trade-off between efficiency and democracy.

Given these initial assumptions, a soft solution based on inter-municipal cooperation is offered to achieve economies of scale and better contracting results (Peréz-Lopéz et al. 2015). The advantage of inter-municipal cooperation is the possibility of selecting activities that are included in municipal cooperation, which means that municipalities can join together to provide services that are characterized by high fixed costs and, on the other hand, activities characterized by high labor costs can be self-directed. There is a relatively broad record concerning Spain, which is also characterized by a high number of small municipalities. Studies (Bel and Warner 2015; Zafra-Goméz et al. 2013; Bel et al. 2012) describe the positive effect of municipal cooperation in waste collection. Peréz-Goméz et al. (2015) point out that most of these studies focus on only one service. In their empirical analysis, they themselves show that the effect may be reversed if other services are included. The assumption of achieving economies of scale in municipal cooperation in the field of waste management in the Czech Republic was also confirmed (Soukopová et al. 2017). In terms of cost per citizen, municipal cooperation in this area means savings for municipalities with up to 1000 inhabitants. In municipalities over 1000 inhabitants, the variable describing municipal cooperation is not statistically significant. In another study (Soukopová and Vaceková 2018), they emphasize the role of internal factors of municipal cooperation, greater savings occur when the cooperation is managed by professional managers and municipal management representatives are involved in the management of the structure. Other pilot projects focused on inter-municipal cooperation in the Czech Republic. The largest project, called Municipalities, focuses on realizing inter-municipal cooperation in the following activities: social services, education, tourism, transport, security, employment and entrepreneurship (Jetmar 2015). Jetmar (2015) lists examples of good practice that have been achieved through municipal cooperation. Despite these partial successes in the Czech system, relatively significant administrative barriers remain, consisting of overly complicated legislation, a lack of funding and low support from the central government. At this stage, it cannot be stated that inter-municipal cooperation means a universal solution to efficiency problems, as the positive effects are documented rather by anecdotal evidence.

Another way to achieve partial efficiency improvements is to revitalize ideas associated with New Public Management. From the economic branch of this ideology, it is possible to reintroduce contracting out, PPP projects, mixed firms and agency. From the managerial branch, there are strategic planning, benchmarking, Balanced Scorecard, etc. Records from the Czech Republic and other CEE countries bring a rather skeptical view of these tools. Soukopová et al. (2017) state that contracting out is associated with statistically significant cost reduction in waste management, while the implementation of PPP increases costs. In the field of managerial methods such as benchmarking, Balanced Scorecard and strategic management, there are only two such empirical studies. Plaček et al. (2019a, b) conclude that the use of these tools in Czech conditions is not associated with higher efficiency. On the other hand, the authors leave unanswered the question as to whether the positive effects translate more into citizens' quality of life. The authors state that these tools are well known in the environment of municipalities, that the municipalities implement them, but that they are not used for management decisions in reality. The reason for this is the overly fragmented policy of quality improvement by the central government and the unprepared institutional environment. This thesis is also supported by other authors dealing with the impact of NPM in the public sector. Dan and Pollit (2015) claim that *"NPM policy has not always been successful to the extent expected and promoted, but there is enough evidence to show that some of the central ideas in NPM have led to improvements in public service organization or provision across different organizational settings. An adequate degree of administrative capacity, sustained reform over time and a 'fitting context' are the main factors that can tip the scale for the success of these management instruments."* The last study (Randma-Liiv and Drechsler 2017) opposes this conclusion, remarking that NPM was conceived as something of a house-cleaning concept: *"it was a reform movement within a well-functioning, if too expensive and bureaucratic (sic!) system. The problem for CEE was that there was no house to be cleaned, but rather one to be built, if 'house' is the metaphor for the public sector as such. To start cleaning before building may be putting the cart before the house, and that is one of the key insights regarding the transferability of NPM coming from the CEE experience."* (Randma-Liiv and Drechsler 2017). In our opinion, greater pressure on the current implementation of mixed firms and PPP projects would be more of a risk; the potential of these instruments could rather be used by local governments in the future, provided that a strong and professional administration could be built at the local level. In our opinion, the management branch of NPM tools has a great potential for benchmarking. In order to maximize the effects of this instrument, it would in our opinion be appropriate to make it mandatory for municipalities, at least in the area of delegated powers of state administration, which is financed by transfers from the state budget.

Another possibility for partial efficiency improvement is the implementation of alternative service delivery (ASDA) concepts. One of the main forms of ASDA currently propagated is the co-production and co-creation of public services. Ostrom (1999) describes it as '…the mix of activities that both public service agents and citizens contribute to the provision of public services," or more narrowly as "involvement of individual citizens and groups in public service delivery" (Verschure et al. 2012). The groups and individuals involved are not just seen as customers receiving the services needed, or as interest groups determining what should be done and then leaving it to public officials to implement it, but as partners who together solve the problems at hand in the provision of public services. Ostrom (1999) claims that coproduction positively influences the efficiency and quality of service delivery, and has also had positive effects on democracy and accountability. In emerging philosophies of governance (inc. collaborative governance/agreements—Brandsen and Johnston (2018), government not only stands at some distance, but often leaves it to policy stakeholders to take the lead. These new approaches typically include the following elements (Osborne, 2010; Strokosh 2013; Miles 2013; Bryson et al. 2014; Bovaird and Loeffler 2015; Tu 2015; Špaček 2016): a greater emphasis on interorganizational networks and horizontal relations, as opposed to top-down, vertical relations in public service delivery; more emphasis on collaboration as opposed to competition or hierarchy; a larger role for businesses and non-profit organizations, or the so-called hybrid organizations; more emphasis on inclusion and participation of citizens, as co-creators and/or co-producers. In their meta-evaluation, Voorberg et al. (2015) conclude that co-production aims at gaining more effectiveness, efficiency, customer satisfaction, and citizen involvement in public service delivery. On the organizational side, its success depends on the existence of inviting organizational structures and procedures, the mindset or attitude of politicians and administrators towards involving citizens, a modern instead of a conservative administrative culture, and the availability of incentives for creating a win-win situation. As for the citizens, their knowledge and skills are important, as is the idea of becoming an owner of the service delivery, the presence of social capital, and the degree of risk aversion. Most important, however, is their conclusion that hardly any information exists about the actual outcomes of coproduced services and whether such service delivery does indeed become more effective and efficient, and results in increased consumer satisfaction. There is also a risk that the new approach benefits those who have least need of it—established businesses and NGOs have more capacity to engage in extensive partnerships than unorganized citizens or start-up businesses. Highly educated, well-connected citizens traditionally find it easier to engage in government-sponsored participation schemes than those at the socio-economic fringes. Such examples suggest that new governance approaches may therefore reinforce existing inequalities. This has also been confirmed in studies related to e-participation (see e.g. Ainsworth et al. 2005; European Commission 2009; Van Dijk et al. 2010). Several analyses indicate that the role of local self-government in co-creation in transition countries may be rather limited; service delivery innovations are predominantly initiated by third sector organizations (NGOs) or citizens themselves. The reason for this situation lies in the traditions and types of governance inherited from the socialist past, and it cannot be changed immediately. Even in developed countries, both bureaucrats and elected politicians who make decisions about innovations in the public sector tend to reject risk (Bason 2010), political thinking does not match economic thinking (Mulgan and Albury 2003) and another problem facing the implementation of the innovation process is the short political cycle (Borins 2008). In transition countries, the limited will of local governments to innovate service delivery modes may also be connected with a lack of responsibility and accountability. The topic is still very new, although coproduction has been an aspiration of public management for several decades. Only recently have attempts been made to understand and implement this through an application of services management knowledge (Osborne et al. 2013), but has been particularly in the context of developed countries, not in transition countries.

In the conclusions of the empirical part of the study, we mentioned the problem of accountability. The Czech Republic, like other post-communist states, does not occupy a very flattering place in the annual corruption charts published by Transparency International. It would therefore seem logical to propose a combination of soft and hard instruments, which would lead to a higher degree of accountability of politicians and officials. We can consider soft instruments as things such as educating the public about the intolerability of corruption and social condemnation of corruption (Orviská et al. 2006). Persson et al. (2013) note that these tools may be more effective than those based on a microeconomic analysis of corruption. These are mainly hard instruments such as increasing control and transparency. Stricter rules and external controls are recommended for the Czech Republic in the field of public procurement (Palguta and Pertold 2017). Bobonis et al. (2016) state that results suggest that audits enable voters to select responsive but corruptible politicians to office. Audit programs must disseminate results when they are most relevant to voters—shortly before the election—and ensure that these programs are sustained, long-term commitments. Plaček et al. (2019a, b) see potential for improvement through the implementation of modern methods using risk analysis in control systems. Kim et al. (2009) note that the implementation of modern IT systems that increase openness and efficiency of public administration has great potential.

In our opinion, these methods can only mean a partial improvement, which still lacks what would be a precondition for the perfect awareness and rationality on which neoclassical microeconomics is built. Current economic theory (Maćkowiak et al. 2018; Steiner et al. 2017; Bartoš et al. 2016) brings new models of information processing and decision making by individuals. This theory claims that market agents are considering the cost of obtaining information and knowingly ignoring some of the information. The public sector should reduce information complexity in its policies. If we apply this approach to the problem of the accountability of politicians and local government officials, we can say that citizens would have enough tools to find out about the management of public funds. These include, for example, click-through budgets that are standard in most cities. The central government also enables the use of the State Treasury Monitor server to obtain complete information on the management of all municipalities, including their contributory organizations, or municipal associations. Another tool is the register of contracts, where municipalities must publish all contracts and orders over CZK 50,000; municipalities are also obliged to publish all contracts on subsidies they provide. Municipalities must also publish and have the final account approved for each financial year, and the management of the municipality must be reviewed as part of the preparation of the final account. Municipalities must also publish all public contracts over a certain value on the contracting authority's profile. As part of the disclosure obligation, they must also publish the amendments to the contracts and the final price of the contract. Politicians and public money decision makers are also required to declare conflicts of interest, stating their income, assets and sources of income. Political parties must also have a transparent account and publish their sponsors. The information obligation also falls on the private sector, as firms must declare the ultimate owners and beneficiaries.

There are non-profit sector applications such as the State Watcher, which searches contract, subsidy and procurement registers and can find links between entities that raise public money.

We can say that citizens have sufficient tools to control and discipline politicians and bureaucrats, but they are unable to understand the complexity of the information they are provided. The solution is to integrate the previous tools into the simplest possible format, to reduce the complexity of the information and the transaction costs of acquiring the information. In the Czech Republic, first attempts are being made to simplify voter decision-making in municipal elections. The project is called the Election Bench. Its main objective is to find out whether improving and simplifying access to information about candidates for municipal councils can activate voters before the elections, and what types of information about candidates are interesting. Another objective is to quantify what programs political movements offer voters and how they differ based on the characteristics of municipalities (Election Bench 2019).

Voters will find information about candidates' plans for their community, their qualifications, experience, worldview, but also about their everyday life. In our opinion, this is the right way to increase the availability of information and, ultimately, efficiency.

References

Agasisti T, Dal Bianco A, Griffini M (2015) The public sector fiscal efficiency in Italy: the case of Lombardy municipalities in the provision of the essential public services. Technical Report no. 691, Società Italiana di Economia Pubblica, Università di Pavia, Pavia

Ainsworth S, Hardy C, Harley B (2005) Online consultation: e-democracy and e-resistance in the case of the development gateway. Manage Commun Q 19(1):120–145

Balaguer-Coll TM, Prior D (2009) Short- and long-term evaluation of efficiency and quality. An Application to Spanish municipalities. Appl Econ 41(23):2991–3002

Balaguer-Coll TM, Prior D, Tortosa-Ausina E (2010) Decentralization and efficiency of local government. Ann Regional Sci 45(3):571–601

Bartoš V, Bauer M, Chytilová J et al (2016) Attention discrimination: theory and field experiments with monitoring information acquisition. Am Econ Rev 106(6):1437–1475

Bason Ch (2010) Leading public sector innovation: co-creating for a better society. The Policy Press, Bristol

Bel G, Warner ME (2015) Inter-municipal cooperation and costs: expectations and evidence. Public Admin 93(1):52–67

Bel G, Fageda X, Mur M (2012) Does cooperation reduce service delivery costs? Evidence from residential solid waste services. J Publ Adm Res Theor 24(1):85–107

Benito B, Bastida F, García JA (2010) Explaining differences in efficiency: an application to Spanish municipalities. J Appl Econ 42(4):515–528

Bobonis GJ, Fuertes LRC, Schwabe R (2016) Monitoring corruptible politicians. Am Econ Rev 106(8):2371–2405

Boetti L, Piacenza M, Turati G (2012) Decentralization and local governments' performance: how does fiscal autonomy affect spending efficiency? FinanzArchiv 68(3):269–302

Bönisch P, Haug P, Illy A et al (2011) Municipality size and efficiency of local public services: does size matter? IWH Discussion Paper no. 18/2011, Halle Institute for Economic Research (IWH), Halle

Borge L-E, Falch T, Tovmo P (2008) Public sector efficiency: the roles of political and budgetary institutions, fiscal capacity, and democratic participation. Public Choice 136(3):475–495

Borins SF (ed) (2008) Innovations in government: research, recognition, and replication. Brookings Institution Press, Washington

Bovaird T, Loeffler E (2015) Coproducing public services with users, communities, and the third sector. In: Perry JL, Christensen RK (eds) Handbook of public administration, 3rd edn. Jossey-Bass, San Francisco, pp 235–250

Brandsen T, Johnston K (2018) Collaborative governance and the third sector: something old, something new. In: Ongaro E, van Thiel S (eds) The Palgrave handbook of public administration and management in Europe, 1st edn. Palgrave Macmillan, London, pp 311–325

Bryson JM, Crosby CB, Bloomberg L (2014) Public value governance: moving beyond traditional public administration and the new public management. Public Admin Rev 74(4):445–456

Dan S, Pollit C (2015) NPM can work: an optimistic review of the impact of new public management reforms in Central and Eastern Europe. Public Manag Rev 157(9):1305–1332

De Borger B, Kerstens K (1996a) Cost efficiency of Belgian local governments: a comparative analysis of FDH, DEA, and econometric approaches. Reg Sci Urban Econ 26(2):145–170

De Borger B, Kerstens K (1996b) Radial and nonradial measures of technical efficiency: an empirical illustration for Belgian local governments using an FDH reference technology. J Prod Anal 7(1):41–62

Doumpos M, Cohen S (2014) Applying data envelopment analysis on accounting data to assess and optimize the efficiency of greek local governments. Omega 46:74–85

Drew J, Kortt MA, Dollery B (2015) What determines efficiency in local government? A DEA analysis of NSW local government. Econ Pap 34(4):243–256

Election Bench (2019) About project. Available online at: http://www.volebnilavicka.cz

European Commission (2009) European eParticipation: summary Report. Available via https://ec.europa.eu/information_society/newsroom/cf/dae/document.cfm?doc_id=1499

Eurostat (2019) Government finance statistics. European Commission, Eurostat, Luxembourg. Available via https://ec.europa.eu/eurostat/web/government-finance-statistics. Accessed 28 Oct 2019

Geys B, Moesen W (2009) Measuring local government technical (in)efficiency: an application and comparison of FDH, DEA, and econometric approaches. Public Perform Manag 32(4):499–513

Grossman PJ, Mavros P, Wassmer RW (1999) Public sector technical inefficiency in large U.S. Cities. J Urban Econ 46(2):278–299

Jetmar M (2015) Meziobecní spolupráce: inspirativní cesta jak zlepšit služby veřejnosti. Svaz měst a obcí České republiky, Praha

Kim S, Kim HJ, Lee H (2009) An institutional analysis of an e-government system for anti-corruption: the case of OPEN. Gov Inform Q 26(1):42–50

Maćkowiak B, Matějka F, Wiederholt M (2018) Dynamic rational inattention: analytical results. J Econ Theory 176:650–692

Miles I (2013) Public service innovation: what messages from the collision of innovation studies and services research? In: Osborne SP, Brown L (eds) Handbook of innovation in public services. Edward Elgar, Cheltenham, pp 72–88

Mulgan G, Albury D (2003) Innovation in the public sector. Strategy Unit, Cabinet Office, London

Orviská M, Čaplánová A, Medved J et al (2006) A cross-section approach to measuring the shadow economy. J Policy Model 28(7):713–724

Osborne SP (ed) (2010) The new public governance? Emerging perspectives on the theory and practice of public governance, Routletge, Oxon

Osborne SP, Radnor Z, Nasi G (2013) A new theory for public service management? Towards a service-dominant approach. Am Rev Public Adm 43(2):135–158

Ostrom E (1999) Crossing the great divide: coproduction, synergy, and development. In: McGinnis MD (ed) Polycentric governance and development: readings from the workshop in political theory and policy analysis. University of Michigan Press, Michigan

Pacheco F, Sanchez R, Villena M (2014) A longitudinal parametric approach to estimate local government efficiency. Technical Report no. 54918, Munich University Library, Munich

Palguta J, Pertold F (2017) Manipulation of procurement contracts: Evidence from the introduction of discretionary thresholds. Am Econ J-Econ Polic 9(2):293–315

Peréz-Lopéz G, Prior D, Zafra JL (2015) Rethinking new public management delivery forms and efficiency: long-term effects in Spanish local government. J Publ Adm Res Theor 25(4):1157–1183

Persson A, Rothstein B, Teorell J (2013) Why anticorruption reforms fail—systemic corruption as a collective action problem. Governance 26(3):449–471

Plaček M, Schmidt M, Ochrana F, Půček M (2016) Impact of selected factors regarding the efficiency of public procurement (the Case of Czech republic) with emphasis of decentralization. Ekonomický časopis, SAP—Slovak Academic Press 64(1):22–36.

Plaček M, Půček M, Ochrana F (2019a) Identifying corruption risk: a comparison of Bulgaria and the Czech Republic. J Comp Policy Anal 21(4):366–384

Plaček M, Špaček M, Ochrana F et al (2019b) Does excellence matter? National quality awards and performance of Czech municipalities. J East Eur Manag Stud 24(4):589–613

Porcelli F (2014) Electoral accountability and local government efficiency: quasi-experimental evidence from the Italian health care sector reforms. Econ Gov 15(3):221–251

Randma-Liiv T, Drechsler W (2017) Three decades, four phases: public administration development in Central and Eastern Europe, 1989–2017. Int J Public Sector Manag 30(6–7):595–605

Soukopová J, Vaceková G (2018) Internal factors of intermunicipal cooperation: what matters most and why? Local Gov Stud 44(1):105–126

Soukopová J, Vaceková G, Klimovský D (2017) Local waste management in the Czech Republic: limits and merits of public-private partnership and contracting out. Util Policy 48:201–209

Špaček D (2016) Public management—v teorii a praxi. C. H. Beck, Praha

Šťastná L, Gregor M (2015) Public sector efficiency in transition and beyond: evidence from Czech local governments. Appl Econ 47(7):680–699

Steiner J, Stewart C, Matějka F (2017) Rational inattention dynamics: inertia and delay in decision-making. Econometrica 85(2):521–553

Strokosh K (2013) Co-production and innovation in public services: can co-production drive innovation? In: Osborne SP, Brown L (eds) Handbook of innovation in public services. Edward Elgar, Cheltenham, pp 375–389

Tavares AF (2018) Municipal amalgamations and their effects: a literature review. Misc Geogr 22(1):5–15

Tu X (2015) Empowering citizens in public services: a systematic review of co-production cases. Paper presented at 2015 IRSPM Conference, University of Birmingham, Birmingham, 30.3.–1.4. 2015

van Dijk JAGM (ed) (2010) Study on the Social Impact of ICT. Topic Report 3 (D7.2). University of Siegen. Siegen. Available via http://ec.europa.eu/information_society/newsroom/cf/document. cfm?action=display&doc_id=673

Verschuere B, Brandsen T, Pestoff V (2012) Co-production: the state of the art in research and the future agenda. Voluntas 23(4):1083–1101

Voorberg WH, Bekkers VJJM, Tummers LG (2015) A systematic review of co-creation and coproduction: embarking on the social innovation journey. Public Manag Rev 17(9):1333–1357

Yusfany A (2015) The efficiency of local governments and its influence factors. Int J Technol Enhanc Emerg Eng Res 4(10):219–241

Zafra-Gómez JL, Prior D, Plata-Díaz AM et al (2013) Reducing costs in times of crisis: delivery forms in small and medium sized local governments' waste management services. Public Admin 91(1):51–68